Praise for John O'Neil

"Understanding the principles of aikido is valuable for any business leader: responding to aggression by blending; recovering your center when the unexpected disrupts; translating a goal into a flow of focused, concentrated energy. John O'Neil's book is a major contribution to broadening the study of business leadership. Not only does he provide leaders with the aikido perspective, but he also crams every chapter with all the practical wisdom he has learned as a successful leader himself. Readers will be delighted with what they discover in this vital book."

—Phillip Moffitt, President, The Life Balance Institute

"John O'Neil is not only an accessible writer but also a psychologist wise in things of the spirit. . . . He introduces his readers to deep insights and ancient wisdom. . . . A sane book for the heart and mind as we move into a world where skill in spiritual Aikido is called for. A wise book for those concerned about a sound spiritual and psychological ecology for the future."

—Reverend Alan Jones, author of
Soul Making and *The Soul's Journey*

"John O'Neil's practical, humane leadership insights are based on real experience with hundreds of leaders. . . . With markets, technologies, and organizations changing rapidly, John O'Neil brings us back to the basics: leaders matter and leadership is an art that can be learned."

—Waring Partridge, Vice President, AT&T

Leadership Aikido

6 BUSINESS PRACTICES TO TURN AROUND YOUR LIFE

JOHN O'NEIL

THREE RIVERS PRESS
NEW YORK

Grateful acknowledgment is given to reprint the following:

From *A Complaint Is a Gift: Using Customer Feedback as a Strategic Tool*, copyright © 1996 by Janelle Barlow and Claus Møller, Berrett-Koehler Publishers, Inc., San Francisco, California. Reprinted by permission of the publisher. All rights reserved.

From an interview with George Leonard. Reprinted by permission of George Leonard. All rights reserved.

Published by Three Rivers Press, a division of Crown Publishers, Inc., 201 East 50th Street, New York, New York 10022.
Member of the Crown Publishing Group.

Originally published in hardcover by Harmony Books, a division of Crown Publishers, Inc., in 1997.

Random House, Inc. New York, Toronto, London, Sydney, Auckland
www.randomhouse.com

THREE RIVERS PRESS is a registered trademark
of Random House, Inc.

Design by Mercedes Everett

Printed in the United States of America

Library of Congress Cataloging-in-Publication Data
    O'Neil, John R.
    Leadership aikido : 6 business practices to turn around your
life / by John O'Neil.—1st ed.
    1. Leadership.   I. Title.
HD57.7.053   1997   650.1—dc21   97-13489

ISBN 0-609-80221-6

10 9 8 7 6 5 4 3 2 1

First Paperback Edition

To my family,
who is always with me in spirit and affection.

Contents

ACKNOWLEDGMENTS

Over the years of studying and practicing the daunting arts and wee science of leadership, I have accumulated many debts from the wisdom banks of friends and teachers. Among my long-term leaders are John Gardner, Warren Bennis, Peter Drucker, Elsa Porter, Juanita Brown, Bob Greenleaf, Charles Hampton Turner, Charles Handy, Bob Schwartz, Jay Ogilvy, John Levy, Frances Vaughan, Roger Walsh, Joe Henderson, Ken Wilbur, and Michael Murphy. And, they just keep on giving.

Another rich source of knowledge and inspiration are associates and clients too numerous to name. I must trust that they know how deeply indebted I am to them.

In recent days, I have borrowed heavily from George Leonard and Phillip Moffitt to get a purchase on the arts and metaphysics of aikido.

Of course, the professionals who offered their talents and sweat were invaluable and much appreciated: Jay Wurts' ideas, words, and discipline were indispensable; Diana Landau and Jan Johnson made order of my confusion with their edits and suggestions; Leslie Stager and Jennifer Kennedy provided research and logistical support of high order; Leslie Meredith and her always gracious and talented associates at Harmony Books/Crown Publishers were a writer's dream, and Muriel Nellis and Jane Roberts at Literary and Creative Artists Agency always kept the faith.

LEADERSHIP
AIKIDO

Introduction

Ai-ki cannot be exhausted
By words written or spoken.
Without dabbling in idle talk,
Understand through practice.

—Morihei Ueshiba, founder of Aikido

Now and then we see something ordinary in a different light that changes our thinking dramatically. Sometimes that new thought develops into a powerful metaphor for a challenging concept. This is the story of one such discovery along my road to Damascus. Somewhere along that road—a twenty-five-year journey through the labyrinth of modern leadership and management studies—a new idea suddenly illuminated everything that had come before. I've turned that idea into the basis of this book.

My place of revelation was a modest aikido dojo in Mill Valley, California. "Dojo," the Japanese name for a martial arts training hall, is derived from a Sanskrit term meaning "place of enlightenment." And so it felt. Men and women of all ages come to this simple room to study under the master, George Leonard, a former editor of *Look* magazine, author of several books, and an old friend of mine. They come to study aikido, an unusual martial art that features self-defense without harming the opponent. Through aikido they are also learning about themselves, their darkest instincts and their great capacity to overcome fear, to find harmony and peace even while under attack.

As I watched the students go through their practice, it struck me forcefully that aikido training and the reverential rituals of the dojo provide a powerful expression for what is missing in most contemporary organizations and in the lives of those who lead them. Those who practice aikido are totally engaged in bringing together their physical, spiritual, and mental gifts, whereas the people I see working in most organizations seem unable or unwilling to experience their full potential as complete human beings—or complete leaders. Most people report that their work lives are consuming but not fulfilling. Even the most privileged of the leaders I work with do not describe the workplace as a source of enlightenment. But through my study of aikido, I've seen how we can change the workplace into a venue in which insight and enlightenment, competition and profit, can coexist and help each other.

From my own experience in consulting with corporations and their leaders, I see how even technically brilliant managers fail in their leadership roles because they have too few emotional and spiritual cards in their decks. Current models of leadership, which emphasize rational thinking combined with action-first and purpose-later instincts, reward the smart-aggressive rather than those who are emotionally and spiritually mature. And the results of such leadership have been devastating.

In the last twenty years we have seen company after company— even whole industries—go from world prominence to payroll-slashing panic, bailout, and extinction. The American auto industry—notably in the Chrysler debacle—provides many object lessons on the dangers of industrial-age leaders becoming lost in command and control.[1] But there are many other examples of slow-footed organizations where power at the top turned good people into arrogant, swaggering despots. Such leaders have brought down airlines like Eastern and Pan Am, tarnished great steel companies like USX and Kaiser, allowed once powerful banks like Barings to vanish, and eliminated great retailers like I. Magnin—all onetime industry giants that, in the hands of bad leaders, could not adapt even in high-demand markets.

While the need for superior global leadership has never been greater, our expectations for leaders have shrunk to an all-time low, leaving workers and managers alike feeling demoralized, frustrated, cynical, and angry. What lessons can we draw from all of this? If the history of the past hundred years has taught us anything, it's that a confrontational, hard-edged, attack-oriented approach to coping with change and conflict usually causes more problems than it solves. In a world beset by social disorder and destructive economic forces, we must devise new codes of ethics and healthy practices for resolving conflict, growing our careers and companies, and governing our lives.

We must seek and speak a new "grammar" that can inform a culture of sustainable growth and cooperation.

Leaders of the future will need to employ win-win ethics and practices to grow enduring, powerful, nimble organizations that bring satisfaction to all their constituents. They will need to wield the tools of self-development to meet the demands of professional and personal life. Those are the central needs this book addresses—by sharing the time-tested wisdom of master leaders, reinforced by a rich body of skills derived from aikido. Any martial art is, first and foremost, a tool for self-discovery and personal development. Aikido—and the leadership practices congenial to its precepts—can promote lifelong learning, self-understanding, harmony of thought and deed, and resolution of strife. These qualities are too seldom seen in today's leaders, but they are crucial to leaders of the future.

THE FUTURE IS UPON US

We all have many models, techniques, and philosophies to choose from as we make our way through life and career. As times become more stressful and the pace of unbidden change increases, the practices and ideas we choose—or allow to govern us by default—become more crucial to our long-term happiness and success. I've come to believe that the volumes and practices associated with aikido will be significant tools for survival, let alone success, in the postindustrial world of the twenty-first century.

For some years now we have, in fact, been hearing about and experiencing what people are calling the postindustrial age. I propose a different name, for now and for the future—the Green Glass Age.

"Green" comes from the recent breakthroughs in biology and genetic engineering that have accelerated evolution itself: the prime mover of life on earth. When this godlike power is coupled to the decades-long growth in environmental awareness in both the industrialized countries and the developing nations—the "green movement" that says we must acknowledge the limits as well as the possibilities of the future—we are fully poised to become true stewards as well as masters of the physical world.

"Glass" is the colloquial term used in Silicon Valley for the silicon wafers and fiber optics that undergird the computer revolution. They are the key to storing and disseminating the vast quantities of particularized information that make the revolution possible.

Together these elements constitute the reality—the technical and intellectual resources—that will fuel the Green Glass Age. Just as Bronze Age technology and the communal life of farm villages created civilization as we know it, so will Green Glass technology and ideals literally redefine what it means to be human. As Kevin Kelly points out in his book, *Out of Control: The Biology of New Machines,* "Not a single aspect of business will avoid being overhauled, either directly or indirectly by . . . network logic."[2] The Green gives us a star to steer by; the Glass provides our vessel.

We require leaders to cope with the stresses of rapid change, network federation organizations that often feel out of control, harsh cross-cultural and social barriers, and the requirements of global thinking. As agrarian leaders had to learn the language and customs of a new industrial age, so must leaders now adapt to the Green Glass Age. They must find new teachers and mentors, learn master practices that will allow them to remain whole while continually reinventing themselves. Aikido leadership can provide a road map.

THE QUEST FOR MASTER LEADERS

Examples of bad leadership abound; we need only glance at the headlines. But this dark picture is illuminated by more than a few bright lights. In the twenty-five years that I've been studying leadership, I've made it my mission to seek out leaders, both historical and contemporary, who endured and remained productive during changing and challenging times. They include inspirational figures from outside the world of business, such as George Marshall, Winston Churchill, Georgia O'Keeffe, and Nelson Mandela, as well as contemporary leaders working in well-known global companies like Intel, Hewlett-Packard, and 3M Corporation. I've also found powerful models in less well-known organizations like A. M. Todd and Sir James Black's laboratory.

So this book is, in part, a report on such leaders, an exploration of their deeply held precepts and practices. It's the story of my decades-long attempt to give the leadership ideal a human face, tangible dimensions we can recognize, and specific practices we can use. In providing cautionary tales of leaders who cause harm to themselves and their organizations, it should also serve as a diagnostic test.

I began by organizing the mountains of personal interviews, transcripts, proceedings, clippings, hastily photocopied articles, and meticulously researched notes I had filed on these subjects over the years. Gradually, the bits and pieces began to form patterns—a mosaic of the coping and decision-making processes used by extraordinary people in a variety of times and places. Strangely, the more I sorted and stacked, winnowed and edited, grouping like with like, the less I felt I knew about how the whole thing came together, the mystery of how the superbly successful and well-balanced leaders I had studied actually molded these practices to fit their different personalities and callings.

I sought these missing pieces in a series of rambling discussions with a variety of enduring leaders and scholars I am privileged to call friend and mentor, from John Gardner and Charles Handy to Warren Bennis and Mihaly "Mike" Csikszentmihalyi. I knew these generous *sensei* (teachers) would treat my queries and ideas kindly (they always had), but I really did not expect the enthusiasm and tangible support—the wealth of new examples and suggestions—they provided. This was a great unexpected consequence of my search. In a very real way, their reactions became the essence of this book.

Like a well-knit, practiced ensemble, though most of them had never met, each extraordinary leader picked up an idea effortlessly where another had left off and developed it further, embellishing it with nuances and fresh ideas from his own experience, resolving dissonances into harmonies of exquisite depth and beauty, before passing it along. I only hope that at least a portion of the genius and virtuosity of these men has been captured in these pages.

Ultimately they taught me that leadership is an improvisational art. It always has been and always will be. We may may pick up bits and pieces of technique from here and there, good ideas that worked well in one situation or failed in another, but it will always be up to us to add our own variation, to derive a tune that suits our timbre.

I believe that this creative process operates at three levels. The first is the big picture, where broad philosophies give meaning to our experience. The second is up close and personal, where we try on specific techniques and use or discard them like garments, gauging their fit. Between these two extremes lies the middle view where most leaders spend most of their time. When necessity demands it and our beliefs give us the courage to do so, we reach into our kit bag of leadership tools and try on something new, hoping for classic style instead of trendy fashion slavery. When the daily grind wears us down too much and we seek to regain our balance, we go back to the bigger picture, rest our eyes on the horizon, and try to refresh our spirit.

In a way, this book is nothing more than a continuation of an endeavor I have long undertaken—to summarize and synthesize the real-life behavior of model leaders into a set of guidelines so that others can effectively learn from them—but I have found this challenging, as these leaders come from so many different fields of endeavor.

Once I grasped the principles of aikido, I began to glimpse an exciting new way of looking at leadership. In seeking the common threads that bind extraordinary leaders, I found that their attitudes and actions, thoughts and practices, tended to correlate closely with the principles and values expressed in this martial art. Looking at the practices of more than a hundred highly productive, creative leaders, I compared them with the aikidoist ideal of harmonious human development. And it became clear that *all these leaders were engaged in practical expressions of the aikidoist ideal of self-mastery as a prerequisite for the mastery of leadership tasks.*

Out of this discovery I've developed the philosophy I call *leadership aikido,* which integrates the philosophy and lessons of the dojo with the real-life behavior of master leaders. It's not necessary to have studied any martial art to pursue it; I've become an enthusiastic student of aikido, and I use it in leadership training, though I don't practice in a dojo. What I'm committed to passing on to readers is the wisdom and power that lie at the heart of aikido and that can be applied very effectively to the world of organizational development and the personal development of leaders. Much of aikido's power is latent within each of us, waiting to be released. This book aims to set you on the path—the way, or *do*—to realize that power in yourself.

THE AIKIDO MODEL FOR NEW LEADERS

We badly need new models of leadership to take us into the next century. Why aikido? After the first moment of epiphany of George Leonard's dojo, I began looking more deeply into the traditions and practices of this unusual martial art. The further I looked, the more parallels I found between the discipline and self-mastery demanded by the practice of aikido and the requirements of sound leadership. Aikido gives us a new language, stimulating metaphors for reintegrating the mind, body, and spirit. Studying it can suggest forms for the full human development that leaders need to experience and promulgate.

In the 1920s the founder of aikido, martial arts master Morihei Ueshiba, developed a life-affirming alternative to the death-dealing combat arts then prevalent in his country. Restoring the original spiritual qualities of *budo*—the way of all martial arts—was his goal. The means he chose was a practice that sought to unite the creative energy of the universe with an individual's life force—a force that, according to Asian spiritual tradition, originates at the center of our being and connects us to the larger world. Both the individual and the universal energy are referred to as *ki*. So aikido translates literally as "the way [*do*] of harmony [*ai*] with the life force [*ki*]." Other phrases often used to loosely translate or describe aikido's purposes are "the power of harmony" and "harmony of spirit and body." *Aiki* is sometimes translated as "confluence."[3] So in thinking about aikido in relation to various aspects of life and work, we can think of making connections, of transforming our personal powers to a higher level by uniting them with outside forces.

A compilation of defensive techniques drawn from many martial arts, Ueshiba's new discipline of aikido literally had no technique for attack. Instead, it offered unlimited ways for a defender to channel an attacker's aggression into harmless directions, avoiding injury not just to the defender but to the attacker as well. Aikido thus provides an especially powerful means for resolving conflict rather than glorifying it. The goal is to avoid domination while achieving one's own maximum potential, to succeed without inflicting unnecessary harm, even when threatened by an unprovoked and dangerous attack. Aikido expert and Zen priest John Stevens emphasizes this self-development rather than the combat side of the art in calling aikido "a kind of martial yoga."[4] Another writer refers to aikido as "dynamic Zen."

In pursuing the connections I felt might exist between aikido and leadership, I turned to George Leonard's book, *Mastery*. There I began to trace the powerful links between the principles of aikido and the lasting success and happiness I had observed in the exemplary leaders

I'd studied. Among the most consistent traits in long-term leaders is their ability to engage in lifelong learning. As George so aptly puts it in his introduction: "With its sophisticated blending moves and full repertory of rolls and falls, aikido is generally known as the most difficult of the martial arts to master. On the training mat, every attempt at circumvention or overreaching is revealed; flaws are made manifest; the quick fix is impossible. At the same time, the pleasures of practice are intensified. The mat, I often tell my students, is the world, but it is the world under a magnifying glass. An aikido school is therefore an ideal laboratory for studying the factors that work for and against long-term learning."[5]

George goes on to note that "Interviews . . . have shown me that what is true for students of aikido is also true for learners in any nontrivial skill: managers, artists, pilots, schoolchildren, college students, carpenters, athletes, parents . . . and even entire cultures in the process of change."[6]

Leadership Aikido aims to help us grow professionally and personally into a new model of leadership by using a set of practices that, like aikido, actually change the inner person. The techniques of leadership aikido can bring beliefs, perceptions, and actions into harmony. Just as aikido students must master inner enemies before they can deal with outside threats, so must leaders find a way (*do*) of harmonizing (*ai*) the mental, physical, and spiritual forces (*ki*) within themselves and the people around them, to achieve lasting success and happiness in both career and family life.

FROM THE DOJO TO THE BOARDROOM

Aikido offers the virtues of any mastery practice plus some unique aspects of moral and spiritual development that are critical to all those who seek leadership roles. I'll explore these throughout the book. To start with, let me summarize a few of aikido's essential characteristics and how they relate to the needs of leaders and organizations:

- Aikido is a combat art whose most profound purpose is to avoid conflict or bring it to a harmonious resolution. In fact, aikido holds that winning is not possible if anyone in the contest—even the aggressor— is harmed. This idea has profound implications for our time, in which the peaceful resolution of conflict must be the highest priority. And the conflicts we face are not just in the arena of business competition; they are also in our families, our communities, and ourselves.

- Aikido is founded on the principles and skills of balance, movement, and dynamic flow. Aikidoists prevail by moving toward and turning away, rolling out of danger, deflecting the opponent's attack, and redirecting its energy, all the while maintaining an unshakable sense of their own center of gravity. Leonard says, "I turn in such a way as to gain my opponent's point of view without losing my own." This is an oversimplification, but it suggests the metaphorical treasures in aikido's physical repertoire—skills that leaders can use in dealing with fast-changing playing fields and players from many different cultures.

- Aikido deals with the same raw materials—our aggressive instincts, our desire for achievement, and our all-too-human fears—that compose the day-to-day fabric of the working world. And it deals with them in a long-term, sustained way, never promising a quick fix.

- In aikido, the dojo becomes an island of concentration where self-absorbed egos can transform themselves into virtually selfless beings. "Selfless," in the lexicon of leadership has a special meaning; it means self-knowledge without the self(ego)-inflation that success in any endeavor can bring.

- Underlying aikido practice is a spiritual and ethical foundation that lends meaning to every movement and posture. Leadership too must build such a foundation if it is to survive the earth-shifting confusion of today's world. As leaders, we need a new ethic to replace the "winning is everything" mentality, with its shadow side of greed and domination. Throughout the book we will look at models of postindustrial leaders who know that the "win at all costs" ethic is harmful not just to competitors but to employees, the environment, and our own long-term growth; it is a short-sighted strategy that is bound to fail over time. In contrast, employing a set of aikido-based business ethics can lead to synergistic benefits for all participants.

- Aikido features a demanding regimen in which, bit by bit, layers of self-understanding are added to incremental gains in technique.

Eventually this synthesis of attitude and action forms an insepara-ble weave, a protective cloak of ideas, ethical standards, and skills. Like the fabric on Penelope's loom, this is a work forever in pro-gress, gaining depth and richness as long as the practice continues. Given enough time the practice itself begins to shape a life that is integrated, replacing scattered pieces seeking reunification. In the same way, the practice of leadership is a lifelong quest for mastery.

INNER ENEMIES AND MASTER PRACTICES

To aikido-style leaders, the whole world is a dojo, a place of enlight-enment offering many paths toward mastery. Though you may have as early companions on your journey the last vestiges of the old attack-oriented industrial-age leadership—overpaid, narcissistic, hypocritical bosses, for example, or irresolute, shortsighted boards of directors—they will eventually see the wisdom of your ways or fall by the wayside; there is simply no other choice. The law of the jungle, so often cited by these people as justification for their predatory practices, is nothing compared to the "terrible swift sword" of economic justice in the Green Glass Age.

Indeed, as more and more constituents demand "big *hara*" (a well-centered or strong-stomached person) in their leaders, the aiki-doist's moral philosophy will become more widespread, producing people who

- Don't need losers to be winners
- Go straight for the truth in any situation
- Keep their perspective—see the whole person in themselves and others
- Value and build heterarchial networks, not hierarchial empires
- Measure success by the full returns their organizations generate
- Seek and fulfill *sensei* relationships, becoming ever better learners and teachers

It's a well-known axiom that in order to get where we're going, we need to know where we are. We must first seek out and deal with some inner enemies that can subvert our best intentions and proudest achievements. The first part of this book describes five of the most common of these enemies—again, drawn from the experience of both aikidoists and enduring leaders. These enemies can be identified briefly as

1. Failing to grow emotionally
2. Failing to make creative connections
3. Failing to empathize
4. Failing to manage ego
5. Failing to overcome alienation and boredom

These inner enemies typically attack when we are least prepared for them, and they often appear in a guise that makes them hard to recognize. They are responsible for many problems that management education usually neglects or ignores. The business leaders who share their problems with me often describe their symptoms in vague terms: "I'm putting in more time and energy and getting less satisfaction," or "I feel out of balance, can't get my family and personal life in sync with the bloody impossible job demands," or "My team needs to come together; they need a shot of tonic." It has been my task to sort out the real troubles, to locate the root problems. And I've found that most leaders tend to mention the same ailments, face the same stealthy inner enemies.

You are invited to discover your own stress fractures and hidden enemies. You can then explore the master practices used by aikido-style leaders to disarm their inner enemies before they can do harm. You will learn how Sir James Black, Nobel laureate in medicine, has remained productive and creative well into his seventies (Johnson & Johnson has awarded his laboratory a new ten-year contract). You will discover how the A. M. Todd Company, a fifth-generation family business, has successfully gone global under leaders trained to be excellent team players, cultivate modesty, and focus on customer needs. You will gain a deeper understanding of how the Intel team has learned to fight (intellectually) for creativity and improved thinking without creating losers.

Aikido calls for the faithful, long-term practice of skills that support and enhance each other, woven on a loom of sturdy principles. Leadership, especially in business, in the Green Glass Age calls for the

same kind of synthesis attitude and action. At the heart of this book
are six master practices that I've identified, guided by the examples of
enduring leaders and concepts derived from aikido:

1. Cultivate self-knowledge.
2. Practice the parodoxical art of planning.
3. Speak the language of mastery.
4. Let values drive your decisions.
5. Turn failure into success.
6. Heed the law of unintended consequences.

Confronted by such practices, what chance do inner enemies like
stunted emotions, muddled thinking, a mania for control, spitefulness,
and alienation have of continuing their evil work?

Periodically, aikido-style leaders also test the spirits that move
them, checking their progress down the road to mastery, an endless
journey made no shorter by its many detours, dead ends, and pitfalls
set for the unwary. Not the least of these dangers is the constant temp-
tation to strike a new deal with the devil—to resurrect an old inner
enemy who promises instant solutions to long-standing problems.

When these seductive sirens call, enduring leaders simply remind
themselves why they first set out on their journey. Are they happy,
prosperous, and productive people, and do the road signs they currently follow continue to point in that direction? Are they using their
limited time on earth to full advantage—wisely, rightly, and honor-
ably? Do new challenges still fortify them, fill them with anticipation
and excitement, even if the outcome is uncertain?

In short, is the process of leading still as energizing and fulfilling
as it was when the journey started?

These questions reveal both the trials and the rewards of lasting
leadership. The techniques, ideas, and ideals of aikido-style leaders
can bring all these benefits within reach, but only if you make the
quest for them an enduring part of your life. Without exception, this
involves a transformation—a metamorphosis—in which you will shed
the old and let your new, more radiant colors shine through, like a but-
terfly emerging from its chrysalis. This process is never easy or pain-
less, but it is the distilled elixir of life. It is the price we pay to give
wings to our hopes and dreams.

At its center you'll see that the end of anything—not just of the Industrial Age but also of our own outdated habits as leaders—means the beginning of something new and better. That is why in an age of monumental discord we can ultimately find harmony, and in the fires of our ambition, the spark of our own renewal.

THE FORCE BEHIND MASTERY

I want to emphasize that the master practices described here are not simple prescriptions that can be programmed into leaders like software into a computer, for use during office hours only. They concern the on-going development of the whole person and of that person in relation to his or her organization, family, community, and world. Like the power that enables a slightly built aikido master to subdue several onrushing opponents, leadership aikido allows the individual leader to come into harmony with universal forces rather than to confront them with head-on aggression. One aikido student, a military hand-to-hand combat instructor, reported that "Aikido did not make me a better fighter; it made me a better husband, a better father, and a better officer."

Throughout the book, case studies will show how individuals and organizations thrive when the whole person is honored, developed, and deployed. The master practitioner knows that nothing really works if the core of the self—the source of all our beliefs, values, optimism, faith, trust, love—is not in place and functioning well. As a leader you must take stock of your core self and seek self-renewal on a regular basis. We will examine many specific methods for doing this, including how to choose a mentor, how to use self-assessment worksheets, and how to construct retreats.

I have had the opportunity to test the theory and practice of leadership mastery in many companies around the world while consulting with their leaders and serving on boards of directors of companies great and small in a variety of industries, including the not-for-profit sector. I was part of AT&T's management team earlier in my career, and more recently I have been privileged to serve that company again as it searches for future structure and leadership following the dramatic trivestiture. Until recently I was president of a large innovative graduate school, the California School of Professional Psychology, another fascinating laboratory in which to study organizations and leadership.

I have introduced the ideas in this book to practicing executives in countless workshops, retreats, consultations, and speeches as well as in one-on-one talks and walks with leaders in many nations. Often my suggestions are greeted with a curious mix of acceptance and resistance—a kind of polite "Well, that's fine for others, but we are a special case." Such tunnel vision usually suggests that I've struck an organizational nerve, a raw wound in need of healing. But the best and bravest leaders, both young and mature, greet with excitement the prospect of growing into a new model, of becoming leaders who operate in harmony with their surroundings and who live lives in balance.

This book is about the future of leadership as I envision it. And I want to see leaders become more like aikido masters and less like fatigued, anxious, bored, one-dimensional taskmasters and "technimanagers." This book is about connecting organizational life and personal mastery. It's about leaders and organizations reaching their full potential by harmonizing their expectations, actions, values, and visions. I believe that when enough leaders begin making those connections in their daily experience, the resulting transformations will reverberate well into the next century. The adventure begins now.

1. Why Leaders Are Failing

> He who will not apply new remedies must expect old evils.
>
> —Francis Bacon

At a conference exploring the future of leadership, a well-known executive revealed in a few words why his style of leadership has no future. "What values inform your decisions?" I had just asked a group of seasoned business leaders, consultants, and scholars. "Just one," he replied tersely. "Shareholder value!"

The answer provoked a storm of protest from others convened around the horseshoe-shaped table in Manhattan's elegant St. Regis Hotel, under the auspices of the *Economist* magazine.[1] First to react was the normally mild-mannered Charles Handy, an English author and business philosopher. Handy, who has witnessed again and again the disasters precipitated by executives who put earnings-per-share above other corporate values, disposed of this statement with one eloquent word: "Rubbish!"

His objection was immediately echoed by a chorus of other voices, some choked with emotion. They talked about employee participation, customer satisfaction, community obligations, and our collective stewardship of the future. Our gentle and professional moderator, Harvard Business School's professor emeritus Abe Zaleznik, could only lean back and smile at the mini-riot my question had provoked.

The mere fact that such a formidable group had gathered to debate the future of leadership is a portent of changing times. The conference aimed to explore how leaders from all walks of life should respond to the planetwide social and economic upheavals that were rocking their organizations, markets, personal lives, and comfortable worldviews. We had several themes: What will the world demand of leaders in the years ahead? What kind of people can best master these challenges? And who will be flattened by the juggernaut of change, which heeds not good intentions, impeccable credentials, or past accomplishments?

Like the dozens of leadership seminars and symposia I lead or attend each year, this one began with high hopes of finding some illumination to help leaders navigate the treacherous waters of our transitional age. But like too many of them, it ended by generating more heat than light. The St. Regis conferees came, as always, in pursuit of professional insight, personal validation and encouragement, practical guidance, peace of mind. Frequently these guiding beacons are obscured by our own egos, prejudices, and preconceptions—the "rubbish" that Charles Handy mentioned.

I also see the proliferation of leadership talkfests as symptomatic of management's never-ending search for solutions "out there"—from expert consultants, technological fixes, public relations spin doctors, or market manipulations. More and more—especially after absorbing some of the wisdom of aikido—I'm drawn to the conclusion that leaders must look inward for answers to many of the problems that seem so intractable, so hard to get a fix on amid the high seas of threat and change.

What do leaders find when they look inside themselves? That varies greatly, but for a start, let me repeat my apparently highly charged question to you: what values inform your decisions? How you answer will say a lot not only about the way you've lived to this point in your career but also about the likelihood of that career extending very far into the next century. In the days ahead, the kind of macho one-line answer offered by our friend at the St. Regis simply won't suffice.

THE MANY FACES OF LEADERSHIP FAILURE

If clear answers to the demands of modern leadership are elusive, the need for them is staring us full in the face. Today's leaders are failing on many fronts. They are failing their organizations and their colleagues, who look to them for inspiration and stability. They are failing society at large when they exert power in ways that betray the ideal of business prosperity for the benefit of all. They are failing themselves, their families, and their communities when their best energies go disproportionately toward their working lives. And ultimately they are failing their shareholders, who gain most in the long run when companies aim for sustained growth rather than short-term market surges.

The symptoms of contemporary leadership failure are especially well documented in this country, and data are starting to appear in all of the other industrialized nations as well. For his book, *White-Collar Blues: Management Loyalties in an Age of Corporate Restructuring,* Charles Heckscher, chairman of the Labor Studies and Employment Relations Department at Rutgers University, interviewed some 250 middle managers at eight giant U.S. corporations, including GM, Dow, Du Pont, and my old alma mater, AT&T.[2] Their perceptions of modern corporate life paint a gloomy picture of the American workplace. Although these managers professed great loyalty to their organizations and leaders—even to the point of subordinating their own well-being to that of the group—that dedication is seldom reciprocated. The result is a pervasive insecurity and inordinately high levels of stress.

In a 1994 global corporate leadership study, Dr. Douglas Ready, executive director of the International Consortium for Executive Research, in cooperation with Gemini Consulting, observed that a "growing gulf" has appeared between a typical organization's need for flexible, resourceful, innovative leaders and the organization's ability to produce them. This gulf is measured by such ominous forces as decreasing trust between leaders and constituents, reduced attention to customer concerns, and creeping organizational atheroclerosis—a "hardening of the attitudes" that prevents creative new ideas from circulating.[3]

My own observations confirm Dr. Ready's findings. Particularly in corporate downsizings, I often see a yawning gap between executives' perception of fairness and that of the workers, and a resulting loss of confidence in the leader-constituent "contract." Both add up to a clear vote of no confidence in the company's future. To illustrate, just look at a few realities:

- *The salaries of top executives compared with the way their companies perform.* William Agee's lucrative 1995 departure from Morrison Knudsen, the once-great engineering and construction firm, shows how wide this gulf can be and how oblivious to it many leaders are. While his company's losses compounded, Agee not only increased his multimillion-dollar compensation package, he also moved the corporate headquarters from Boise, Idaho, to California's Monterey Peninsula to enjoy its leisurely lifestyle. Even if Morrison Knudsen's stock had been riding high, this self-serving move would have been hard for constituents to swallow. Enraged stockholders finally forced Agee's removal in 1995, then won class-action and other lawsuits against the company, resulting in big changes in corporate governance and operations.[4]

- *Leaders who air dirty linen in public, then send the laundry bill to constituents.* If you think dissing a rival is dangerous in South Central L.A., try doing it at Disneyland. I refer to the flap between Disney Studios chairman Jeffrey Katzenberg and top boss Michael Eisner over the latter's perceived lack of respect. Instead of resolving personal squabbles to the interest of stakeholders in their billion-dollar-a-year business, Katzenberg jumped ship to form DreamWorks SKG with entertainment moguls Steven Spielberg and David Geffen—a potentially damaging competitor for Disney. That Katzenberg reportedly walked away with a $50 million bonus, simply for not showing up at work the next day, did little to calm Disney stakeholders.[5]

- *Leader hypocrisy and use of official disinformation.* Harried leaders often feel pressured to put a happy face on a dire outlook. A case in point: throughout the late 1980s and early 1990s, the retail giant K mart lost increasingly big chunks of market share to its aggressive archrival, Wal-Mart. Instead of revitalizing its core sales function, K mart's leaders went shopping for other speciality businesses—office supplies, electronics, and sporting goods—while touting "breakthrough" store concepts that somehow never materialized. By 1994 harsh reality had forced them to spin off many of these ill-conceived ventures—but not before they'd lost most of their customers to Wal-Mart and left their shareholders to handle the cleanup on aisle five.[6]

- *Isolated leaders: a formula for disaster.* An increasingly common symptom of the insulation of leaders and the hubris it can spawn is white-collar crime at the highest levels. A notorious example is the Barings Bank scandal. At England's oldest merchant bank, atrophied leadership allowed one rogue trader, twenty-eight-year-old Nick Leeson, to literally—and fraudulently—bet the bank on high-risk Asian futures. When those securities finally went south in 1995 and losses soared to over a billion, they took the centuries-old institution with them. While aggressive leadership isn't necessarily equivalent to banditry, white-collar crime is one way that some deeply frustrated, ambitious, and gravely misled people occasionally try to make their mark when all else fails. But the real problem is the isolation of leaders from the gritty day-to-day work of the enterprise.[7]

- *Leaders who prize image over substance.* Despite increased competition and uncertainty, too many leaders think that if they avoid risks and keep dissenters quiet, they won't be criticized by stakeholders—until the next big wave swamps the boat. These dolittle skippers fly colorful flags and spout hollow slogans. Meanwhile, the firm's value and integrity sink out of sight, threatening to take with them jobs, vendors, and other community interests. One such leader was Robert Brennan, owner of First Jersey Securities. Brennan nurtured his public persona as a latter-day Horatio Alger, decorating an aggressive penny-stock investment business with an array of flashy good works, from making generous political contributions to donating horses for New York's budget-strapped mounted police. Using inspiration speeches—in person, on videos, even on T-shirts—he hawked his self-improvement program to employees and customers alike: encouraging self-confidence, courage, honesty, responsibility, impatience with one's own shortcomings, determination, and enthusiasm. The problem was that Brennan took little of his own good medicine. He ruthlessly punished salesmen who questioned his questionable methods, which, as revealed by an SEC lawsuit, included securities fraud and market manipulation. Eventually the balloon burst and his company was forced by a federal court to pay $71.5 million to the thousands of small investors it had bilked.[8]

How Did We Get Here?

We can readily trace to their roots these symptoms of widespread leadership failure. In a nutshell, the social and economic environment in which leaders operate is, and has been for nearly two decades, in the process of profound change, but leaders are not responding as they need to. Most leaders remain mired in models of leadership that arose and flourished during America's 150-year era of frontier exploitation and industrial growth.

In the 1950s, the good old days of the mature industrial era, if people upheld their end of the employment contract, they were guaranteed a job for life. They studied, collected the right credentials, worked hard, kept their noses clean, and got ahead. If their skills and accomplishments merited it, they managed others and their resources and results were multiplied. Good leaders were expected to achieve big things. People expected to conquer the world—and why not? Their parents, schools, TV shows, books, and movies plied them with myths of success American-style. The westerns promoted a two-fisted good guys–bad guys leadership style. America's romanticized western frontier quickly became equated with a freewheeling brand of free enterprise that, despite all of its flaws, is being passed on to the developing world, which is eager to embrace it.

The leadership model that emerged from this long period of industrial growth and prosperity was characterized by an untrammeled sense of the possible, by a belief that both resources and markets were inexhaustible, and by a management style based on conflict and dominance. The organizations that grew up around this model were hierarchical, with all authority emanating from the top down through levels of managers and workers. Management came to be seen as a science, its objectives reducible to statistics and analysis. Leaders themselves were seen as almost superhuman, driven to win at all costs, and sacrificing their personal lives in the name of profits, status, and the immortality of the empire builder. Unfortunately, from what I have seen we have also exported this style of leadership to much of the developing world.

But the features that created and perpetuated industrial-age leadership are on the decline. Profound shifts in the availability and cost of resources and the nature of labor and markets are threatening the assumptions that industrial prosperity was founded on. We are currently in the grip of profound changes on many fronts: technological, economic, social, and organizational. These phenomena are well documented, so we need note them only briefly: the silicon-based information revolution, the globalization of enterprise and communications, the wrenching shifts in global realpolitik resulting from the collapse of the Communist bloc, the alarming rise in militant fundamentalist religions, and the looming crisis of population growth versus resource management and environmental quality. And this is just the broadest sketch of the forces that will shape the next century.

The industrial age was an extremely vigorous and successful stage in the evolution of leadership arts, but it's clearly coming to a close. In crafting the kind of leadership that must replace it, we'll return to the principles of aikido. It's useful to note that aikido was preceded in Japan by a tradition of fighting arts originally designed to inflict injury and death on the battlefield. Then, around the turn of the century, observing Japan's dangerous obsession with military might and conflict, Morihei Ueshiba recognized that a shift in approach to the martial arts was called for—a more subtle kind of discipline and mastery.

THE TRIALS OF TRANSITION

The end of a century is always a notable event, particularly the end of a century that has been as packed with change and progress, violence and terror, like ours. In a 1994 speech at Philadelphia's Independence Hall, Czech President Václav Havel said that "Many things indicate that we are going through a transitional period, when it seems that something is on the way out and something else is painfully being born. It is as if something were crumbling, decaying, and exhausting itself while something else, still indistinct, were arising from the rubble."[9]

The distinguishing features of transitional periods are a blending of cultures, a plurality of ideas, and the collapse of once-consistent value systems. New meaning is gradually born from the encounter of many different elements, but meanwhile, the world as we experience it seems chaotic and confusing. To some extent, our current situation is the legacy of two centuries of unbridled growth and experimentation; other aspects of it are completely unprecedented. All in all, this new landscape will undoubtedly appear daunting to the pioneering first wave of Green Glass "corporate immigrants."

For a taste of what's in store for us, just look at the communications revolution caused by the humble fax machine. Not only has it drastically changed the flow, volume, and pattern of global mail, but those who know say the overthrow of the Communist government in Poland—the first thread of the Iron Curtain to unravel—would not have been possible without a network of fax machines passing information among dissidents at very near the speed of light.

Knowledge is power. In their power to subvert the old and invite the new by the rapid decentralized flow of information, computers and telecommunications—especially with new fiber-optic technology—literally know no bounds. Truly the levers of power have never been closer to the hands of individuals. This conjunction of new technology and new freedom with the need for new forms of leadership is no accident. One drives the other just as day follows night.

Another aspect of globalization worthy of note is the spread of industrial-age ambitions, along with new technology, into the developing world. As millions more people join the struggle for the good life, Western-style, tremendous stresses will be put on resources, markets, and government controls. Third World industrialization has staggering implications for what our leaders will be called upon to do. A new epoch with more diverse players and entirely new rules is irrevocably upon us.

In the workplace, our struggle to deal with worldwide change is exacerbated by the last quarter century of demographic change in America. The *Chicago Tribune,* in a 1995 survey of labor and census statistics, insurance industry studies, and consumer research reports, arrived at the startling conclusion that the once-thriving American middle class has disintegrated into three sickly components:

1. *The aging traditionals:* Having come of age at the end of the Great Depression, the hardy survivors of World War II enjoyed the salad years of the American dream. Their incomes and expectations flourished during the 1950s and 1960s, the greatest sustained economic boom in our history. In recent years their fading recollections of affluence and stability have become the standard by which we judge our present condition—and find it wanting.

2. *The cheated children:* The "second middle class" is the group of baby boomers who came of age during their parents' era of affluence, only to find later on that they had inherited a spiraling national debt, an economic "world war" nobody knew how to win, and fears of corporate downsizing that have etched a permanent scar on the national psyche.

3. *The anxious X Generation:* Taking a cue from their disillusioned boomer parents and employers, the twenty- and thirty-something contingent finds under- and part-time employment the rule, not the exception. Even those who have managed to keep their jobs during corporate restructurings and cutbacks seldom have the cash to buy a house or start a family. While they quaff gourmet coffee and channel-surf, they know they will be the first American generation to remain poorer than their parents.

The common denominator that unites these factions, according to Edward Luttwak, author of *The Endangered American Dream,* is the "unprecedented sense of personal economic insecurity that has suddenly become the central phenomenon of life in America."[10] Managers now define a fast-track career as one without too many layoffs, setbacks, and lateral diversions. The corporate ladder climbing of the previous thirty years has turned into a game of hopscotch: two steps back and three to the side for every triumph and promotion. Everyone's job is more precarious; this is true not only for the workers on the line but also for the puppetmasters who pull the strings, though they have options the others lack. Stress, in a word, has become the dominant force in our lives, the one that shapes our differences and widens the gaps between our classes.

"There's a phenomenally high level of stress in this place," reported one manager in the Heckscher study. "People are hurting, yet they're so dedicated to this place that they'd never admit it." Another lamented that, despite top leadership's reassuring platitudes, "this isn't a family, this is a business."[11] Too often Heckscher's interviews reveal the true costs of ruthless resizing in the name of competitiveness. It may indeed yield temporary gains for the company, but it leaves survivors living in fear that the next round of cuts will carve them, bloody and shivering, out of the corporate womb.

Even worse, a poll by the Lutheran Brotherhood found that this fear of "radical jobectomy" is actually greatest among those who should feel best insulated from its effects: people with high incomes, good educations, and enviable job titles—professionals in the prime of life, at the top of their game—in other words, those who should be our fearless leaders. It's hard to keep your eye on the prize, and your nose to the grindstone, when you're constantly looking over your shoulder.

COMPARING OLD AND NEW MODELS OF LEADERSHIP

From today's precarious perspective, industrial-age, frontier-style leadership and the system of values it represents seem as dated as silent movies. The machine age that flourished from the happy conjunction of need, money, and manpower has all but run its course. In our new environment, dominated as much by scarcity as by opportunity, such ingredients as speed and reliability of service, customer satisfaction, continuous quality improvement, and process efficiency will be the hallmarks of survival, not to mention success. As our past assumptions about markets, workers, suppliers, and transportation give way to new Green Glass Age realities, leadership must evolve to keep pace. Following is a summary of the fundamental contrasts in some key areas between industrial-age leadership and leadership for the Green Glass Age:

General Situation

Yesterday's Leaders saw apparently unlimited resources, which required low-skilled workers who could fit into the organization. They had little concern for environmental issues and they faced clearly defined markets.

Tomorrow's Leaders see resources as finite and rapidly changing in character and value and require highly skilled technical people to create value and competitive edge, e.g. silicon chips. They face complex regulatory and social constraints and markets easily accessed by many competitors.

Goals, Ambitions, Style

Yesterday's Leaders saw shareholder values as preeminent and other stakeholders were given grudging attention. Capital, labor, and consumer markets were to be dominated, if possible. Competitors were clearly defined and were to be eliminated.

Tomorrow's Leaders see all stakeholders as important and that strategies and behaviors must be adaptive and opportunity driven. They are early adopters of technology and science, good shepherds of resources of people, and view the world as full of potential partnerships and alliances.

Organization Structure

Yesterday's Leaders saw the organization as power-layered hierarchies with top-down relationships characterized by command and control.

Tomorrow's Leaders see network federations with power dispersed so each unit achieves maximum capabilities and maintains good, healthy practices. All units are connected by a common story of purpose, values, and shared agreements.

Attitudes and Education

Yesterday's Leaders saw management as quantified science with the primary objective the measurement of quantifiable results; education was focused on techniques and skills.

Tomorrow's Leaders see management as a blend of intuition, wisdom, science, and value holding. They will promote cross-cultural understanding, diversity, creativity, esprit, and the development of leaders throughout the organization.

Identity

Yesterday's Leaders saw themselves as commanding, aloof, and alone—a combination of mystical power and a common touch. Too often they were compulsive, driven by money, ethically edgy, and focused on power. Their answers were found outside the self.

Tomorrow's Leaders see themselves as teachers, mentors, team players—the transmitters of a common, healthy culture with strongly articulated and practiced values. They are models of the highest ethical standards, learning for mastery of self and a well-balanced life.

Clearly the distance that must be traversed between the leaders of yesterday and those of tomorrow is considerable. For the most part, though, leaders aren't rising to the challenge. Most are busy trying to stay on well-traveled roads when they should be charting new paths through the terra incognita that confronts our culture and economy. For leaders schooled in old myths, the new world is a frightening one, filled with foreign dragons and domestic swamps. Fear of the unknown often causes leaders to equate risk avoidance with success, to congratulate themselves on disasters avoided rather than on victories won—a formula for extinction if there ever was one.

The typical behavior pattern of corporations in a declining industry well illustrates the scope of the problem. As income dwindles, profits sag or disappear. Worker morale decreases, and the cost for a mediocre product goes way up, causing consumers to walk away. What do company leaders do? They start by delivering stump speeches—propaganda taken right from their own brochures and annual reports. They talk about "getting closer to the customer" and "empowering employees," while engaging in ritualized and sanitized downsizing. (Remember, if a company has to tell you how much it cares about you, it probably doesn't.) In fact, these initiatives further alienate employees and drive more customers away. As product quality sinks, leaders increase controls and hire more hard-nosed supervisors, further demoralizing workers. As ever more customer problems go unresolved, the leaders add another layer of customer-service representatives, which only further insulates the bosses from the markets they're supposed to serve.

Poll after poll shows a steady decline in satisfaction with the performance and character of leaders, not just in the business community but also in politics, nonprofit organizations, and the professions. Highly qualified physicians, for example, are often seen as the last people we want in charge of our health care system, and our judicial system is frequently described as "too important to be left to lawyers"— the formal officers of our courts. As politicians increasingly avoid making tough legislative decisions, hoping that courts or circumstances will relieve them of having to take a stand, voter initiatives are becoming the primary agent of political change in some states. This doesn't mean that such grassroots initiatives are wrong—far from it. It only shows that traditional leaders are now most often seen as part of the problem, not the solution.

Ironically, some of the leadership qualities that once tamed a frontier and built a nation still retain much virtue. Who can condemn hard work, an indomitable spirit, and unflinching persistence in the face of great odds? Isn't there something praiseworthy about a fighter who eats stress for breakfast and doesn't even spit out the bones? But the ultracautious mind-set of many leaders contains little of the optimism, faith, and grit that built the first American frontier.

It's not enough just to bear down harder, drive oneself and one's associates at a more frantic pace. On closer inspection most such "heroic" figures have chinks in their shining armor. When, we must ask, does dedication become obsession? When does tireless effort yield chiefly emotional exhaustion, coloring every decision, professional and personal, the muted gray of despair? When does ambition turn selfish, burdening big dreams with heavy guilt? As I pointed out in *The Paradox of Success,* our society is filled with leaders who have won at work while losing in life. "What does it profit a man," asked an obscure Judaean mystic two thousand years before our industrial age, "if he gains the whole world but loses his soul?" We're still trying to answer that question.

Of course, we followers haven't been much help. As times become more uncertain, tradition-minded workers, middle managers, customers, and spouses project their fears, frustrations, and insecurities onto leaders, who have always been vessels for our collective spirit. We inject each leader's rational decisions with our own increasingly irrational expectations, leaving both parties disappointed. We consider leaders who bend or break under this double load not only failures but betrayers of our hopes and dreams.

AIKIDO-STYLE LEADERSHIP: START BY LOOKING INSIDE

As the old ground rules and assumptions about effective leadership give way, the new precepts, principles, and guideposts that will replace them are just emerging. How will we choose which new rules to follow, which habits to adopt, and which actions to take? Which values from the past are worth keeping and which must we shed—like an eagle's down—in order to soar higher?

Although we sometimes use clinical metaphors in speaking of leaders—"her enthusiasm was infectious" or "his dejection spread like the plague"—we can't put leadership under a microscope. Despite the contributions made to organizational studies by social scientists, leadership—especially today—is more art than science. This is especially true when issues like ethical behavior and cultural resiliency are considered. To adapt to our new circumstances—expanding markets, shrinking capital, foreign partners, constituent demands, and so on—leaders must learn the subtle skills of embracing opposites, dealing with paradox, accepting ambiguity. Where before leaders saw competition, even conflict, as the natural route to glory, they must now craft collaboration.

The leader's worst enemy lies not "out there" but within the confines of old habits and beliefs. You may have a right to think the world is flat, but that doesn't make it true, and it certainly won't speed your ships on the spice route to the Indies. In the liminal world of blended cultures and contradictory values, we must learn to question, and occasionally abandon, our comfortable notions of black and white. We do so not by abandoning our core values but by allowing others to be faithful to theirs. In this way we may reconfigure the building blocks of our ethical system—the mortar that holds our networks and organizations together.

Since I found no ready-made models for leadership in this startling new environment, I began looking for examples that struggling leaders could use to organize their thoughts and to serve as templates for action and as a gauge to evaluate results—in other words, new metaphors to convey not just the process but the purpose of leadership. The discovery of aikido was the key I'd been looking for. Aikido is a discipline of coordination, not conquest. It contains valuable tools for helping people contend with such age-old predicaments as virtue versus expediency, or doing good while doing well—issues at the very foundation of a leader's character and long-term well-being.

One of aikido's founding principles is that success grows from harmony of the inner self with external forces, more than from technique or strength or drive. The chief threats to this harmony are fear (often experienced as the avoidance impulse), anger (leading to confrontation), and machismo (often expressed in bluffing). Both men and women are vulnerable to these reactions. The aikido *sensei,* or teacher, is adept at spotting a fluttering fear that tenses muscles and puts harmony out of reach. Technique and training are important, and being strong on the mat is important—but neither will substitute for a composed inner self.

Today's leaders have no shortage of tools and techniques to solve external problems. The standard fixes for modern organizations include powerful communications and database tools, systems design and development, and infusions of resources and capital. Yet the landscape of leadership is overgrown with competent, well-trained managers who are simply unable to move forward in their leadership roles because they haven't paid enough attention to the practice and mastery of self-development.

The success of future leaders will hinge on their competence in areas such as team-building and communications skills, creativity, strength of character, and vision. Cultivating true expertise in these delicate, powerful arts—all of them linked to the development of the whole person—is a matter of long practice. Critical to this practice is an awareness of your inner enemies, which are much the same as those the aikidoist faces; we'll come to grips with them in Chapter 3.

A LEADER IN TRANSITION

Scholars have produced many lists of leadership attributes, some more useful than others, and we'll refer to them at various points in this book. For the moment I want to identify a few specific tasks that distinguish the needs of future leadership from the industrial-age version. To illustrate, I'll use the struggles of a fictitious chief executive officer to bring enlightened leadership to a painful corporate restructuring.

Charles Emory,[12] a fifteen-year veteran with Cyclops Financial Services, is caught in a dilemma similar to the one that many of today's leaders face. As restructuring peeled away layers of management, he saw that his company's future would depend on people with vision, men and women who could take action and energize others, more than on administrators and functionaries, regardless of their credentials or titles. Charles unburdened himself to me at a critical point in the process: "I need more leaders, not more managers—and certainly not more bureaucrats. So far, our track record in developing such people is miserable. We must push harder. We simply can't afford to have our own Barings Bank problem."

This CEO recognized that *a leader for the future must seek leadership at every level of the organization, make use of the best creative energies of every member, and find followers who can also be leaders.* Any observer of organizations knows that some "leaders" are simply good managers with power and that many "managers" are outstanding informal leaders, whatever their titles.

Yet for all his insights, Charles's problems ran deeper than even he suspected. To truly succeed in the new global market, his organization had to do more than simply identify and nurture fledgling leaders. It also had to *find ways to distribute its centralized power throughout a growing and complex network of leaders,* many of whom came from and reflected radically different cultures, outlooks, and values. The old-style industrial-age leadership models he had been raised with not only couldn't help him meet those challenges, they actively worked against them.

In short, what Charles needed but couldn't find was practical guidance on how leaders can dismantle those inherited hierarchial building blocks and reassemble them as global webs, where power is diffuse and resides closer to those who directly face the currents of change. For a network to function properly, all nodes must be healthy, resilient, and capable of coordinated but independent action. In a network every action affects all the players, every loss or gain is seismically transmitted to all parts. It's as if a spiderweb is tapped, instantly radiating signals through the miraculous fibers. Leadership in networks involves the art of pulling, persuading, testing, always with a shared purpose and vision.

The CEO's challenge was not just to foster participation, to empower employees or reengineer the company, but to rethink the fundamental relationships among all of the people involved: to redefine old notions of winning and losing, succeeding and failing. This process may begin in the corner office or in the boardroom, but it means nothing until it reaches the manufacturing line, the suppliers' and distributors' warehouses, the retail sales floor, the schools and colleges that provide our workers and leaders, and the hearts and minds of the workers' families. Charles had overlooked the simple fact that without willing participants, or followers, there are no leaders, only taskmasters, preachers, and bullies.

BUILD DYNAMIC LEADER-FOLLOWER RELATIONSHIPS

One reason good leaders have become so scarce is that fewer people these days consent to be led in the old traditional ways. A clue to this phenomenon lies in the sometimes tortured vocabulary we use to discuss followers.

First and foremost, leadership implies a dynamic relationship. It does not exist in a vacuum, and it is always changing. It is primarily a sociological, not a psychological, phenomenon, although psychology plays an important role in understanding what makes both leaders and followers tick. Listed below are some of the more popular euphemisms for "follower" that have surfaced in recent years. Where these terms signify genuine changes in attitude and behavior at all levels, they're a move in the right direction. Too often, though, they're mere window dressing that promotes cynicism, not commitment. Which ones have you seen? Which can you see through?

- *Team member:* Old-style leaders thought they could have it both ways—commitment from below and control from the top—by telling workers they were not employees in a hierarchial structure but members of a competitive team. Unfortunately, most traditional managers failed to provide the quality leadership needed to make the team metaphor real, so people understandably grew cynical about this particular ploy.
- *Associate:* The use of "associate" is an attempt to make employees feel more professional and thus more self-directing and accountable in their daily efforts. At Disneyland, for example, workers who meet the public are referred to as "the cast." If they think of themselves as performers, the theory goes, they will become more focused on customer satisfaction—a valuable asset if your business is entertainment. Similarly, big retail firms sometimes call their sales clerks associates in an attempt to add stature to jobs that the public, executives, and workers themselves regard as menial.
- *Stakeholder:* This term, used widely during the 1980s, is perhaps the most inclusive term for follower. A stakeholder is anyone who has a vested interest in the organization and what it does, including the side effects of its operations. From this perspective, a leader is a stakeholder, too, and this democratizing effect is one reason this term has gained currency among organizational theorists and enlightened practitioners alike. Of course, a person needn't be a member of an organization to be a stakeholder, so the word loses precision when made synonymous with "follower."
- *Constituent:* I've found this to be the most useful word for "follower" in the Green Glass Age. For some, "constituent" casts a political light on the leader-follower relationship, and that's not entirely bad. In politics, a constituency is a body of people from

whom a lawmaker or leader ascends and to whom that person is accountable. While the idea of reciprocity is not new in leadership, the notion that a leader outside of politics is somehow beholden, legally and morally, to those who are lower in the organizational hierarchy is often viewed as heresy. To be candid, that's one of the reasons I like it; so it's the word I'll use in place of "follower" for the remainder of this book.

The key idea behind "constituent" is consent. A person needn't be among an organization's anointed elite—in a top managerial position, for example—to play a significant leadership role, and a constituent may be only distantly involved with the leader's formal chain of command. What creates constituents is perceived membership in the leader's group and a shared belief: an identification with that group and a consequent willingness to act in its behalf. If that belief is strong enough, it becomes commitment, and constituents work to achieve mutual goals, whether or not the leader or peers are around to prod them on. Without such commitment, constituents act, at best, in mere compliance with the leader's directives, and devote little psychic energy to overcoming obstacles. This is the true, though usually unstated, social contract among constituents, and leaders ignore it at their peril. Sadly, most employees (followers) in organizations today are not true constituents.

One of the hardest lessons for old-style leaders to learn is summed up by the leadership scholar and writer James O'Toole, who writes, "Leaders must begin by setting aside that culturally conditioned 'natural' instinct to lead by push, particularly when times are tough. Leaders must instead adopt the unnatural behavior of always leading by the pull of inspiring values. The difficulty lies in that imperative 'always.'"[13]

ETHICS, AESTHETICS, AND CHARACTER: THE DNA OF LEADERSHIP

Finally we come to the preeminent task for those who would lead us into the next century: *New leaders must cultivate systems of ethics and aesthetics* that they can practice and pass on. This idea of leader as artist or moral architect may sound odd to people steeped in industrial-age mores, but it is the chief criterion by which future leaders will be judged. Key to the art of leadership is taking the measure of every decision based on a clear understanding of how ethics apply and to what extent lasting benefits will flow from the decision.

Ethics and aesthetics determine the nature of the leader's relationship with everyone around him or her—associates, constituents, board members, competitors, and those in personal life. They are the primary tools with which you can forge harmony between the personal *ki*, your own life force, and the universal *ki*, the forces outside. As the aikido master locates a center of gravity from which to practice, so must the leader develop an ethical and aesthetic "center of gravity" that will keep the organization in harmony, regardless of external attacks or changing environments. The leader's center may also be thought of as character—an old-fashioned but serviceable word.

Being a martial art, aikido deals with personal encounters from the standpoint of conflict, but it uses a much more subtle and complex definition of conflict than the industrial-age mentality does. Aikido approaches conflict in a revolutionary way, offering a rich body of knowledge and theory on how to deal with it. In fact, aikido's founder defined four "ethical levels" of conflict that seem to correspond well to the challenges facing aikido-style leaders:

1. On the lowest level, an unsuspecting and blameless defender is attacked without warning, the way a mugger assaults a victim. In business and politics, its analogue is economic or legal predation and exploitation—dog-eat-dog competition that shows no mercy and desolates both people and the environment.

2. The second level is what we might call aggravated assault. Here, the defender may provoke an attack by arguing with or taunting the attacker, sharing blame for the resulting violence. This level is comparable in business to "Don't get mad, get even." Office politics—and the politics of special interests—often orbits around this dynamic.

3. At the third ethical level, a blameless defender turns the tables and defeats the attacker. Outside aikido, this might be regarded as justifiable homicide, self-defense, or "winning is everything." Even though the defender may be justified, however, one party ends up

being injured. This can be extended to the idea, in sociopolitical terms, that the end justifies the means: as industrial-age leaders justify actions that make some people worse off in order to help a chosen few, or as they sacrifice family happiness and a balanced life in the name of increased productivity and career advancement. The attack-oriented martial arts, like karate, view this as the highest and most moral level of conflict.

4. Aikido masters see a level beyond the win-lose dynamic. To them, the fourth level is the highest and most ethical form of conflict resolution. In combat, a defender operating on this level diffuses or diverts the attack in such a way that *neither defender nor attacker is harmed*. As aikidoist Adele Westbrook says, "Only through neutralization of an aggressive action, rather then the aggressor himself, can harmony of existence be restored."[14] This fourth and highest ethical level offers the kind of win-win solution that leaders in the Green Glass Age must seek. Decision-makers should consider and, if possible, advance the interests of all constituents. More than anything else, it is the dimension of ethics and aesthetics that raises leadership to an art.

After giving a talk along these lines at a prominent business school, I was chided by a top accounting professor for even raising such issues in conjunction with leadership. "If you can't measure it," asked the exasperated academic, "what's the point of bringing it up?" His attitude is shared by many who are still imbued with the industrial-age mentality. They have become addicted, through time, tradition, and textbooks, to an overly rational, technique-dominated outlook that relegates the human spirit and intangibles like ethics and character to the back shelves of leadership study.

Character is not personality, nor is it the sum of our credentials, professional experience, or political skills. It is not even deep commitment to a goal, high energy in its pursuit, and unswerving loyalty to a person or an organization who shares our beliefs. These things all existed under the old-style industrial-age approach to leadership and still exist today. While they are often necessary for lasting success and well-being, they are not, by themselves, sufficient to achieve it.

When fully realized, character is the engine that drives these other qualities and chooses their direction. I regard character as a level of integrity and mental-spiritual well-being sufficient to get one through life's darkest trials and most glamorous successes. When that character begins to influence others, we have the beginning of leadership. Most failures of leadership, at least as I've observed them, are usually failures of character: a lack of resistance to the inner enemies that constantly seek to undermine us. To put it in terms our numbers-loving accounting professor would appreciate, character is not a scalar quantity (one that varies only in magnitude, like inches on a ruler), but a vector quantity, like the path of a guided missile, which gains much of its significance from the direction it takes.

Here are some other signposts for spotting leaders with highly developed character:

- *They don't need losers to feel like winners.* They are empathetic toward, not contemptuous of, others' failures, and they feel humble after their own victories. They are grateful to parents and teachers, and even to rivals and past antagonists, because they realize that important lessons can be learned from even the worst defeat.

- *They don't skate on the edges of truth; they gravitate toward its center.* They may try to explain failures, but they seldom rationalize them and they never prevaricate. If they put a spin on a disaster, it is to highlight the usefulness of the bruise, not to put the black eye on somebody else or make failure seem like success.

- *They don't confuse the person with the accomplishment or with the position.* They know a person is not the sum total of a résumé or paycheck. They take pleasure from their own achievements and share the pleasure of other achievers, but they never forget that perfection is only a direction, not a final destination.

- *They don't forget their human responsibilities.* They cherish and are grateful for the web of warm relationships that sustains them: family, friends, and community. And they use that web as a model for the other interpersonal networks they create. Helping those who have helped us, like helping those who cannot help themselves, validates our own good fortune and gives our joys and rewards a new luster.

All in all, leaders of good character hold themselves constantly ready for judgment by a higher power, even if that tribunal is nothing more or less than their own standards and beliefs. If future leadership models do not account for character, they will fail just as surely as those held over from the industrial age are failing us today.

The good news is that good character can be developed. All it takes is an acknowledgment of your human origins, a desire to learn from experience, and a willingness to become all that nature made you. As we proceed, you'll see how this path toward mastery unfolds.

2. The Face of Aikido-Style Leadership

[In aikido] the self is open, fluid, flexible, supple, and dynamic in body, mind and spirit.

—Kisshomaru Ueshiba

Not long ago, in Melbourne, Australia, a group of high-level leaders from business, the public sector, and nongovernment organizations took part in an unusual exercise. Gathered in a lovely Victorian mansion for a retreat to review their leadership, they turned a high-ceilinged ballroom into a makeshift dojo and took turns practicing basic aikido movements involving wrist holds and body rotation. The exercise culminated in a compelling demonstration of how an attack can be either resisted—usually in vain—or turned gently into a harmless encounter, with both participants moving harmoniously in the same direction. For some of these outwardly macho leaders, the demonstration was a powerful and surprising illustration of their potential to turn an aggressive competitor into a collaborator—and enjoy the process.

Aikido-style leaders are using a similar approach to form strategic alliances that enhance their practice of leadership. At a 1995 workshop for Silicon Valley CEOs, my attention was caught by one man who moved about the room completely at ease, chatting amiably with everyone, even those who might constitute future competition. He was Phil White, president of Informix, the world's fastest-growing global database company. His company's remarkable success is attributed to White's harmonious moves in putting together strategic partnerships with major high-tech firms including IBM, Hewlett-Packard, Sun, and Hitachi. He brings such value to his partnerships that companies are apt to go with Informix even if they are capable of developing databases in-house or with other firms. White's methods have made him one of Silicon Valley's most respected leaders, acknowledged as such by *Fortune* magazine in 1996.

The ability to turn conflict into harmony—identified in Chapter 1 as the fourth and highest ethical level of conflict in aikido—is central to the leader's task in our age. So are certain other skills and qualities closely related to the aikido model. In this chapter we'll look at the actual practice of aikido in closer detail, then see how the same elements translate into present-day leadership skills.

Since the practice of aikido takes place in the physical realm, you might wonder how it applies to the largely mental and psychological exercise of leadership. But it won't be hard to see the parallels unfold, for several reasons. First, the physical actions of aikido depend on the total commitment of mind and spirit to the task. Kisshomaru Ueshiba writes that "the unity of *ki*-mind-body . . . is the critical essence of aikido both in principle and in actual movement."[1] Second, as I suggested in Chapter 1, effective leadership in our age cannot be static or slow to respond to change. Today's leaders must think of themselves, in a sense, as artists of perpetual movement, ever prepared and poised for new challenges and opportunities coming from any direction. What we need now is a form of kinetic leadership—an idea that has a great deal in common with aikido.

WHEN GOOD INTENTIONS
STUMBLE OVER OLD MIND-SETS

Most current leaders grew up with and still believe in industrial-age models of leadership. They reckon the future by looking at the past; they think and communicate just fast enough to keep up with the present, not anticipate the future. To be sure, many leaders see the need to change their organizations, and they are willing to allocate resources toward it. Most, however, don't have a clear sense of what direction the change should take. Naturally inclined and constantly advised to be proactive, they often take steps that prove wasteful or even harmful. They don't start by looking deep within themselves, at their aspirations and apprehensions.

The experience of one executive in an international electronics firm illustrates the perils of action for its own sake, uninformed by introspection and a full commitment to change. His firm had begun an "empowerment" program for its thousands of technical-service reps. Its admirable aims were to "get closer to the customer" and make the front-line techies feel more accountable, creative, and self-directed. Because many of the company's products used cutting-edge technology, and because breakdowns could be costly for customers, these tech reps were under great pressure to respond to frequent, urgent calls for help.

Unfortunately, at the time the program was launched, the company was downsizing its middle management and reorganizing many operations—anxiety-provoking measures even without new-product problems. As a result, a communications gap opened between corporate headquarters and the first-line reps. Also, the chairman announced a "total quality initiative," expanded his direct surveillance over the technical reps, and increased the number, complexity, and frequency of reports required from the field. Less and less was left to the discretion of the "newly empowered" first-liners.

This situation eventually created discord among workers and managers trying to respond to conflicting demands. The reps split into two camps: those who still tried to get the job done, regardless of the system, and those who were content to play the paperwork game because that was what the company rewarded. Middle managers who survived the "right-sizing" formed alliances with superiors and subordinates they thought they could trust, regardless of who officially reported to whom. Soon the company began functioning literally on two sets of books: a formal executive information system that was almost entirely window dressing, and the informal networks that actually got things done. In other words, the more data the top executives tried to squeeze out of their employees, the less they knew about their business. The more things they tried to control remotely, the more things got out of hand at the local level.

At the conference where this young president and COO told his sad tale, I asked what he took from the experience. "Well," he replied, "I guess none of us really knew what empowerment meant. My human resources people sold me on this thing called empowerment training, but it never really did what we needed, which was to create an atmosphere of trust and initiative. And for my boss, the chairman, the lack of control was just too hard to take. My boss lives by control, even in his personal life. His need for control subverted my attempts to create trust, to let people feel their own power."

The chairman had never really *delegated* authority at all; instead, he *relegated* it to a system, substituting paper for people and keeping authority where it always had been—at the top. When the going got tough, as it usually does during a change, he got anxious and let his old instincts take over—that is, he tried to lead with the "push" of more controls rather than the "pull" of shared values. Real empowerment and mutual trust can be realized only through decentralization of power and voluntary assumption of accountability. However laudable the intent of the company's initiatives, the timing was ill-chosen and the appropriate leadership qualities were lacking.

Most of us who work in groups face similar dilemmas every day. When old systems of coping are changed by circumstances or design, we feel as if we're caught on an ice floe. Wherever we look—into the executive suite or down the lines on an organizational chart—cracks suddenly seem to open wide beneath us. When our ice floe heads toward the waterfall—facing product quality problems, for example, or the threat of global competition—mistrust increases and anxiety turns to panic. We make bad decisions or implement good decisions badly, and we substitute blind instinct for reasoned intuition, as the anxious chairman did.

Reshuffling top-level staff, launching new programs, and drumming up catchy slogans are among the things we do when we don't know quite what to do. Such knee-jerk responses to change are one reason we often overshoot the mark as leaders and then, like a pendulum, find ourselves retreating, driving our constituents crazy. To those addicted to action, as most industrial-age leaders are, monkey motion is a great substitute for thought. "Do something, even if it's wrong" becomes a desperate strategy for leaders seeking to revive organizations stricken by postindustrial trauma. But all the reaction they may get is the squeeze of a hand that's already dead.

THE CALM CENTER IN THE WHIRLING SPHERE: MOVING TOWARD AIKIDO-STYLE LEADERSHIP

Action implies the use of energy. The art of aikido focuses on using energy to bring attackers and defenders into harmony—and what works for individuals can work for organizations, too. Intellectually, this notion of marshaling energy to unite and achieve individual and group goals is easy to grasp, but people steeped in industrial-age thinking often find it difficult to put into practice. They feel ill at ease examining deeply held beliefs about competition and the self-image of winners and losers.

How can we tell purposive action from action for action's sake? What principles should guide the choices we make? To answer, I'll start by briefly sketching a scenario that's a world apart from the undirected flailing of many companies, including the electronics firm we just observed.

Aikido students in a bright, clean dojo sit in the classical *seiza* pose, backs upright, hands on knees. They begin a practice session by bowing in respect to the founder of the art and to their teacher, the *sensei.* They may go on to practice certain individual exercises, notably the centered stance called *hanmi,* and a series of smoothly energized forward and backward shoulder rolls, similar to somersaults. Then they pair off and work on a wide range of movement techniques for attack and counterattack, all of them proceeding from a fundamental principle of spherical rotation.

The *nage*—the "leader" of the pair—is always the defender. He or she responds to an attack by moving in a circular fashion around a stable center of gravity. As described by Kisshomaru Ueshiba, the son of aikido's founder, "when the opponent moves forward, one avoids the linear thrust and enters into the opening outside his vision. . . . The point here is swift, sure footwork where one's center takes over the opponent's center . . . and when he loses his center, he also loses all power. Then he is subdued swiftly and decisively. . . . [T]he emphasis on spherical rotation gives the visual impression of a smoothly flowing, choreographed dance."[2]

The end result of such an encounter, if performed properly, is that the attacker—sometimes several attackers in advanced practice—is thrown to the ground, where he can be kept helpless, though uninjured by a wrist- or handhold.

To a spectator, aikido can be deceptively uneventful because of its lack of apparent violence, but it is no less effective than other martial arts. Achieving the impression of a "smoothly flowing, choreographed dance" depends on the mastery, hard-won through long practice, of closely interwoven physical and mental skills.

Central to both the physical art and the philosophy of aikido is *centering*—the sense of wholeness and sureness one gains when body, brain, and spirit work in harmony with one's environment. Aikidoists find that the centering gained from their practice brings great benefits to other areas of life. And centering also can grow out of other kinds of committed practice. Since this concept is so fundamental and important, it seems wise to explore it in more detail here, particularly as it applies to leadership.

In the West, we often talk about the center of the human body, in reference to our physical center of gravity, the point around which our weight is more or less equally distributed. This physical center lies somewhere in the lower abdomen, slightly below the navel—our first point of connection to life. The center of gravity is important in martial arts—and indeed in other sports as well—because it dictates our degree of balance. If our center of gravity gets too far ahead of us, behind us, or off to one side, we lose our balance and must scramble to recover it—or fall down. This is the key to many of aikido's defensive techniques. If attackers become overextended—and a defender using aikido encourages this—they lose their balance and become vulnerable.

Anything that raises the center of gravity makes a person less stable. Just imagine teetering on a tall ladder or walking around with a heavy box balanced on your head, and you'll get the idea. Conversely, anything that lowers the center of gravity makes one more stable and harder to move. It's tough to knock someone over if he or she is already close to the ground. Therefore many techniques in martial arts require lowering one's center of gravity. This usually involves widening your stance, bending your legs, and so on, so that you will remain fully balanced and in control while executing a surprisingly wide range of movements.

But aikidoists also speak of *ki,* which Kisshomaru Ueshiba defines as "the world-forming energy which also lies at the core of each human being, waiting to be realized."[3] He goes on, "By virtue of the subtle working of *ki* we harmonize mind and body and the relationship between the individual and the universe." They conceive of this energy emanating from one's center, and the use of *ki* as crucial to mastering both the physical and mental skills of their art. How does this elusive Eastern concept relate to the rational, easily grasped idea of a physical center of gravity? Are we back in the land of metaphor, or metaphysics, or is something physical happening here as well?

In fact, the mind-body connection is real, and it's more obvious than you may think. You can demonstrate it easily to yourself without subscribing to any metaphysical beliefs. First, temporarily set aside all of those mechanistic notions you've learned about the production of energy through conventional physics. There is no "engine" in our abdomen that emits a special force, like some kind of strange electrical current. There is no special *ki* gland or organ that produces measurable phenomena, beyond the neural impulses, muscular contractions, hormonal secretions, and other normal manifestations of physiological functions that science has known about for years.

What may be new to you, and what has only lately become the object of serious scientific study, is the power our minds can exert over many physiological functions. In his book *Mastery,* George Leonard gives us a simple way to demonstrate the mind-body connection:

> Try this: stand normally and draw your attention to the top of your body by tapping yourself a couple of times on the forehead. Then have a partner push you from behind at the shoulder blades just hard enough to make you lose your balance and take a step forward. Next, stand exactly the same way and draw your attention to your center by tapping yourself a couple of times about an inch or two below the navel. Then have your partner push you exactly the same way with exactly the same force as before. Most people find they are more stable with their attention on their centers.[4]

Some master aikidoists with years of centering experience claim they can make themselves virtually immovable using similar techniques. True or not, the margin for argument is only one of degree. The fact is, centering works. As demonstrated in the techniques of biofeedback and meditation, our minds can control a surprisingly wide range of bodily responses, just as our body's condition often influences our mental and emotional state.

Ki can be defined in different ways, but for our purposes it's useful to think of it as the force, the current of energy, that animates the network of mind-body-surroundings. When activated by a master in the martial arts, *ki* energy is responsible for physical feats that often strike us as miraculous. From the perspective of leadership, *ki* is both a physiological force and a mental tool that allows us to gain more control over the mind-body connection, thereby increasing our ability to change attitudes and behavior patterns that are influenced by it.

When mind, body, and spirit are disunited—for example, when we are being hypocritical, telling our constituents one thing while practicing another—we fracture that unified center and lose our balance, just as when our physical center of gravity is too far displaced. Our fall may be physical—that is, the stress from an imbalanced life may lead to headaches, stomach troubles, or insomnia—or it may be mental, causing us to misstate or to speak in halfhearted, confused, and inconsistent ways. If we are uncentered in our personal lives, with great discrepancies between how we live and how we feel, we may hesitate to commit fully to relationships (or commit to only unhealthy relationships), develop secretive or deviant behavior, or bottle up great rage. Seriously disunited or uncentered people are great candidates for substance abuse and make very erratic performers. They do not become enduring leaders.

THE TOOLS OF LEADERSHIP AIKIDO

For leaders seeking mastery, the physical skills of aikido can be understood metaphorically, the mental or spiritual ones quite literally. Since it's not my purpose to teach aikido, I choose to focus on those that relate most directly to the leader's tasks: in resolving conflict, in maintaining calmness and clear vision in the midst of chaos, and in focusing action effectively.

Using Trust, Intuition, and Control

Practitioners of aikido find it difficult to analyze and convey precisely what makes the art so effective. Much of the achievement in aikido, as in other traditional Japanese arts such as sword-making, "is due to an intuitive quality known as the working of *kan,* and this can be acquired only through the accumulation of years of training," notes Kisshomaru Ueshiba. "For *kan*-intuition to work," he continues, "one must experience a creative tension stemming from single-minded concentration on the work in progress. . . . [T]he ultimate essence of aikido . . . is such that as long as one strives on the path of training with the goal of achieving it, the realization will come sooner or later. This kind of trust . . . will unlock the heart of aikido and bring the ultimate essence to realization."[5] In other words, mastery in aikido comes as a form of intuition that can be experienced but not really described. And it comes only after years of faithful practice in which one is sustained by trust.

Trusting one's intuition, trusting that one's focused practice of leadership over time will bring the desired results, is difficult for leaders who have been trained to believe that their efforts are subject to scientific analysis, rigorous controls, and numerical evaluation. But trust is the essence of leadership as an art. Master leaders can trust their intuition because they have patiently honed it to a sharp edge. They can also trust their relationships with colleagues and collaborators, because they strove to develop the ethical and aesthetic qualities of those relationships. At times when the future is unclear, intuition—call it educated guessing or gut feelings—can be far more useful than formal logic.

More often, alas, leaders give up on trust and intuition for the illusion of total control, especially when they are under pressure, like the company chairman in the preceding account. It is tough to give up the certainty of control that worked in the past, such as hierarchical management structures. And relinquishing control will always produce anxiety before it produces success. That's where trust comes in again: trust that one's efforts will succeed, even if quick evidence is not manifested.

Postindustrial leaders need to trust in more than their own experience; they must be guided by how well their own experience fits into a larger global picture. They know that the whole is often more than the sum of its parts, that nobody has a monopoly on good ideas, and that sometimes you have to let go and trust someone else's way of doing things. This is not a new idea, even in the West, but its real power is only now becoming widely appreciated.

Take for example the Todd Company, which for more than five generations has quietly based its global operations—extracting, processing, and selling essential oils—on local partnerships that cater to the needs and tastes of regional markets, not on the preconceptions and dictates of a headquarters elite. Their business relationships are based on trust derived from consistent quality, fair pricing, customer service, and close personal contact. When young cousins join the firm, they learn to work directly with growers and customers, and they gradually establish lasting bonds with their counterparts who provide raw materials or who buy their products.

For example, when customers began requesting just-in-time inventory support to stay competitive, the Todd Company complied immediately, writing off the additional costs. What they lost in the short run, they will make up for many times over in long-term, large-scale results. By all measures, the company scores high in growth, diversification, profit, capital improvements, and technological enhancements—not just over one or two years but decade after decade. Enduring success like this occurs only in an environment of trust, where meeting supplier and customer needs is not only expected: it's the norm. And it creates ties that span generations.[6]

Staying Flexible, Rolling out of Trouble, Landing on Your Feet

Some of the basic skills of aikido cultivate the ability to be resilient, to avoid an attack by literally rolling out of its path, either forward or backward, then coming upright in a low, centered stance. Paradoxically, this action—known as going to the ground—can give the aikidoist a remarkable sense of strength. As one woman student comments, "I couldn't even do a somersault when I began aikido, so when I took my first forward roll, I felt like my day was made. Within half a year my body became light as a ball when I was thrown. I think aikido made me stronger as a person." Staying flexible and organizationally light on your feet, knowing when and how to sidestep trouble, and bouncing back quickly are key attributes for successful leaders and organizations of the future.

Industrial-age and Green Glass Age leaders employ two substantially different approaches to managing their careers. In the old days, apprentice leaders could rely on a fairly stable command-and-control hierarchy. Once they learned their way around its sources of authority, and around the office politics, they could expect to move up the corporate ladder, staying within the same system for most of their careers.

In the future, though, even old-style corporate "intrapreneurs," if they expect to succeed, will have to think and act more like real entrepreneurs—taking real risks, marshaling independent resources, and making lasting alliances based on mutual respect as well as temporary need. In fact, Charles Handy predicts that by the year 2000, half the working population will be employed outside traditional organizations.[7] Already, almost a third of working-age Americans are employed as temps, part-timers, or independent contractors. In Europe, that number is close to half the workforce.

Similar contrasts can be seen in yesterday's and today's organizations. Old-style enterprises succeeded because they bent markets to their will. Postindustrial firms will succeed because they themselves adapt to changing markets. Industrial-age companies planned in linear fashion, one move building on another: design the product, develop it, then take it to market in an orderly way, utilizing economies of scale and other "scientific" marketing principles, such as the ability of mass production to reduce the cost of each unit. This approach actually created our modern consumer economy, led in part by Sears Roebuck's nineteenth-century concept of finding out what people wanted, then getting it to them no matter what—in a way that made them feel good about themselves, the product, and the retailer. Unfortunately, the very success of this approach eventually produced an institutionalized, cookie-cutter mentality that isolated Sears—and other big retailers, like J. C. Penney, who followed its model—from their customers. When postindustrial retailers like Wal-Mart began viewing their markets as an endless series of detours rather than as one long superhighway of progress, they began building their business around a philosophy of continuous experimentation with their supplier-partners. In consequence, the old-style firms like Sears rapidly lost market share and customer loyalty.

With a new focus on customized products and quality rather than cost competition alone, tomorrow's leaders will base their plans on open-ended scenarios that unfold in a wide variety of patterns, leaving plenty of room for improvisation, side trips, and diversions. As Ueshiba says, "The person in accord with the principle of universal change moves with lightness and agility."[8] Likewise, the organizations they lead will tend to be smaller, self-managed, quicker to respond, and more resilient, gaining economies of scale by collaboration, through networks tailored to specific territorial, product, or functional needs.

One current example of this collaborative environment is Cellular One, a highly successful joint venture formed by competing telecommunications companies. In a constantly de- and re-regulated environment, it's hard to tell how long this particular alliance will last, but the method that propelled Cellular One to prominence can be seen in similar experiments elsewhere, and more are on the way. It's noteworthy that Susan Swenson, a female aikido-style leader who must be well centered and flexible, gracefully directs this collaborative venture.

Questions of Balance

In talking about centering we saw how important it is for the aikidoist to develop an awareness of balance and the ability to stay balanced even when in whirling motion. The art does not demand that one be perfectly balanced at all times. It is more fluid than that, allowing for both rising (a form of yang) and falling (a form of yin). The key is allowing oneself to get out of balance, in confidence that it can shortly be recovered.

Such questions of balance come into play constantly in the practice of leadership today, though they did not greatly concern industrial-age leaders. On the frontier, there was only one perceived direction of movement: forward. Today, though, leaders and organizations need to consider balance in resource use, in evaluating economic return against full return in the lives of their constituents and in their own lives.

Industrial-age leaders are used to thinking in terms of economic return, in a narrow sense. Is the business making enough to justify the trouble of running it, or would we be better off putting our money in T-bills? And if the company is making a profit, is that profit all it could be? By answering these questions in a way that served investors, leaders assumed they were serving society too, since nobody would buy unsatisfactory products, and since the profits generated the capital needed for new investments.

Postindustrial leaders, on the other hand, know we are all responsible not only for our own success but to some extent for the quality of life experienced by those around us. They recognize that the traditional ingredients of economic return are being supplanted by other criteria that can have just as much impact on a company's long-term health. I call these new criteria full returns because they measure not only profit but economic growth, product safety, ethical conduct, resource conservation, and social awareness—standards the modern market actually uses to pick long-term survivors.

There is perhaps no better example of such a survivor than Hewlett-Packard, a firm that employs tens of thousands in nine states and sixteen foreign countries. H-P has gracefully built a business on finding the best people and nimbly moving from market to market—from manufacturing electronic test gear in the 1940s to medical instrumentation in the 1960s, then to personal computing in the 1970s and 1980s and on to advanced high-tech systems in the 1990s. Its leaders have pursued a path to enduring success by being clear and consistent about values, always balancing issues of quality, profit, ethics, and human needs, and by being flexible about products, processes, service, and technology.

Industrial-age leaders tend to think of employees as "labor costs" rather than productive assets. While a fundamental conflict may exist between the owners' right to control their property and the workers' right to enjoy the full benefits of their labor, that conflict can more constructively be seen as a balancing act rather than a contest. For every industrial-age company like Continental Airlines, whose bare-knuckles leadership by Frank Lorenzo in the mid-1980s set a new low in labor relations, there are people-centered organizations like Hewlett-Packard and the Todd Company, which are finding new ways to resolve old conflicts. A study of six thousand randomly selected Du Pont employees, conducted by an independent Boston research firm, found that such enlightened work-family options as job sharing, flex-time, childcare, and elderly relative care resulted in more productivity among the workers who availed themselves of these programs. Researcher Charles Rodgers concluded that "This study shows that management practices that respond to the needs of the labor force are very effective as tools to make the workforce more committed and more engaged."

Successful Green Glass Age companies won't be run like health clubs or social service organizations, but their constituencies will be broader and their leaders will be held more accountable for what their organizations do to our society as well as for it.

Critical Timing

> The martial arts considered intelligence foremost because intelligence involves the ability to plan and to know when to change effectively.
>
> —Sun Tzu, *The Art of War*

Master leaders must fully understand the dynamic relationship between preparation and execution. The leadership art of planning links the amount, style, and intensity of practice with the correct focus and timing for action. The old joke in marketing and product development concerns the brilliant planner who prepared long and hard and finally introduced a product called 6-Up. When it comes to timing, there's no such thing as "almost right."

In aikido, the defender seeking a black belt is attacked in rapid succession by three seasoned black belts. He or she must remain calm, maintain a low center of gravity, and be alert for each attack. Timing of response is critical, since there is scant opportunity to appraise the opponent's tactic, get ready, calm the mind, and feel one's feet on the mat. Instincts honed by countless hours of practice must take over, allowing the defender to gauge the timing of each response in milliseconds.

Most business decisions seem to be rationally conceived and supported by a deliberate planning process. But wise leaders, like Intel CEO Andy Grove, know that timing is anything but an exact science. When is the perfect moment to introduce the next-generation chip? If you bring it out too early, you lose millions in your Pentium inventory. Delay too long, and your competitor moves ahead.

Although Grove claims, tongue in cheek, that paranoia is the secret of leadership success in the seismic world of Silicon Valley, the truth is that planning, preparation, and finely honed timing instincts give Intel its edge. Its leadership team prepares more rigorously than competitors to vector in on the swirling future of computing and telecommunications for well-timed product introductions. No one is allowed to get comfortable at Intel. People's assignments shift every 1.8 years, on the average. Managers are required to take part in aikidolike verbal sparring, in which ideas and plans can be attacked and defended without harm resulting; a stronger third position usually emerges from the fray.[9]

The environment at Intel might be compared to a dojo; lots of time is spent in preparation, searching for computer enlightenment, and feeling out critical timing. As Sun Tzu said of the martial arts, intelligence to plan and change is what's prized.[10]

Seeing Clearly and Noticing Well

It was . . . just a matter of clarity of mind and body. When the opponent attacked, I could see a flash of white light, the size of a pebble, flying before the sword. . . . All I did was avoid the streams of white light.

—Morihei Ueshiba

The founder of aikido describes other occasions "when the center of *ki* is concentrated in one's mind and body" and he could intuitively see the thoughts—including the violent intentions—of an opponent. In one case far removed from the rituals of the dojo, he was traveling in Inner Mongolia in 1924 when his party was attacked by Chinese Nationalists. Ueshiba is said to have avoided the oncoming bullets merely by a slight shifting of his body.[11]

Using the techniques of centering, calming, and focusing *ki* can enhance any leader's ability to read the intentions of others and thereby disarm any who might pose danger. It can even enable a person to foresee larger trends in business and society, to great advantage. Someone who learned how to "see clearly and notice well," partly through his study of aikido, is Phillip Moffitt, a quintessential entrepreneur for our age. Moffitt, with his partners, bought the faltering *Esquire* magazine in the early 1980s and restored it to its former vigor.

Moffitt, a newcomer to the parochial world of New York publishing, was the subject of virulent media attacks during his tenure as *Esquire*'s owner and editor-in-chief. Instead of fighting back directly, however, or allowing his center of gravity to be shifted by the attacks, he saw through to the provincialism at their core and deflected them by pursuing a vision of a magazine unlike all the others he was expected to imitate. Further, he demonstrated an almost uncanny ability to sniff out and publish stories on trends that would soon sweep through the nation's consciousness—topics like mind-body connections, male sexuality, and extending life through nutrition.

At the end of the decade, Moffitt sold the Esquire group, and he moved to California, where he founded a software applications company called Lightsource—and gained his black belt in aikido. In his new role as president of the Life Balance Institute, he has brought his clarity of vision and mindful awareness to fostering aikido leadership among business and professional practitioners. It was Moffitt who led the seminar on aikido-style blending in the Australian workshop I mentioned earlier in the chapter.

With a strong background also in yoga and meditation, Moffitt is well aware of the need to see oneself as clearly as one perceives others. When asked what he has learned from his own transition to a mentor of leaders, Moffitt says, "There is an almost magical interplay between self-knowledge and the discovery that in every situation the leader has options. So often leaders self-destruct because they are possessed by unacknowledged anxiety, which narrows their vision so they see only one option to the specter of failure. Aikido teaches two things superbly: it helps one find one's own ground so fear can be acknowledged and released, and it shows one how to find options so the most harmonious way can be chosen."[12]

The Power of Focused Intention

Aikidoists know that focused intention—the highly disciplined channeling of *ki* energy—can be far more potent than brute muscular strength. Aikido's founder, Morihei Ueshiba, had been a legendary expert in several other martial arts but realized with advancing age that they were too dependent on strength alone. This, in part, led him to develop aikido. As Terry Dobson relates in *Aikido in Everyday Life*, "He saw that all his training, all his knowledge, was founded upon the principle of physical strength. He could hit harder, move faster, and dodge better than his opponents. But for how long? Like the aging gunfighter in American Westerns, Ueshiba was a ripe target for every younger, faster, stronger warrior who came along."[13] George Leonard assured me that the master Ueshiba's greatness came after he was seventy years old.

The language of industrial-age leaders was replete with swaggering male imagery of strength and violence. The dependence on aggression and raw power can work for a while, but focused attention is what works in the long run. Lee Iacocca, famous in the auto industry for his macho talk, was quoted on the subject of Japanese imports invading the United States: "We are going to kick their asses back into the Pacific."[14] Not only did his prediction go wrong, but also the industry eventually had to bow to the superiority of exports.

More recently, much press attention has focused on the Wild West tactics of the cable industry, especially those of John Malone, chief of TCI. Notoriously brusque, tough, and commanding, he made good copy for the business magazines. His empire was vast and his power to stop other giants like Ted Turner and the baby Bells from poaching on his turf was the stuff of old robber-baron legends. Yet, ultimately his style has not made TCI a great leader in the telecommunications business. In fact, the company is in retrenchment, operating losses are running high, and Malone is slashing staff and putting service-enhancement promises on hold. Those he once frustrated now have the power to hold him in thrall.

Even casual observers of an aikido encounter are amazed to witness how smaller or apparently weaker masters of the art can render helpless much larger opponents. Phillip Moffitt describes his own experience of young, muscular black belts going against the older, wiser, supple bodies of masters: "It was remarkable how little effort the masters used to disarm the attackers. Their energy was so powerful and graceful, and their ability to use the energy of the attacker so perfect in timing and execution. The throws were lightning-fast, and the masters were utterly calm, relaxed, and joyous. The falls look hard, but every attacker reported that it was like landing on a cloud—now that's harmony."[15]

Another image that conveys the power of focused intention is the ability of a slender reed or splinter of wood to pierce a solid tree, when blown by the force of a typhoon or tornado. Ueshiba himself says, "Anyone should be able to hold another person down with one finger."[16] Of course, this is easy to say but may call for a lifetime of practice to realize.

Ben Cohen, the co-founder and currently chairman of Ben & Jerry's Ice Cream, is a leader who flourished through the power of focused intention. Ice cream is and was Ben's ruling passion. He and his partner succeeded in carving out market space for their small Vermont company despite intense, and illegal, retailer pressure from the market giant Häagen-Dazs. Their success was due partly to a fierce devotion to product quality, a canny sense of the ice cream–loving public's tastes, and a tongue-in-cheek approach to their image that set them apart. They made great strides in a relatively short time because they concentrated fully on a single goal, followed their best instincts, and learned what they needed to learn about business—instead of starting out with the idea of creating a food-retailing empire.

Ben Cohen also illustrates the important distinction between focused intention and the obsessive-compulsive behavior that overtakes so many talented leaders. The person who is an obsessive-compulsive is simply not in charge of significant portions of his or her life, but is under the control of a demonic striving that flings aside considerations of family, community, self-development, and small pleasures. Whereas a person with focused intention, as demonstrated by Ben Cohen, brings conscious effort to the task of harmonizing working goals with these other values. The leader who uses it acknowledges that fairness, learning, aesthetics, nature, and relationships are always to be honored. Ben's social advocacy is well known, and he is also devoted to his son, his friends, education, and sculpture. But his core interest—making a good product that brings people pleasure—has not dimmed. In making the transition from CEO to chairman, he has remained involved in product development; after I last met with him, he was off on his bicycle to tour stores, sample products, and meet salespeople and customers.

John Malone of TCI recently took a long sabbatical from his day-to-day role, a self-imposed exile on his boat in Maine. Perhaps it will help him adopt a calmer, more centered approach to his work. By all accounts his intelligence is exceptional, so surely he is capable of learning that the strength of focused intention will be a more effective tool in his business future than the brute force of old.

BEYOND WINNING AND LOSING

While the blush of victory is sweet and brief, bitter defeat can leave scars that last a lifetime. A glance through any history book or the headlines of any newspaper will show how yesterday's vanquished often become—or at least struggle mightily to be victors. From this perspective, win-lose, go-for-the-thr always produce lose-lose outcomes in the long run. The energy created by such contests is never completely dissipated.

The shortsightedness of industrial-age leaders causes them to value short-term victories too highly, no matter how they are obtained and despite the long-term problems they create. Postindustrial, aikido-style leaders, on the other hand, believe only lasting victories are desirable. They know that not all conflicts must be viewed as contests—which by definition require a loser.

If Lee Iacocca was the pinup model of the conflict-driven industrial-age leader, a contrasting example of an emerging aikido-style leader may be Nelson Rising, CEO of Catellus Development Corporation. Catellus, the successor company to the Southern Pacific and Atchison, Topeka & Santa Fe railroads, is an enormous owner of real estate: Rising's job is to manage and develop $1.8 billion in land and income property in eleven states. No one could accuse Catellus or Rising of having a wimpy background. The company is the progeny of rough, tough railroad ancestors; Rising, when I first met him, was an aide to John Tunney, the scrappy former U.S. senator from California (who is the son of heavyweight fighter Gene Tunney). But Rising shows signs of becoming a leader with a true win-win philosophy of succeeding by collaboration, as the following story illustrates.

Catellus owned a 50-acre parcel in the heart of downtown Santa Fe, the site of the town's historic rail yards. The property was coveted by the city for an urban park and civic structures; however, in booming Santa Fe it was immensely valuable and eminently developable for commercial uses. Developers like Catellus tend to have two natural enemies—no-growth local governments and environmentalists—but Nelson Rising entered into negotiations with Santa Fe leaders and their broker in the transaction, the Trust for Public Land, with a view toward selling the land to the city if terms could be worked out.

Rising's explanation of his actions is an instructive example of aikido-style leadership in action. "I think development can be a very creative and positive process," he said. "It doesn't have to be rape, pillage, and plunder . . . [but] it became clear to me that Santa Fe did not want this development and that no amount of persuasion would change that. I concluded that if there was a way to structure a

what it needed while protecting my
...at we should do."[17]

...Fe got its land and Catellus made out well
...ing, "we received cash, and we'll receive tax
...nd was sold for less than its current market
... where a potentially costly dispute was resolved
... parties. Such win-win scenarios don't happen without e... ...e will and a focused intention must be there to even
get the a... ...ment off the ground.

The Anatomy of Mastery

The aikido-style skills described above are indispensable tools for leaders pursuing the path of mastery. Another set of concepts that will serve developing leaders well is a kind of vocabulary of mastery formulated by George Leonard. Leonard identifies five key aspects of mastery in any field: *instruction, practice, intention, edge, and acceptance.*[18] Let's look closely at each one:

1. *Instruction:* At its lowest level, the instruction is the transfer of knowledge, but it also means handing down a tradition, inculcating an attitude, and developing a particular worldview—that of the master. In the master-apprentice relationship, this sort of instruction must always come from a specific person, even if that person lived centuries ago and is known to you only from books. To attempt to achieve mastery alone, without instruction, is to risk getting stuck in old mistakes. I encourage any leader in search of mastery to begin by searching out teachers and mentors, a task we'll address in Chapter 4.

2. *Practice:* This is not practice as musicians and athletes use the term—the repetition of fundamental techniques in order to build skills—but practice the way it is used by the best physicians: the lifelong search for perfection in an art for which they have been trained. Of course, the conduct of such practice is full of ups and downs, lateral diversions, and broad plateaus where personal and professional stagnation hang in the air like vultures. Perseverance is the only remedy, and once you've experienced break-

ing through to a new level, you may even come to enjoy the plateaus.

3. *Intention:* Every action has a purpose, and that purpose must relate to the philosophy underlying the act. This is sometimes difficult to see in isolation, but intention usually becomes clear when we view an action as part of a larger pattern. For example, martial arts instructors usually require students to observe certain rituals at the beginning and end of each practice session. Novice often consider this a nuisance—until they realize that such rituals, when conscientiously performed, imbue the student with both humility and self-discipline—important requisites for any master.

4. *Edge:* An edge is the place where something stops, like the edge of a knife or a table; but an edge can be sharpened and extended—by whetting the blade or inserting a leaf in the table. In the quest for mastery, this means working to the limits of your own capability while learning specific techniques and then extending those boundaries once you've mastered them—at least to the degree that you are able.

5. *Acceptance:* Leonard's term for this last quality is "surrender," but I've found that "acceptance" comes closer to what the best leaders—and perhaps the great masters in many other arts as well—do in practice. Acceptance means that they subordinate their ego to the demands of their art and lay it as an offering on the altar of success. In doing so, they admit that they are no greater than the discipline they hope to master; indeed, they accept that they will always be smaller than the art's potential, though they become the grandest master of all.

Leonard puts great store in "practice" as a noun: something you do for its own sake as a regular and integral part of your life, not something you do to achieve a specific goal. "For a master," he says, "the rewards gained along the way are fine, but they are not the main reason for the journey. Ultimately, the master and the master's path are one."

Another master, Mihaly Csikszentmihalyi, a brilliant researcher in the areas of happiness and creativity, wrote a groundbreaking book about the state of "flow"—a fine example of *ki* in action.[19] Most people who attain competence in a difficult task experience flow, often quite unexpectedly. A person "in flow" acts with a high degree of effectiveness and assurance, often achieving great outcomes while guided by intuition alone. Time seems to stand still during flow, and the person experiencing it often feels euphoric, even ecstatic.

It's not that all rational processes stop during the flow state—far from it. It's simply that the conscious mental and physical processes needed to learn and perform a certain task, or combination of tasks, are so fully integrated that they become unconscious, allowing a master to perform at a very high level almost automatically and for extended periods of time. Surgeons have reported feeling "in flow" for hours during a challenging operation, as have pilots in combat, athletes in championship games, and jazz musicians and public speakers "on a roll." Jim Whitaker, the first American to climb Mount Everest, insists that his life since Everest has been lived in a more or less continuous state of flow, whether he is climbing mountains, tending to his business, or engaging in a wide range of social and political activities.[20]

Obviously, flow is possible only for those people whose mind-body energies are well centered and focused. When these forces become disunited, flow stops, though it can be rekindled quickly with practice.

Attaining a high level of leadership mastery requires both conscious practice at specific tasks and an unconscious "letting go" and opening of the self to outside influences. George Leonard's vocabulary of mastery can serve as a template for the tasks we set ourselves. Even the greatest talent left unshaped by self-discipline and caring instruction can remain wasteful and unproductive.

But our self-guided course in mastery must leave room for the unpredictable. I had a friend who flew thousands of miles on a regular basis to take lessons from a great and famous teacher. I asked one day what he and his teacher discussed during these rare and expensive sessions, and my jubilant friend replied, "Oh, photography, fly fishing, natural history, cooking, you name it—a hundred things and sometimes nothing at all." When I remarked that both his enthusiasm and his out-of-pocket expenses seemed a little high for the services rendered, he shot back, "Not at all! I'm getting double my money's worth: it's good for my soul as well as my mind—a can't-miss investment!" I had learned a little more about mastery.

We are in charge of our own learning, our therapy, our growth. If we get very good at that task—leaving room for wonderful accidents and respecting the power of serendipity and synchronicity—the rest will take care of itself.

DEVELOP YOUR *HARA*

The Japanese have a term, *hara,* that expresses the effects of positive *ki* in a well-centered person. *Hara* means "stomach" or "belly." It is also used in a metaphorical sense to denote tolerance and motivation—the way we speak of someone "having the stomach" for a difficult task. Martial arts master Herman Kauz explains that "In describing a way of functioning that is down-to-earth, big-hearted and reflective of a broad and deep understanding of human life, the Japanese speak approvingly of a person acting from his *hara* or of having a big *hara.* . . . It implies an acceptance of the idea that we are connected with the world and with one another. We are not separated from the rest of life."[21]

A central task for you, or for any leader, then, is to develop and shape your *hara:* the ability to center and harmonize the energy produced by your mind, body, and spirit so as to better cope with your environment—the part that nourishes you, and the part that tests you. The transactions involved in growing *hara* may be small—a ritual greeting, perhaps—or large—a formidable task that demands all your resources and concentration. But big or small, with each transaction you are working toward the same end: to protect yourself from worldly dangers, yet leave the world better off for your having passed through it.

Practitioners of aikido and other martial arts are able to work on their *hara* in the sheltered environment of the dojo; some academics have a similar privilege. But most leaders don't operate in a dojo, the warm, secure womb of a great teacher's classroom. The wider world must become our dojo, the place of enlightenment where our self-directed journey toward mastery can unfold. In this workplace-as-dojo leaders must train themselves to discover *hara:* in their mentors and superiors, in colleagues, in those who may emerge as future leaders, and of course in themselves.

Simply put, *hara* can be seen wherever it operates. I often compare the homes and workplaces of master leaders to the typical aikido dojo. They are typically relaxed, good-humored places where both master and students nourish their strength, develop new skills and insights, and grow their *hara*. This is in contrast to the typical karate studio, where the atmosphere is often rigid, stressful, and competitive—like the offices of many industrial-age companies. Here are some qualities that demonstrate *hara* in operation.

The person with *hara*

- *Has an abiding sense of purpose.* This is different from strong goal orientation or the single-mindedness of an overcommitted workaholic. For example, those who talked with Jonas Salk, a great medical leader with an unrelenting schedule, often sensed the basic altruism that lay just below the surface of everything he said, no matter what the topic. Not every discussion eventually turned to medical research, but it was clear that a genuine desire to better the human condition ran through every fiber of Salk's being—a powerful common thread that united his thoughts and actions and pulled him through many of life's hills and valleys.[22]
- *Always seems to be in balance, even in the midst of chaos.* People with well-developed *hara* can move quickly and decisively but seldom seem rushed or flustered. Their emotional and spiritual center of gravity is very stable, providing an excellent platform for action. They take the long view of life's challenges, and they consider both triumphs and tragedies to be only one part—and a transitory part at that—of the master's journey. What matters to them is practice: doing what they do.
- *Views teaching or mentoring as a joyous obligation to his or her art.* Obviously one can become a master and never take a pupil. But the most valuable master leaders are always accessible to students with the proper motivation. They see the development of other leaders as an obligation—their duty to repay society for what they have taken out. In this light, teaching is but a further step in a master's own development, another avenue for learning, a way to test ideas and discover new techniques and viewpoints.

An example of an aikido-style leader with a strong *hara* is Alex "Pete" Hart.[23] Hart is vice chairman and CEO of Advanta, a network of financial service activities from credit cards and mortgages to dating services, which he refers to as "relationship business." Headquartered in an obscure suburb of Philadelphia, Advanta was honored in 1996 by Hambrecht & Quist as the fastest-growing financial services company in the land—from $3 million to almost $3 billion in assets over twelve years.

Despite having gone through Harvard on a football scholarship, Hart speaks in a gentle, open manner. His language is carefully considered and never vulgar, his demeanor modest, never bellicose, but his intentions are clear and focused, and the *hara* behind them is steady and powerful. "Our job," he says, "is to deepen and widen our service relationships with every customer."

A former president of MasterCard, Pete left that post for the smaller and less well known company for two reasons: to be part of growing a creative business, and to do so with partners he could enjoy and rely on.

The founder and chairman, Dennis Alder, describes Advanta's approach to sharing and cultivating leadership, and his own approach to life: "I started a small business so I needed a lot of help as it grew. I decided to split up the responsibility so I could devote more time to my family and community responsibilities. Pete had the ideal background to be the CEO: strong financial services, marketing, and global partnership experience; and a feel for running a large enterprise. Besides all that, he is a pleasure to partner with."[24]

This is the voice of tomorrow's leaders, and in the chapters to come we'll see many other examples of *ki* in action: of people working to develop their *hara*. Before leaders can aspire to this level of mastery, however, they must confront the inner enemies that seek to foil the full expression of *hara* in even the most gifted. Still later we'll see how these subversive forces themselves can be foiled, aikido-style, and made productive allies in your life.

3. The Five Internal Enemies
Locating the Blocks
to Leadership Mastery

> Love your enemies. It makes them so damned
> mad.
>
> —P. D. East

Over many years of working with leaders and organizations, I've observed that failures of leadership can be traced far more often to internal causes—diseases of the soul—than to any external forces like competition or markets. These inner enemies are aspects of the self that we usually keep under wraps. They are revealed when our darkest emotions surface, when creativity is stuffed away, or when excessive pride clouds our vision. They may attack during the chaos of change or, even more insidiously, while we are enjoying the heady pleasures of rapid success. No leader is naturally immune from these inner beasts, and no organization—be it a small family business, a foundation, or a global empire—can thrive if they remain undetected and unconstrained.

Certain of these inner enemies are so common to leaders of all kinds, in all places, that it's important to identify them and study how they operate. The five most dangerous internal enemies are those I call the Jabberwock (the failure to grow emotionally), the Flat-Earther (the failure to make creative connections), the Predator (the failure to manage ego), the Mirror-Seeker (the failure to empathize), and the Prisoner (the failure to overcome alienation and boredom).

MARTIAL ARTS AND THE FIVE ENEMIES

At the time in my life when I was trying to get a focus on the inner enemies in situations of organizational leadership, I was also learning more about the martial arts and aikido. One of my most intriguing discoveries was the writings of Yagyū Munenori, a sixteenth-century swordmaster in the house of Tokugawa. This old master declared that the goal of all martial arts training is to overcome what he called five diseases—human frailties we all are heir to:

- The desire to win
- The desire to rely on technique
- The desire to show off
- The desire to dominate others
- The desire to remain passive

To these he added a sixth, probably the most dangerous disease of all: to become free of these desires. Munenori knew that, though we may fight mightily to free ourselves of the first five failings, we can never do so completely, and that a quest for absolute virtue, taken to the extreme, can be as tyrannical as any vice. As with any congenital disease, our lifelong burden is to live with these human frailties, minimizing them as best we can.[1]

While our terminology differs, I found that Munenori's list of "soul diseases" correlated well with the internal enemies I was locating in leadership situations.

Let's take a closer look at the five internal enemies that must be tamed in order to achieve leadership mastery in the Green Glass Age:

1. *The Jabberwock (The Failure to Grow Emotionally):* Named after Lewis Carroll's poem about a monstrous birdlike creature, whose only form of communication is a mindless squawking, this enemy is revealed in leaders with limited emotional capacity, usually caused by arrested emotional development. Stunted emotional growth is often seen in people with great natural talent who rise to a certain level of competence and fame—in athletics, the arts, or business—then suddenly stop growing. Often they believe the rules that govern the rest of us no longer apply to them; some-

times they descend into self-destructive behavior. Munenori's "desire to show off" is the work of this enemy, as are other negative and self-defeating responses to life's challenges. As one manager said of her surly boss, "He has an even disposition—always angry." We can think of leaders afflicted by this enemy as having a low EQ (emotional quotient).

2. *The Flat-Earther (The Failure to Make Creative Connections):* This enemy is responsible for leaders whose perceptions and creativity are seriously restricted by their own experience and by reliance on proven formulas. They have adapted quite well to a flat earth and see little reason to venture out. The Flat-Earther is the part of ourselves that favors comfort over challenge, sameness over diversity, and doctrinaire thinking over open inquiry. Leaders harmed by this enemy often become overdependent on technique, as Munenori cautioned against. In times of rapid change, such leaders may disguise a lack of clear purpose by keeping things in constant motion, showing an obsessive need for action. Another symptom of this "disease" is the use of tired, impotent slogans in place of compelling, insightful language and open, direct communication.

3. *The Predator (The Failure to Manage Ego):* Leaders under the sway of the Predator have allowed natural pride in their success to swell into arrogance, or hubris, the ancient Greeks' term for the fatal flaw that can cause a leader's downfall. The Greeks believed that overweening pride prevented learning and therefore was subject to violent, horrific punishment—as in the tale of Oedipus, for example.[2] It is not surprising, then, that the most successful organizations and leaders are the most prone to damage by this inner enemy. The Predator feeds the desire to win and to dominate others, another disease spotted by Munenori. Failure to manage ego produces a mind-set in which one believes solely in one's own vision, an authoritarian drive to stay on top by keeping others down. A generation of leaders prized for their capacity to dominate others is one legacy of the industrial age. But there's no surer way to inhibit creativity and long-term success than to force others to work to the limits of a single mind.

4. *The Mirror-Seeker (The Failure to Empathize):* The leader who becomes self-absorbed cannot understand the needs and wants of others, including family, associates, customers, and friends,

because everything is filtered through the needs of self. Too often, by the time people discover this enemy they have driven off all those who mattered to them and are surrounded by those who agree with them. Mirror-Seekers place too much value on their achievements, titles, trophies, social standing, and wealth. This affliction appears when we don't listen thoughtfully to others and catch the feelings behind their words. Today's leaders must look deeply into the needs and wants of customers, investors, associates, and partners, and act accordingly. "I win–you lose" thinking robs us of empathy and leads us to see others as adversaries fit only to be conquered. Demonizing a competitor is one way to ensure that our own inner demons stay in charge.

5. *The Prisoner (The Failure to Overcome Alienation and Boredom):*
   After years of hard work, many otherwise healthy and well-adjusted leaders become jaded and alienated from the world they helped create. Long-standing frustrations or an inability to tolerate plateaus can immobilize even the most gifted. Ennui, cynicism, and inertia may become a substitute for growth. When leaders fail to pursue fresh learning ventures and instead rest on their fund of accumulated wisdom, they become trapped in staleness, prisoners of their own atrophied curiosity.

GROW THE LEADER, TAME THE JABBERWOCK

The growing-up process is full of milestones: earning a driver's license, graduating from school, casting one's first vote. We assume that the maturity needed for each new privilege has been gained through experience or education. But what happens when maturity has not kept pace with experience? We all know people who drink too much, drive irresponsibly, and fail to fulfill the obligations of good citizenship. If we're lucky, the damage done by people who betray society's trust is confined to themselves. Too often, though, the price for immaturity is paid by others: the innocent motorist, the abused spouse, neglected children, the community at large. And in the case of leaders with low "emotional quotients," the organization and the people in it must pay the price.

Whenever we let an emotion take over, no matter what it is— sadness, manic cheerfulness, or any other feeling that never found its proper place in a balanced life—the mature, rational, intuitive decision-maker and moral problem-solver we are capable of being gets buried in the sandbox.

Many rapidly promoted leaders with superior intelligence and great power find themselves playing with too few cards in their emotional deck. Immature leaders often mask or rationalize their behavior, but a day of reckoning usually comes. Take, for example, one fortyish IBM executive I started to coach some years ago. He knew office systems inside and out, had a good track record, and was being groomed by the company for bigger things. People referred to Jack as "dynamic," which sometimes means temperamental, though in our sessions together I had seen only the consummate corporate professional.

One Friday morning his secretary called to cancel our afternoon appointment. When I suggested we reschedule, she got evasive and said it would be best to "wait until things settled down." Alarmed, I made a few calls and discovered that Jack had been put on medical leave and was under a physician's care. Only later did I hear the whole story.

Hurrying down Madison Avenue—running late, as usual, for an important client meeting—Jack had snagged his elegant pin-striped trousers on one of Manhattan's ubiquitous trash bins, tearing a gaping hole in the fabric. "I've dodged ash cans for years," he groaned when we next spoke, "but not this time." He described how he had stopped, stared at the torn pant leg in disbelief, then howled and thrown down his briefcase. He began kicking the bin, cursing the fates. As cautious pedestrians gave him a wider berth, he wrestled the bin across the sidewalk and hurled it into the street. Struggling to compose himself, he then picked up his briefcase and went on to his meeting looking very un-IBM-like: hair mussed, tie askew, pants ripped, jacket reeking of garbage. He made it as far as his client's reception room, then collapsed, sobbing, into a chair. The next day he was on Prozac.

Like most breakdowns, this one didn't happen by accident, and certainly not without warning. What people in his department had been willing to rationalize as quirks of a "dynamic personality"—mood swings, a mercurial temper, abusive behavior—now were revealed for what they were: the unmistakable signs of a teenager trapped in a middle-aged body. Jack's education, experience, and worldly sophistication allowed him to pass himself off as a mature individual, even a superior leader, a person worth emulating. Inside, however, lurked a scared and scheming adolescent who had never figured out how to deal with his frustrations—a condition that only grew worse as he rose higher. Fortunately, Jack's downtime turned out to be relatively short; he had scared himself enough to seek counseling and pay attention to its value.

Of course, as a case of arrested development, Jack isn't unique—among other executives I've known. The symptoms of immaturity vary with each person's circumstances, but they always result in self-destructive behavior: for some it's drugs or drink, for others it's depression. Interestingly, many emotionally handicapped people were child prodigies or highly gifted individuals who ended their careers prematurely because they were not prepared to manage life's ordinary successes and failures. Conditioned by early success to assume the dice will always roll their way, they cultivate brilliance rather than resilience, and even small setbacks can set off inappropriate responses. They respond to bad news by brooding and feeling betrayed instead of analyzing the situation and taking positive action. Such leaders set themselves up to fail in ways that would scarcely occur to their more mature contemporaries.

Here are some other arrested emotions in action. How many have you seen in others? How many can you spot in yourself?

- *Abusive interpersonal relationships.* Unfiltered, seething anger is a common symptom of emotional immaturity. Emotionally abusive people are like playground bullies. Although we're told that bullies are really big babies at heart, that doesn't help much when the bully is our boss or some other powerful person. Indeed, while bullies do cope and relate well in some situations, they frequently get very good at aggressive, confrontational behavior—one reason they resort to it so often. Smarter bullies dismiss criticism by accusing others of being envious, of being failures, or of not understanding how the dog-eat-dog world really works.

  An example of the successful yet abusive leader is Paul Kazarian, the "mad genius" who saved Sunbeam-Oster from bankruptcy in the early 1990s, only to be jettisoned shortly thereafter by his own board.[3] To investors Kazarian was a godsend: a brilliant administrator with an uncanny ability to both save and make money in a very competitive market. But to his employees, according to news reports, he was a tyrant whose autocratic style went way beyond hard-nosed efficiency to childish abuse: smashing telephones, firing BB guns into empty chairs at meetings, making lewd remarks to women, rousing key executives in the middle of the night for "crisis meetings" when no crisis existed. Kazarian's reign of terror ended when a handful of more mature executives offered Sunbeam's board of directors a choice: staff resignation en masse or the CEO's head. Surprised and sobered, the board showed their wunderkind the door. Sadly, Kazarian either disdained or dismissed the charges, apparently learning nothing from the experience.

- *Acting out inappropriate impulses.* Some people go out of their way to make themselves the focus of every conversation, no matter how awkward the situation. Sometimes their tactics are merely annoying. We've all met the office clown, the practical jokester, or the garishly dressed clotheshorse. In others, however, this trait is more menacing: the sexual harasser or the cheat who takes credit for another's work. This is bad enough when it occurs in workers, but when a leader succumbs to such childish impulses, the whole organization suffers.

  One way to handle such attention-starved people is to reinforce the behavior you want, ignore the actions you don't like, and gently channel the person's energy—aikido-style—into more productive directions. For example, self-dramatizing leaders who dominate discussions and meetings often calm down if their audience stops responding. Sometimes a strong staff group can break the cycle through direct confrontation. But a coach or mentor can often be more direct in suggesting new styles and approaches. Once the pattern has been broken, such leaders—often very talented public speakers—might be encouraged to participate in community groups, trade organizations, or local politics—places where a taste for center stage is an asset.

- *Psychosomatic illness.* The symptoms of a psychosomatic illness are real enough. Study after study shows how painful and debilitating conditions like allergies, asthma, migraine headaches, rheumatoid arthritis, and a variety of gastrointestinal disorders can be triggered or aggravated by emotional upset, more proof of the powerful mind-body connection. While genes play a part in one's susceptibility to psychosomatic illness, much of it can be mitigated by a healthier, more balanced approach to life—the "centering" that good leaders show by their example and encourage in others.

- *Amoral or immoral conduct.* Many writers on leadership skate past the issue of character development. In my experience, however, one of the biggest obstacles to enduring success is a leader's moral lapses. A fully developed moral sense is a mark of adulthood, and the lack of one is a sign of lingering immaturity. Without a well-tempered moral sense leaders are easy prey for the temptations that arise from success. Their achievements may make them feel exempt from inconvenient bourgeois notions of fair play, honesty, and moral consistency. Examples abound, from decadent Roman emperors to modern politicians with lamentable "zipper problems," and no amplification is needed here. Leaders with lax or nonexistent morals almost always self-destruct and lose their effectiveness—not to mention their friends, families, and allies—sooner or later.

There is no single, simple way to tame the Jabberwock and achieve instant emotional maturity, but here are some specific ways to get the process started:

- *Slow down the emotional response and give reason a chance.* Mature people understand the law of averages: if you do something habitually, you will eventually encounter all possible variations on its consequences. If, for example, you have a habit of running late, like our impatient IBM executive, don't be surprised or enraged when traffic delays you even further. Practice calming your mind, centering your thoughts, and accept responsibility for problems you helped to create. Don't conclude that inanimate objects, indifferent salespeople, or irritating bureaucrats are out to get you personally. Rehearse various reasonable, rational responses to situations your illogical emotional impulses may get you into. If running late is your Achilles' heel, find alternate routes to appointments or reschedule meetings at more convenient times. Gradually modify the types of behavior that have gotten you in trouble or taxed your emotional reserves, until those reserves are high and the troubles you encounter cease to be self-made. Above all, don't assume that childish emotions can't be controlled. They can. It takes practice.

- *Channel emotional energy into positive directions.* Like

the aikidoist turning an opponent's momentum to his own advantage, find appropriate outlets for an outsized sense of competitiveness or injustice, a need for attention, or simply a passionate temperament—community work, industry activism, public speaking, amateur theater, sports, or martial arts. The options are endless. Find one that suits you.

• *Find a truth-telling mentor.* When time or conditions do not permit self-exploration and reeducation, harried leaders can often enlist an emotional "guardian angel" to help them weather a difficult time.

A good example is public relations consultant Gershon Kekst, a widely respected, mature, and straight-thinking man who acted as conscience and moral advocate to Steve Ross of Warner Communications during the tumultuous Time-Warner mega-merger of the late 1980s. So clear, scrupulous, and valuable was Kekst's advice that he was chosen to speak at Ross's memorial service years later, where he was nicknamed "the rabbi" by the attendant reporters. Like any good rabbi, Kekst—an old friend of long standing—is a splendid teacher and scholar. He loves to tell stories and parables and insists that his clients respect words and get their stories right. Those who have worked with him speak of his toughness and discipline; his understanding, caring side; and his passion for getting the best out of those around him. He makes friends with some of his clients, but he can be a stern, exacting friend. In the peculiar world of public relations, he is a moral standout, a reliable mirror for his clients. Rabbis have not done their work unless they make people think. Kekst honors his clients by making them look more closely at their utterances and their thoughts.[4]

The section on choosing a *sensei* in Chapter 4 continues the discussion of mentors.

THE FLAT-EARTHER: HOW WE BLOCK CREATIVITY AND COMMUNICATION

Ideas absorbed early in life circulate constantly in our subconscious, crowding out more creative impulses and ideas. Or we may have learned one way of functioning in career situations that worked for a

long time but that holds us back when we need to move on. Lead.
controlled by the Flat-Earther enemy are in danger of having their
vision narrowed, their thinking confined to traveling in circles, and
their communication reduced to endless repetition of old formulas or
obfuscating nonsense.

When the problem gets serious enough, a person may go on talking
simply to reassure himself and to prevent the intrusion of uncomfortable
ideas. Years ago, while helping a large retailing firm revitalize its operations, I met Tracy, a merchandising executive. He had just received a
plum assignment: special assistant to the president, a high-visibility job
the firm typically used to groom its general managers. Our initial meeting had been brief, but Tracy impressed me as an outgoing, energetic
person who was totally dedicated to the company. I was astonished
when, only a few days later, he was reassigned to a far less prestigious
job in fulfillment—an organizational backwater. Something very bad
had obviously happened. I was curious to find out what—and why.

At our second meeting, I expected to find Tracy a shaken man, or
at least dejected, but he greeted me with a big smile and a hearty handshake, just as he had a week before, and immediately started telling me
all about his new job. Before he got too far, I interrupted him and
asked, as discreetly as I could, what had caused his sudden reassign-
ment. He made a face and said he had asked his superiors that very
question, but nobody "in charge" would give him a straight answer. He
said he finally found out, though—from his wife.

When I asked what she had told him, he immediately changed the
subject to what was wrong with the corporate culture and how long-
standing rivals had sabotaged his one big chance. "Amazing!" I said.
"And how did your wife know about all of these things?"

"What?" Tracy blinked, as though he had already forgotten his
original answer. "Oh, she doesn't know about any of this. She said my
problem is that I don't listen to people. I guess she's right. She knows
me pretty well. I told her I'd work on it. Anyway, as I was saying . . ."

Needless to say, my question had been answered. Tracy's biggest
enemy wasn't a corporate rival; it was himself. He had a noisy, distract-
ing inner enemy cluttering his mind with half-baked theories, name-
dropping, aimless gossip, and banal platitudes—all substituting for
reflective discourse. Whenever anything happened that threatened his
self-image, he simply overwhelmed it with empty rhetoric. He unconsciously dominated every conversation until he wore his colleagues

is wife's potentially career-saving advice was all but blotted out the sheer volume of his babble. Like the Energizer bunny, he kept talking and going until he was at risk of falling off the edge of his narrow path.

As I got to know Tracy better, I saw that he had certain things in common with other failed leaders I had known. When he started out in the business, Tracy's charm and enthusiasm had been enough to carry him through. Co-workers thought he was brilliant, if talkative, and supervisors promoted him regularly—often to get him out of their hair. When he finally arrived at the executive suite, however, his fast-talking patter just wasn't enough. Top leaders want and need fresh ideas, clearly expressed. Tracy didn't have these to offer. Instead, his experience shows how clinging to familiar territory and a comfortable self-image can become a habit, restricting productive thinking. Tracy came to believe that the sheer quantity of his ideas was more important than the quality, so every stream of thought became a waterfall—good ideas gushing out with the bad, submerging listeners and leaving them gasping for air. Eventually he was offered a job in sales, which seemed to fit his gregarious nature. But he turned it down; perhaps it didn't measure up to his inflated expectations. The last I heard, he had yet to find a position well matched to his talents.

Only clear thinking gives us the option of clear communication— a leader's most valuable tool. Without it, creative connections are overlooked and errors of omission, and commission, multiply. The worst of these errors are missed opportunities—a joint venture not investigated, a promising product not considered, a good solution left unrecognized. Poor communications, like a faulty railroad switch, can derail a fast-track career or the best organization, especially one that is under the pressure of change.

Vocalizing one's thought processes can be equally dangerous for a leader. Too often, leaders who favor extemporaneous speaking come across as tentative or unsure because they externalize their inner debate on complex issues. Spontaneity can be a potent leadership tool, particularly in creative settings like private brainstorming sessions and team-building retreats, but the public presentation of those conclusions should always be well fashioned, focused, and persuasive. As a leader, you must listen to yourself at least as closely as you listen to others. Take stock of your own ideas and make sure you appreciate the impact of your words, and of the way you say them, on your listeners. The more familiar you are with your own thought processes and responses, the better able you will be to communicate them to others.

Here are some other ways in which leaders fail to make creative connections and what can be done to overcome a flat earth perspective:

- *Big picture or big blind spot?* We all know leaders who pride themselves on seeing the big picture—often to the exclusion of all else. They think relevant details are somehow beneath them and that as long as they define the grand strategy, the tactics will take care of themselves. In one sense, this attitude is justified: some leaders fail because they get bogged down in minutiae that should have been left to others. On the other hand, Albert Einstein reminded us that "God resides in the details." Only when operations are well managed can the big picture reliably take shape. There is no substitute for sweeping vision *and* getting hands-on with operations.

- *Big praise for small minds.* Leaders with unresolved power needs and low receptivity to new ideas often reward best the people who challenge them least, creating a culture of sycophancy. Eventually the objective information any leader needs to function is entirely cut off. Their organizations go down in flames even though all the dials in the cockpit read correctly. Widespread agreement among leaders may look and feel good, but too much harmony can be fatal. Japanese companies, in particular, have struggled for years with this problem. As one Japanese executive told me, "Public agreement is good, but private agreement is foolish." This insidious problem can't be solved if our best tool for correcting it—the leader's mind—is not making the proper connections or is full of distortions. The aikido leader makes sure that fair fighting takes place so ideas aren't smothered in political correctness.

From the martial arts perspective, flat-earth thinking is clarified best through the process of centering. When thoughts, feelings, and actions are united, a leader comes across as strong, consistent, and purposeful. The way to consensus among constituents may be time-consuming and rough—contrary opinions must be heard, differences resolved, and all views given a fair hearing—but once agreement is reached, the organization can begin to function as a unified whole, without the dangers of syco-phancy or noncommitment. As a catalyst and symbol for that unity, the leader's thoughts and words must always point the way.

THE PREDATOR: WHEN CONTROL BECOMES STRANGLEHOLD

The Predator is the enemy that encourages the ego to fly out of control, that tempts leaders to solidify success by dominating others and to control situations to the point where creativity is stifled.

Usually it is the stress of a high-level challenge that unleashes the Predator. People respond to stress in different ways. Research shows that as our level of stress increases, we often think and act in ways that differ considerably from our usual patterns. In other words, great stress not only changes us; it can create an entirely different person. When we attempt to lead others while we ourselves are lost, the results can be disastrous.

A few years ago I served as leadership consultant to an investment banking firm that had invested in a hot software company. The president of the software company had just hired a hyperachiever—a real technical wizard—from a rival firm to head his engineering department, and expectations were high. Obviously, part of the president's motivation was to influence our evaluation. The company already had a good track record and the addition of a rising star could only make it better. When we finally met, I found the new director to be a surprisingly soft-spoken, accessible young man who seemed as willing to listen as to lead.

All went well for the first few weeks—but the honeymoon abruptly ended when two of the company's top applications engineers quit without warning. Close examination showed that their biggest complaint had to do with sudden changes that had swept through their department. The first thing the new chief engineer had done was to impose draconian controls on all his salaried workers. Designers now had to keep detailed records of how much time they spent on a specific task within each particular project. The new boss—call him David—also prohibited "cross-talk" among engineers assigned to different projects. They were all told to "stick to their knitting," and that directive stuck in the craw of the oldest, most valuable workers.

"He's killed the very things that made this department great," one of the lead engineers muttered. "I just can't do my job with the boss sitting on my shoulder." Another echoed his complaint. "We're a team, and we always have been. A new coach can't just waltz in and tell the quarterback to stop talking to the receivers or order the backfield to ignore the tackles. It's crazy."

On hearing these comments, David only shrugged, saying that in his experience, the best teams were characterized by discipline and a strong goal orientation. He felt the engineers wasted too much time helping each other on unrelated projects instead of focusing on their own assignments. He was adamant about the need to track individual contributors, assess the effectiveness of their managers, and make accurate cost and schedule forecasts. The more controls he implemented, however, the more employees resisted. By the end of the first month, two more senior staff members had resigned and others had asked for transfers. Within another month, the exodus had been joined by several people in tech support—a virtual palace revolt.

The president was baffled by all this. He wanted to support his new man, of course, but was appalled by the gradual evisceration of what had previously been a group of solid performers. He put all personnel actions on hold and spent several days camped in the department, listening to complaints, calling in advisers, and scheduling meetings far into the night. After a long morning closeted with David, he announced that David would be moved to a newly created position as director of advanced research, where he would be out of line management—and out of the limelight. The president then appointed a senior manager to act as temporary engineering director until a permanent replacement could be found. Thus the crisis was contained, but not without a lot of damage—and a heaping portion of humble pie served up for all concerned.

What went wrong with this match that should have been made in heaven? When I asked David, the displaced engineering director, his response was tepid, almost casual at first, as if this sort of thing happened to him every day. But the longer we spoke, the more animated he got and the more revealing his answers became. "I don't regret a thing," he said. "I did what I thought was right. I thought that was why I'd been hired. They [the founders, including the president who had hired him] just didn't back me up."

Then, even as I watched, the self-possessed Dr. Jekyll gave way to Mr. Hyde. David slammed his fist on the table: "I mean, here's this big department filled with malcontents and backsliders just waiting for me—an outsider—to fall on my face! They had a nice thing going before I came along. Success is ten percent inspiration and ninety percent perspiration, and these guys had forgotten how to sweat. They'd sit around drinking Cokes, talking about the Forty-Niners. Then when you stuck your head in to ask how things were going, they'd tell you they were working the problem. You know—real high school stuff. They weren't dummies. They'd just forgotten how to work."

At last we seemed to have arrived at the root of the problem. David was confident enough in his own powers, but was unwilling to trust his subordinates. Under the tremendous stress of joining a new company in a very responsible job, and at a time when the whole firm was being strictly evaluated, he found himself resorting to behavior patterns that were unfamiliar to him and inappropriate for his new constituents. The mere idea that his team might fail, that *he* might fail, was too much for him to bear. Rather than adapt to the culture of a mature work group with a proven track record, he chose to assuage his anxieties by initiating tight new controls that alienated everyone and isolated the department's informal leaders—people whose initiative might pose a threat to David's authority. By throwing a wet blanket over a well-established creative group, he smothered the very spark that had made them successful.

This case illustrates how easy it is to release the predator inner enemy when we feel:

- *Alienated:* David was new to the work setting and probably could have used closer support. The predator surfaces quickly when we are afraid and feel alone.
- *Slighted:* Small slights can be easily magnified when we are anxious. We need to learn how to remain calm, centered, and more purposeful in response.
- *Criticized:* George Leonard says all new students will push back when first pushed. In aikido, this impulse must be tamed to open up more options when feeling attacked.

David wanted more control over what he saw as an unstable situation. Some of the most participative executives turn into real tyrants when the going gets tough, and their organizations almost always suffer because of it. Does this mean that the need for control is meaningless or unimportant? Of course not. But when old instincts or new fears threaten creativity, we must find aikido-like moves to accomplish what controls are meant to do: assure quality, protect stakeholders, and allow us to meet our obligations in an orderly way.

The leader with a healthy ego should be aware of the fine line where control becomes excessive and counterproductive, and should be able to relax his grip. But if the Predator is in charge, any sign of trouble is likely to make this leader tighten down still further.

THE MIRROR-SEEKER: WHERE LACK OF EMPATHY CAN LEAD

Hate is a powerful emotion, a lonely scavenger that feeds off wounded egos. It requires a certain detachment from the hated object, a shutting down of empathy, in order to function—the way nations depersonalize and monsterize an enemy during war. We seem to tell ourselves that if we get too close to a despised person, we might begin to see that he or she is human just like us, making our thirst for "noble vengeance" or "just retribution" seem less noble and less just, and therefore harder to sustain.

Leaders who deal in hate and recrimination are not content merely to win; they must plunder the self-esteem of the losers they create. As a result, such leaders are often seen as dreadful people, even by their followers. If a vengeful leader is also the victim of flat-earth thinking, as many are, the sense of righteousness that blinds them also obscures reality, and any feedback they get about their hellish reputation comes as a total shock.

Often, however, Mirror-Seekers are fully aware of their spiteful feelings. They may even take pride in them and boast of their ability to "do unto others before they do unto me," crediting their success, and their enemy's failure, to their superior Machiavellian instincts in a dog-eat-dog world. Believing in the futility of compassion and distrusting the power of goodwill keeps the spiteful inner enemy in power over the Mirror-Seekers' souls, even when the cause for anger has long since disappeared. Here's the story of one such unempathetic and hate-filled person. Do her actions seem familiar?

Evelyn was a successful editor at a prestigious New York publishing house. Although not the best at picking best-sellers, she prided herself on her business acumen and became a self-styled money maven in her department. She delighted in taking new editors under her wing and helping them craft deals with high-powered agents, paperback publishers, and others who sought to license their books. In short, she became a master of the deal, a virtuoso in technique.

A few months before I met Evelyn, her firm had been purchased by a foreign conglomerate. The new owners scoured her company looking for like-minded employees (namely, those who cared more about the bottom line than aesthetics) and promptly promoted them to positions of power. In many cases, these new executives became overseers of people who only days before had been their supervisors, colleagues, and mentors. By virtue of her reputation and ambition, Evelyn was among this elite.

As an adviser during the transition, I heard Evelyn's name mentioned early and often—usually accompanied by muttered curses, shaking heads, and looks of frustration. When I began to make inquiries, I discovered that, almost as soon as she assumed her new post, Evelyn had caused to have terminated various people who had given her grief over the course of her career. People who had disagreed with her on even the smallest issues—a book jacket design, the number of cities on an author's tour, and so on—found themselves polishing their résumés. Evelyn was the consummate corporate sniper, and her aim was deadly.

After a while, I had collected an impressive file of "Evelyn stories." One very senior editor who had been Evelyn's mentor when she first arrived in editorial was kept waiting for hours, like everyone else, whenever he tried to see her, only to be informed on many occasions that their meeting had been canceled because Evelyn had more important business to attend to. While Evelyn furnished and refurnished her large private office with expensive antiques, she told her editors to lay off their assistants and use freelancers instead to "save unnecessary costs." The few co-workers she still associated with walked around on eggshells and met my inquiries with sighs, shrugs, and silence. "You'll have to ask Evelyn about that" became their mantra.

When I finally got an interview with Her Majesty, as she'd become known, and tactfully acquainted her with these facts, she tossed her head and laughed. "Oh, people around here are so thin-skinned!" she said. "They're just jealous. I'm sure you've seen it all before. They'll get over it. And if they don't, they know their way to the door. Nobody's chained them to this company."

We talked for almost an hour, and the more she spoke, the more I sensed great sadness behind Evelyn's bravado. She was smart and ambitious, to be sure, and I was just as impressed as her new bosses with her obvious business savvy. But beneath it all, I detected a very fragile person: a gifted practitioner in her chosen field, but one whose quest for true mastery seemed stalled on an endless plateau bounded by her own insecurities—and by rage.

Pain is a very subjective thing. Setbacks and irritations that merely annoy some people can be devastating to others—who will do anything to prevent them. In Evelyn I detected an easily wounded soul whose sensitivity to stress demanded the persona she had forged for self-defense. She wanted anyone who might threaten her to know she was a person to be reckoned with. Inside the spiteful monster, however, huddled a wide-eyed little girl afraid of having her pigtails pulled or being teased for wearing the wrong dress. In fact, Evelyn sometimes apologized after abusing people, claiming she "wasn't herself" or blaming pressure from above. Of course, nobody was fooled. She wanted it both ways: to behave as she wished—to give in to a vindictive inner enemy—but to still be liked.

I would love to say that Evelyn eventually found her grail—learned humility and forbearance, and gained the relaxed confidence only well-centered souls enjoy—but that hasn't happened yet. Since her new corporate bosses were several times removed from the action in her division, they saw only Evelyn's glowing financial results and ignored the turmoil in her staff. Today Evelyn is a corporate officer—swimming daily with the sharks. She has few allies and, as near as I can tell, almost no friends.

Evelyn's story is all too common. Character flaws once kept hidden by friends, family, and co-workers are now trumpeted in headlines, on talk shows, and in business school case studies—and that's probably all to the good.

After parlaying a start-up company into a billion-dollar business, the late British publishing magnate Robert Maxwell plundered his constituents' pension funds and buried himself and his heirs in a crushing mountain of debt. His mysterious death in a yachting accident in 1991 left his two sons legally liable for his excesses. This "inheritance" is what most hurt his wife Elisabeth Maxwell, author of a book about life with her hard-driving, hard-hearted husband. In a February 1995 interview, she described as an intimate observer the internal forces that led to his downfall. "[T]o see my sons' careers in ruin, knowing their character and the kind of men they are, is unacceptable and unforgivable," she told the interviewer. "It's strange, toward the end of his life he wanted no constraint of any kind. That was really the irony, you know. To communicate between two human beings is a very humble level, and an extremely complex affair. He didn't like doing it. . . . He was really a very sick man at the end of his life."[5]

In a strange way, Maxwell may have been lucky: leaders in the vengeful clutches of the Mirror-Seeker usually do not go lightly into their sunset years. Few such people lie on their deathbed wishing they had been meaner.

Mirror-Seekers are hard to help unless their lack of empathy can be spotted early. Like the classic narcissist, they cannot hear anything that threatens their carefully constructed self-image. So, the trick is to spot this enemy early and remain extremely vigilant. Stephen Covey offered a quick test for spotting mirror-seeking, empathy-depleting behavior:

- Can you listen to others and give them such clear and sensitive feedback that they feel heard? If you cannot do this, keep practicing until you can really hear what thought and emotions they are trying to convey.
- Is it possible for you to truly understand another's point of view, even when it is abhorrent to you? (Covey was able to help people who were on opposite sides of the abortion debate actually empathize with the other persons' perspective to the point of tears.)
- Can you really hear your enemy regardless of what they say? If you can override the natural tendency to stop listening to those you consider vile, foolish, wrong-headed, you can claim being empathetic.

In aikido, the idea of blending energy with the attacker (the enemy) is considered a basic art. This is a form of empathy. If you can answer the above questions affirmatively, you are keeping the Mirror-Seeker under wraps. But, be mindful how easy it is to become like Evelyn or Maxwell. Sometimes we are only a promotion away. That is why the aikidoist never stops practicing, facing the inner enemies.

THE PRISONER—FREEING OURSELVES FROM ALIENATION AND BOREDOM

The last, and perhaps the deadliest, of a leader's inner enemies is the grim warden who locks us away inside ourselves. The walls of this prison are stale routine; its bars, the boredom and ennui caused by taking the path of least resistance, assuming only the most predictable risks, and settling for their even more predictable rewards. As they hang pathetically in self-made manacles, these leaders gaze longingly at the exciting world the rest of us inhabit and that they have somehow lost the courage to rejoin.

I had known one such leader, Carl, for over two decades, one of those clients who had become a close friend. The CEO of a large materials handling and shipping company, he had been a dynamo at the beginning of his career—a leader not only of his own firm but of charities and industry associations as well. A robust outdoorsman and environmentalist, he at one time even considered running for public office. Recently, though, his pace had slackened considerably—not just the scope of his many activities, but his zest for them. While fundamentally strong, his company had taken some hits in the market and was receiving uncharacteristic bad press. I thought this was why he asked to see me, but as I quickly found out, it was the last thing on his mind.

When I walked into Carl's austere corner office after an absence of several years, my first impression was that he had been sick. Posture can be a good sign of a person's mental state, and he telegraphed his piteous condition well before he opened his mouth. He seemed too small for his big executive's chair, shrunken inside his well-tailored suit. It seemed to take all his strength to stand up, shake my hand, then gesture to the armchair beside his massive desk. I sat, he slumped, and we spent a long moment just gazing through the window at the spring greenery surrounding his corporate headquarters. This passive weariness was distinctly un-Carl, who even in the face of adversity always tackled his troubles head on. I wondered if he'd been diagnosed with some serious disease or was distracted by a personal problem, perhaps in his marriage or with one of his grown children. But something else was wrong. It was as if something inside of him had died.

"You know, John," he finally said, "a day doesn't pass but I think about getting out of here. No . . . I mean it. Nothing here excites me anymore."

I jokingly replied that this was his chance to run for state senator, as he'd long threatened. But I couldn't get a rise from him. He went on grumbling about his lack of enthusiasm for work and for the prospect of retirement: "If I get one more snapshot of a paunchy guy in a straw hat grinning next to a marlin, I'll puke!" How did other men manage to retire happily? he wondered.

"It's easy," I replied. "You just say, 'that's enough.' Then you walk away from what you hate and toward something that you love."

"That's the problem. I don't know what I want to do. I only know this isn't it." Carl then gave me a sad, brave smile. "What went wrong, *compadre*? Where do I go from here?" My once-confident friend looked like a lost little boy, totally engulfed in the mists of ennui. Ideas that used to excite him now weighed him down like anvils. Commitments that had filled his life with meaning—business, community work, political interests, family activities—now seemed meaningless.

After spending a few days with Carl, I sensed that his staff was well aware that something was amiss. His quiet nervous breakdown was beginning to take its toll on the company as well as on Carl himself. Truly, he was incarcerated in a cell of depression, a bottomless pit that only looked blacker and deeper the longer he gazed down into it. How had this happened?

The main symptom of this wasting disease of the soul is alienation: a sense of estrangement and isolation from all those things that used to provide positive meaning in a life. A broad and bleak plateau seems to stretch out unexpectedly just when we thought we had reached the pinnacle of our career. Having mastered most of the techniques of our profession, once-demanding work becomes routine, the stimulation of new challenges becomes scarce and therefore noticeable by its absence. Although new peaks to climb may be in view, they appear distant and impractical. We rightly sense that something important has gone out of our lives, and we gradually begin to view life as a disappointment, even

unfair. We raise our defenses and go through the motions of leading others even though our enthusiasm is hollow and our cynicism is conta-
gious. Eventually our tools for coping with even the most elemental
aspects of life begin to rust and our most cherished dreams lose their
luster. Our lives may go on for many years, even decades, but for all intents and purposes, we've already ceased to exist.

Carl's self-imprisonment eventually cost him his job, alas. To
relieve the tedium he became not only restless but reckless. His unconscious self could not be restrained, and so he put the company into
some adventures that were clearly off plan and beyond the firm's core
competence. When these forays became too costly, the board fired
Carl, to his great surprise. At first he was angry and defensive, and
then he realized what others had seen before: he needed an entirely
new kind of challenge. So Carl went after one of the projects his company had jettisoned, and in doing so, he created a new learning curve
for himself. He also created a whole new role: that of mentor to a very
bright young woman, his daughter. The combination of a new venue,
fresh learning tasks, and a redefined role restored the vitality his inner
enemy had robbed him of.

Here's a short list of ways we can work at keeping the Prisoner
at bay:

- *Stop and smell the roses.* Many leaders run out of gas on the ennui
  plateau because they forgot to replenish their emotional fuel tank
  on the way up—and because they failed to slow down and enjoy
  the scenery. Here are a few simple ways to smell the roses:
  1. Change your way, time, and method of going to and fro.
     Once a week go to work very early and then walk home.
     Ride a bike on small errands and see how many new things
     you enjoy along the way.
  2. Make firm, regular dates with people you care about. Add
     one new person to your lunch list each month for a year.
     Change your dates with loved ones to include new adven-
     tures such as picnics or a ferryboat ride.
  3. Read a book by a new author or about a new topic once each
     quarter. Join or form a book group with people you really
     enjoy.
  4. Learn to do one new creative thing with your hands; gar-
     dening, cooking, and sketching all qualify.

- *Look for another peak to climb.* Mastering one field of endeavor is fine, but as your resources grow in that area, so will your ability to apply them to other fields, to undertake new journeys. Why not shift your sights and aim for another peak? True, you will have to develop different techniques, but the lessons you've learned about mastery will continue to serve you well.

  Whatever you do, don't be satisfied merely to relive or repeat past triumphs, and don't allow your choices to make themselves by default. The true master leader is always curious, peering beyond what he or she knows well. The expert in computers will benefit from pursuing biology; the banker would do well to read in the classics or social sciences. Master leaders know that new learning is the best safeguard against the dread enemy of staleness.

- *Renew your core commitments.* Any pursuit of mastery must include efforts that go beyond our personal well-being. When your passion for daily life seems to slacken, let compassion take up the slack—compassion for yourself, your family, your constituents, your stakeholders, and the environment. This, I think, is the ultimate larger purpose. Fulfilling our promise as human beings is certainly the greatest challenge most of us will ever face.

Again, aikido gives us a life-affirming way to begin seeing all of existence from a non-self-centered, compassionate point of view. In the foreword to Kisshomaru Ueshiba's treatise on his father's life and work, translator Taitetus Unno reminds us that "Aikido . . . realizes this universal love through rigorous training of the body. The hard physical discipline, however, cannot be separated from mental development and real spiritual growth. While many people may fall short of this goal, the crucial element is in the process of training, which is beginningless and endless. And while on that path, in a most unexpected moment, the ultimate realization of aikido as the Way of Life—beyond any martial art—may dawn."

Leaders who have achieved true mastery of themselves and a harmonious fit with the world around them are highly distinctive individuals. Although their methods can be learned and emulated by others, great leaders employ them in ways that are uniquely their

own: full of energy, virtuosity, and originality. They ins[...]
sonal loyalty that transcends the bonds of rank, duty, an[...]
Their constituents feel changed by having known them a[...]
approach the same task, or follow other leaders, in quite the[...]
way again. Leaders like these get the very most from their resour[...]
human and material; they also stretch the organizations, industries[...]
or institutions they lead, leaving them transformed for the better.
Truly great leaders change the way we view the process of leadership
itself.

A Self-Assessment Exercise for Leaders

Perhaps you recognized some aspect of yourself or your behavior in
relation to one or another of the inner enemies I've described in this
chapter. Most leaders are afflicted by more than one of them over the
course of a career. It's worth noting that the enemies sometimes
operate in tandem. Emotional immaturity (the Jabberwock), for
example, can encourage flat-earth thinking or the need for excessive
control. And someone in the grip of the Prisoner may lose empathy
for others and become a Mirror-Seeker. Keep in mind, too, that you
may overcome one enemy at a certain stage in your career, only to
be attacked by others later on. The Jabberwock and the Predator
are more likely to strike younger leaders in the first flush of success,
while those who are farther down the road may fall prey to the
Prisoner.

Practicing rigorous self-observation, as any aikidoist knows, is
critical to spotting inner enemies at work before they gain the upper
hand. In addition to studying the enemies profiled in this chapter and
staying alert to how you may manifest them, there are some very specific, useful tools for determining where you stand in your quest for
leadership mastery—and life mastery. Before going on, take a moment
to experiment with the following "sort, think, and feel" exercise,
which I often use in my leadership planning sessions. Its goal is to help
you strengthen your effectiveness and maximize the satisfaction you
find in your personal and professional life. All you'll need is a clean
sheet of paper, a pencil, and about half an hour, but the benefits you'll
find can last a lifetime.

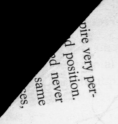

ur Worksheet

et of paper: one vertical line down the center,
across the middle, forming four equal quad-
uadrant "Career Satisfactions"; the top right,
he lower left, "Career Dissatisfactions"; and
Dissatisfactions." That's all there is to it.
...ts simplicity fool you. To get the most out of the exercise, you'll have to think seriously about these four key aspects of your
life, both on and off the job.

Step 2. List Your Career Dissatisfactions

Begin with the lower left quadrant. Under the heading "Career Dissatisfactions," list those things you like least about your career. We start
here because people facing periods of stressful change usually know
more about what they don't like than about what they do. Getting negatives out of the way can also help you accentuate the positive later on.
Be sure you list things you actually dislike, not just the things you feel
you don't do well. The two are not the same.

A typical list of career dissatisfiers might read like this:

- About 80 percent of what I do is dull routine; I seldom learn
  anything new.
- I relate positively to few, if any, people in my office.
- I suffer more stress than my job is worth.
- I hate it when people do what I ask just because I'm "the boss."
- I like working with small groups, but I get tongue-tied before a
  crowd.
- I wish people would keep their personal problems to themselves.

Make your items concise, but be specific. Focus on things that make
you feel bad rather than things that merely go wrong.

Step 3. List Your Personal Dissatisfactions

Now move across the page to the quadrant on the lower right. List
those things about your personal life—in relationships, in your use of

free time, in recreation and hobbies, and so forth—that leave you unsatisfied. Again, your answers should focus on feelings, not on some outside measure of success or failure. "I don't enjoy tennis as much as I used to," for example, is a better answer than "I'm unhappy because I keep getting beaten in my tennis club's championship."

Here are some typical responses for personal dissatisfiers:

- I don't spend enough time with my friends and family.
- All my energy is gone by the end of the day.
- It seems like I haven't read a good book in years—I start, but never finish them.

Step 4. List Your Satisfactions at Work

Now move to the upper left quadrant of the page and list those things that you enjoy most on the job. With the negatives out of your system, it should be easier to focus on the things you really like.

Typical work-related satisfiers include the following:

- I like projects where I learn something new every day.
- I like winning, and winning as a team feels best of all.
- Despite what everyone says, money is important. I really feel good when I get a raise!
- I enjoy seeing people's eyes light up with enthusiasm!
- I enjoy leadership books and seminars.
- It feels good to know that my team has solved a really tough problem.

If your list of satisfiers is shorter than your list of dissatisfiers, don't worry. That doesn't make you a pessimist—just somebody who's ready for change. Leave a little extra space at the bottom of this quadrant. You'll use it later in Step 6.

Step 5. List Your Satisfiers at Home

Now move to the upper right quadrant and list those things in your personal life—away from the pressures of work—that give you the greatest pleasure. Some high-achieving people have trouble separating their private from their professional lives, but in this case, be sure to leave business at the office. For example, don't say, "I enjoy my department's holiday party," even if it doesn't feel like work, when what you really mean is "I enjoy going to parties." Again, save a little space at the bottom of the quadrant for use in the next step.

Here are some typical personal satisfiers:

- All my troubles melt away when I'm cycling cross-country.
- I get a kick out of building things; I like working with my hands.
- I really enjoy my book group. What nice, bright people!

Some people stop the exercise here, and that's fine. Certainly, working through each quadrant is therapeutic and what you've written says a lot about your life. But the real value of the lists lies in their potential to be reexpressed as goals—what you're willing to do right now to make your home and work life better.

Step 6. Move Dissatisfiers to the Satisfier Lists by Rewriting Them as Positive Goals

You can turn the negative statements on your dissatisfier lists into positive goals by combining them with the positive statements on your satisfier lists. Using the typical lists of career dissatisfiers and satisfiers we generated above, we got these new goals:

- Eighty percent of what I do from now on will involve learning something new.
- By referring to my co-workers as a team, I'll relate to them more positively.
- When a stressful project comes up, I'll negotiate a bigger reward.
- I'll take more time to explain to people why I've asked them to do something.
- I'll volunteer to give presentations more often to improve my public speaking.
- If someone brings me a tough personal problem, I'll refer him or her to a support group.

Repeating the same process with the personal di⸝
get this list:

- I'll take at least two bike rides each month ⸝
- I'll spend an hour in my workshop each moⸯ
  fresh.
- I'll schedule my book group meetings early each month to avoid
  any conflicts.

By now you've probably spotted the real purpose of the exercise: to
reduce the number of dissatisfiers and increase the number of satisfiers in every aspect of your life. By expressing each dissatisfier positively, you write your own prescription—an action plan—for change.
By combining these less satisfying items with activities that already
make us happy, we give ourselves a better chance, and more incentive,
to make them work.

Although this process may seem deceptively simple—almost a
trick—experience shows that it really works. Psychologically, we are
reinterpreting our life's story to come up with a different script—a
new way to play scenes that, in the past, have left us dissatisfied, unfulfilled, anxious, fearful, or angry.

Although this ends the basic exercise, I'd like to add one final,
optional step—one you can take as many times as necessary.

Step 7. Review Your Lists Every Time You Make a Significant Life Change

Obviously, big life-changing events—a new job or termination, a marriage or a separation, the birth of a child or the departure of a child for
college, to name just a few—can unbalance even the most centered
people. If you wait until new dissatisfiers build up before revisiting your
lists, you may subject yourself to more stress and strain than necessary.

Instead, think of new problems and challenges (potential dissatisfiers) as opportunities to create new satisfaction. Don't wait until negative feelings develop and need to be converted through remedial
action: preempt those dissatisfactions by approaching every challenge
with a positive attitude, using techniques you already enjoy and understand.

4. Find Your Balance as You Set Out to Practice the Art of Leadership

> Do what you love. Know your own bone, gnaw at it, bury it, unearth it, and grow it still.
>
> —Henry David Thoreau

In aikido philosophy, this sense of centeredness—of connection to life and to the time and space around us—is the soul. It is that point at the core of our existence where the instantaneous becomes the eternal, where "then" and "there," past and future, become "now." Usually we're aware of that blissful synchronization only when it doesn't happen: when our life seems to have taken a wrong turn and we don't know what to do about it. Instead of letting our energy, and the energy of people and things around us, flow easily through that center in a way that reflects our will, we divert too much of it to peripheral concerns, to things less central to our well-being. Happiness and fulfillment become increasingly distant targets, and our pursuit of them seems more tiring and frustrating. Paradoxically, the harder we push, the more distant our destination becomes. Fortunately, this paradox points the way toward our salvation—our return to grace.

Kisshomaru Ueshiba, son of aikido's founder, Morihei Ueshiba, says that this negative condition is essential to recognizing and rebalancing ourselves after we have undergone substantial change.[1] *Ki,* or the Chinese *chi*—the life force at the center of aikido—after all, has a dual aspect: part positive, part negative. The two must coexist to be in balance. People who believe their lives are all positive are living in the proverbial fool's paradise. Rather, *ki* operates as yin and yang, darkness and light, each aspect supporting the whole needed for harmony.

Read allegorically, this means that the light and dark forces reflected in our nature are created when we are born, are groomed and shaped as we grow up, and follow us for the rest of our lives. Only by solving life's riddles, overcoming its hurdles, and finally discovering this truth within ourselves—as Ulysses and the other heroes have done—can we neutralize the enemies that trouble us, like the spiritual travails brought on by greed, envy, spitefulness, alienation, and a desire to control that which is not ours to command.

Intuitively, this aikidoist philosophy—linked as it is to similar common stories of journey, test, and salvation known in other cultures throughout the world—is very appealing. But intellectual acceptance of its ideas is one thing; using those ideas to change your life is another. For this we must turn to the examples of enduring leaders who have successfully tested the spirits in their own lives and then used that knowledge to move on.

THE AIKIDOIST'S PATH TO RENEWAL

Like good health, we notice the virtues of a balanced life mostly by their absence. As leaders, when an inner enemy takes control and we feel emotionally depleted, uncreative, insensitive, ego-dominated, and numb to life's joys, we stray from the road that brought us to our success. We fear that our epic journey, begun with high hopes and promise, has somehow been shunted off onto a back road; that we will never reach our productive and creative potential.

Several years ago I participated in a brief seminar for corporate and academic leaders. Its ostensible goal was an exchange of views: to give practicing leaders the latest thinking in organizational theory and to provide management scholars with an update on life in the trenches. There was the usual mix of introverts and extroverts, joiners who liked the process of give-and-take, and those who had come mainly to lecture others but who wound up dominating the discussion. Learning and growth are possible in such circumstances, but you've got to listen carefully and read between the lines.

One corporate leader gradually emerged as quite unlike these others: a mild-mannered young woman who on more than one occasion completely stopped the backward slide of posturing, self-congratulation, and pontificating by asking insightful questions. What a joy it was to see her more outgoing elders pause, visibly rethink their often outlandish positions, then march off in an entirely different and more fruitful direction. Gradually, what had begun as a somewhat embarrassing contest of credential polishing and pedantic storytelling turned into a productive exchange of perspectives—the reason we had assembled. This was effective leadership of a very refined and economical sort, so I made a point of getting to know this able and self-possessed young leader better. She was Christie Hefner, CEO of Playboy Enterprises, heir to Hugh Hefner's eclectic empire of lifestyle publishing and other ventures.

In subsequent discussions, my high esteem of Hefner only increased. I was impressed by her wide range of interests, from business and the media to issues of the global environment and women's rights, and by her genuine mastery—or approach to mastery—over them. While most executives defined their lives in terms of their organizational responsibilities and career ambitions, Hefner described hers as a never-ending process of learning—about herself as well as the world—a process that, whatever her success to date, had not been without frustrations.

"How do I get really good, wise teachers," she asked, "people I can spend time with, much as I do with the good advisers I have in business?" She wanted more than simple recommendations about books and seminars; she was after associations that would challenge and inform her, take her to places she knew instinctively were part of her journey as a leader. As we talked about retreats I became increasingly aware of the unique circumstances that had shaped this young leader's life. Growing up under the tutelage—and shadow—of an American icon like Hugh Hefner was more than an educational experience; it was very close to a mythological rite of passage—an epic journey of Homeric proportions. Not only was she forced to come to grips with the issues that bedevil all aspiring leaders (Who am I? What do I want from life? What do I have to offer?), but she also had to steer a narrow course between the rocks and cliffs of her own talents and ambitions, on the one hand, and her father's enormous celebrity on the other: the Scylla and Charybdis that have destroyed many celebrity offspring who sought to make their own mark on the world.[2]

The method that she and other similarly engaged and enlightened leaders devised for doing this is worthy of consideration by those who seek to maintain their identity while the world tries mightily to remake them:

1. *Seek variety in all you do.* Sameness—in our surroundings, tasks, and associates—brings lassitude, which stifles learning. Just as bland food suppresses the appetite, so variety of experience—the spice of life—is the raw material for growth. Unless we know what's on the menu, we don't know what to ask for.

2. *Ask "So what?" Then find the answer.* Hefner takes pleasure in looking past the numbers, the facile arguments, and the obvious rationales for a decision to find out what really makes it tick. Why have we defined the situation as a problem? Is there an opportunity, as well as a solution, hidden inside it?

3. *Surround yourself with the best available advisers.* Hefner asks, "Why not build the organization around the very best people, those who have the right values, the right stuff for the future? I have really good business advisers and exercise trainers, but where can I find top-quality people for my personal development?" For a leader, this is not narcissism. If the leader fails to grow, the constituents fail, too, at least for a while, so it's in everyone's best interest to make sure such leaders are healthy, vital, and well informed. But the leader must take ownership of the learning challenge, create an interesting array of possibilities, and find the provocative teachers to match the list.

4. *Remember that purpose is more important than time.* Most leaders get locked into stultifying routines and dead-end tracks because they focus on one goal or a few issues to the exclusion of all else, particularly when the pressure of time is a constant companion. Hefner's solution—one that is used by many overtaxed and overtired executives—is to delegate authority, not just to save time but to create time for taking on new and more creative problems. Under the old way of thinking, leaders wanted absolute certainty that the outcome would be predictable. Under the new way of thinking, leaders seek diverse, not cookie-cutter, solutions. Green Glass Age leaders seeking rejuvenation and renewal should delegate authority to those who share their sense of purpose.

5. *Form new alliances to get away from old patterns.* To become leaders, most people must meet and disarm at least one inner enemy. If these enemies would stay vanquished, it would be a perfect world, but they don't. To endure, you must grow, and to grow, you must change. As our ancestral stories tell us, as soon as one challenge is mastered, another rises to take its place, just as day follows night.

An inventor-entrepreneur overcame a high need for control in order to grow his company from a suburban garage to a major player in his industry. Knowing he was the best engineer in the company, he realized that unless he allowed his constituents to make their own mistakes and be responsible for correcting them, they would never develop that synergistic group learning curve from which truly great organizations are born. So the founder took a long breath, drew back, let his "children" grow—and found that his own wealth and reputation grew along with them.

Eventually it was time for him to take his company public. By now the firm had diversified into products and services well beyond the founder's expertise. He was no longer a mere sponsor of shared leadership; he was its partner and interdependent with it for the firm's continued success.

This is not a pleasant place for most control-oriented founder-leaders to dwell. It evokes all the insecurities and frustrations that drove them to entrepreneurship to begin with. Founder-leaders may feel challenged by the host of new legal, financial, and marketing experts, all of whom have their own agendas. In this case, our CEO sensed his old inner dictator stirring, restlessly hatching plots, conspiring to seize power once more from the more mature and enlightened leader he thought he had become. His solution was to create even more distance by setting up a laboratory for creative, hands-on projects, which he finds challenging and pleasant.

Leaders at such crossroads can find many ways to avoid addressing the real problem that confronts them—evolving to the next higher level of their own personal and spiritual growth. The only solution that works (and by that I mean lasts) in these cases of "spiritual amnesia" is to use the power of those restless inner enemies against themselves, aikido-style, so that you can get on with your growth.

INTEL'S BALANCING EXERCISES

Intel conducts periodic checkups aimed at detecting inflated pride and releasing any dangerous high pressure through humor, special counseling, and team feedback. One thing they've learned is that these relief valves themselves must not become so routine or so familiar that they themselves become part of the problem.

The model that works best here is the periodic contests held between aikido schools—a counterpart to the tournaments held among aggressive, attack-oriented karate academies. If you find yourself asking why a noncompetitive sport like aikido would have any contests at all—congratulations. You're beginning to think like an aikido-style leader! An aikido match isn't a match at all; it's a demonstration. Those involved strive not to defeat their opponents, but to show the audience the skills, joys, and accomplishments they've gained in a communal, supportive, and good-humored environment. Winners are judged not by whom they defeat but by how much they have learned and by how well they can demonstrate that learning to others.

Intel director and education expert Ann Bowers describes techniques for driving out inner enemies and testing the organization for balance:

1. *Balance your press releases with a hard look in the mirror.* "People are great at selective listening. When we feel insecure, we focus on the slightest hint of criticism. When we're feeling great—as successful, talented leaders often do—we hear, see, and read only the things that support our exaggerated view of ourselves, and we chalk up the critical comments to the stupidity, shortsightedness, or sour grapes of others. It's hard to learn much about yourself or to see long-term changes coming when you're busy running the universe."

    She goes on, "By having a team at Intel of respectful peers at the top," Bowers says, "they could complement and challenge each other." This means establishing and using a team of truthsayers, not sycophants, a habit carried forward by its current CEO and co-founder. "Andy Grove loves to be challenged and he sees the others as real peers." I recall Bowers's late husband, Bob Noyce, coinventor of the integrated circuit, echoing her view when he said of this team, "They really enjoyed their work and could have fun while arguing and working very hard. The word is 'balance.'"

The glue that holds such teams together through good times and bad is trust, which rewards good people and helps make all people better. Ann herself is adamant about respect. "Respect means pushing people to do better and trusting them to do the best they can," she says. It also means augmenting their natural talents with good training and letting them fail in a supportive environment. "At Intel," she affirms, "failing to learn is the biggest sin."

This philosophy was put to the test in 1994 when a flawed Pentium chip made headlines around the world. Many pundits began to denigrate the company on the spot, but Intel's eventual openness and candor in handling the incident, and in applying what it learned to its re-marketing efforts, helped the company bounce back with astounding speed. At this writing, subsequent Pentium sales have wiped out the costs of the fumble, and Intel now commands over 75 percent of the microprocessor market.

2. *Set high standards and stick to them.* "What's so interesting about Intel," Bowers says, "is that they are always pushing way beyond what their customers are asking for. They lead their customers." Pentium sales have already eclipsed the company's previous best-seller, the 486 microprocessor, the sixth generation of which is twice as fast as its prototype, and a seventh-generation chip is already on the way. Late in 1995, Intel beat competitors like Cray and nCUBE to win a coveted Department of Energy contract to build the world's fastest supercomputer using a core of 6,000 Pentium Pro microprocessors.

Advance thinking like this means more than market leadership: it means survival in the Green Glass Age. Such standards must apply not just to job performance or team-based problem-solving but also to interpersonal relations, including the way you treat yourself. Self-awareness is a perishable skill that dwindles without use.

3. *Create rituals for resolving conflict and settling disputes.* One reason people fear and avoid conflict is that each dispute puts them on untested ground. If they view conflict as a win-lose contest

instead of an aikidoesque search for harmony, they feel threatened, and that creates stress. At issue is not only the outcome of the disagreement but also their personal pride, their self-esteem, and their reputation within the group.

Bowers believes these collateral issues always take center stage when people are forced to settle disputes with verbal fisticuffs, political backstabbing, or executive power plays. In these cases, all people learn about themselves is the depth of their own mean spirit and ability to manipulate a situation—hardly the stuff from which long and happy lives are made. What's needed, she thinks, is a system whereby the assets of the entire group are made available to help resolve disputes among any of its members.

"By getting people to challenge each other, the culture says, 'We respect your ideas and opinions.' It promotes diversity and works against group-think. Andy is great at getting people to improve their efforts by fair challenges." It's only fair, then, that members of the group return the favor by acting as mediators, issue researchers, adjudication panelists, or facilitators, or by doing whatever it takes to help the conflicting parties stay focused on the facts and not the fight. This is where the ritual aspect comes in. The great value of rituals is that they give us something to do while we're trying to figure out what to do. They provide a sense of spiritual direction when things are most uncertain, tapping the hidden power of our subconscious to mediate and design solutions that are often inaccessible to minds preoccupied with battle.[3]

TESTING THE SPIRITS

Most spiritual crises begin with a question mark, not an exclamation point. Confident people accustomed to success feel most threatened by doubts, not challenges, problems, or even failures. Here are some of the questions these leaders fear the most:

- *Is my faith no longer justified?* Is it strong enough to see me through? Faith in anything is a matter of belief, not proof; so the mere act of questioning it is evidence that something is amiss. This applies not only to religious faith but to faith in institutions like companies and governments and in ideologies, philosophies, and idolized individuals.

- *Am I running on chemicals or adrenaline rather than natural energy?* This question comes up most often after an extended period of stress when we begin to feel that we are simply going through the motions or running hard just to stay in one place. It's also a question we ask when we notice—or when it is brought forcefully to our attention by a loved one or through an accident— that we've become dependent on drugs or alcohol to get us through the day. Mindless or habitual activity is the enemy of true accomplishment, yet both consume loads of psychic and physical energy. It's unnerving to think that our life force is trickling away like water over a dam—nourishing little and bringing light to no one, including ourselves.

- *Am I just getting the wrong answers or am I asking the wrong questions?* Mental and emotional burnout is marked by an inability to focus on what's important, to prioritize, to separate goal-setting from wishful thinking. You have good reason to worry if you find yourself working frantically to solve the wrong problem or to achieve goals you no longer care about. When you lose the star you normally steer by, the edge of the earth looms perilously close.

- *Why has my trust turned to mistrust? Why has my affection turned to jealousy or to anxiety?* Survivors of the corporate wars who go on to great success often find themselves substituting obedience for trust, calculation for cooperation, when dealing with peers and subordinates—afflictions familiar to great leaders in every age. Industrial-age leaders talk about the loneliness of command, never realizing that such isolation is brought about by their own attitudes and actions, not by the feelings of constituents who want to be more involved, trusted, and self-directing. Even so, feelings of isolation can cause you not only to doubt your constituents but often to question your own humanity as well.

- *Who is that person in the mirror?* I've seen this happen to leaders in crisis many times: they begin a story, usually a favorite tale of triumph or adversity—a founder's myth or a common story upon which the corporate culture is based—only to have their eyes glaze over, their smile fade, and their voice quaver when they get to the moral of the story. When leaders no longer recognize themselves in the essential narratives that drive their lives and bind their constituents together, something indeed is terribly wrong.

The list goes on, and you could probably add other questions of your own, but they all reflect the same fundamental condition: life for such leaders has become unbalanced; it has drifted off-center and is wobbling, threatening to topple or fly apart at the seams.

When questions like these surface in leadership conferences, seminars, or retreats, I usually recommend one of the following ways to help such troubled leaders redefine their lives and get back on track or, failing that, to find new territory to explore:

1. *Talk to your mentor, or* sensei—*or find a new one.* Mentors and trusted advisers—especially those with whom you have established a true *sensei* relationship—act like scouts, riding ahead and reporting the nature of the forces that will soon confront you but which are temporarily hidden by the fog in which you are enveloped. Your mentor can also be your magnifying glass, making apparently insignificant and overlooked but potentially troubling factors life-sized; or your telescope, bringing visions of distant hopes and dreams within reach.

   The most important thing, however, is that no leader should feel that he or she must face a large-scale crisis alone. I am always surprised (though I shouldn't be) when I hear that a leader in crisis doesn't have this kind of confidant. Most assertive, successful people either don't feel the need for a mentor or think that turning to wise counselors when things go wrong is less honorable, or more demeaning, than looking for teachers who will help them excel.

   If your problem is profound, your *sensei* should practice a kind of well-tempered tough love: supportive enough to assure you he or she is on your side, but challenging enough to make sure your long-term best interests—which the *sensei* often sees more clearly than you do—are also given a voice in the proceedings.

   When your counselor becomes your friend, it's easy to lapse into a comfortable camaraderie where your mentor gives you support unconditionally and avoids bringing up topics or taking positions that will bring you pain. Conversations here tend to be superficial and reassuring. Your mentor assumes that the world is wrong, not you, and generally helps you play the game of "ain't it awful" instead of playing a devil's advocate. Of course, this attitude (or outlook?) won't serve to help you in the long run.

Your spirit guide in such crises should not be a dilettante or a close friend with too much personal baggage in the relationship. It should be someone who is objective and caring enough to focus on your renewal before turning the exchange into therapy for himself. If your current mentors or advisers seem inadequate for this task, don't be afraid to look around for new ones. That usually means asking trusted associates for people who have helped them in similar situations. As all aikidoists know, the best masters can always be found—and judged—by their students.

Phillip Moffitt was successful in business from the age of twenty-one, creating numerous publishing ventures. He was named one of *Inc. Magazine*'s entrepreneurs of the 1980s. At forty, he switched his interests to leadership and the mind-body connection, and he began to seek out new teachers, including George Leonard for aikido.

At any given time, Moffitt may have two or three master teachers on subjects ranging from meditation, psychology, mind-body healing, yoga, and physical performance. He says, "I was starting over and in disciplines where many people get off the track. My teachers give me both knowledge and a reality check."

Here are guidelines for choosing a mentor to help you get back on track:

- *Look for the best teachers in the field.*
- *Don't expect one teacher to know everything.* Even the best teacher has blind spots, biases, or gaps in life experience. The more effectively your network of advisers can fill in these holes, the broader your resources for renewal will be.
- *Be respectful but not shy when you talk with your teacher.* Many leaders would rather walk on hot coals than ask for help, even when they need it most—and especially when they feel the pangs of a gut-wrenching personal crisis. If you are absolutely genuine with your teacher, he or she will be earnest, and most helpful, to you.

- *Commit yourself totally to your own development.* Too many leaders—especially executives in large organizations who are used to achieving their objectives through others—do well at locating and establishing *sensei* relationships, then drop the ball when it comes to putting the lessons they learn into practice. Positive change means positive action, and lasting change means continual practice—in the George Leonard sense: an activity pursued primarily for its own sake.

2. *Retreat to the dojo—or find a new one.* A dojo is a place of enlightenment. To martial artists, it's the training studio. It's any place that gives us a sense of connectedness to feelings, ideas, and events that are larger than ourselves. While it can be a particular country, city, village, building, room, studio, garden, desert shack, swimming hole, jogging path, mountain cabin, sailboat, resort hotel, camping tent, or even a favorite chair, it is always a state of mind—a place where practice makes perfect, where rituals gain meaning, where a higher reality seems possible. For Michael Murphy, founder of Esalen and author of the best-selling *Golf in the Kingdom* (a meditation on the Zen of mastery disguised as a sport-travel book), a Scottish golf course became the spiritual proving ground.[4] And I have heard of stranger dojos!

When George Leonard first opened his aikido studio in bucolic Mill Valley, California, he realized he was making a life-long commitment to his art and to himself. Like all dojos, his became a place of reverence and renewal that in no way preempted the joy, good humor, frustration, and hard work that goes into building any business or mastering any significant endeavor.

"The dojo is a wonderful place to go," George says. "I work in my house, so I leave my writing and family life I so treasure and enter another place where I am completely absorbed. I switch gears. I go deeper into myself. Mastery is a long process and so very slow at times, when progress comes, it is surprisingly quick and satisfying. All mastery requires the discipline to detail and ritual we associate with the dojo."[5]

Mastery of the self, in all its changing hues, is no exception. The role of the dojo as a place for practicing the art of leadership doesn't change when the person pursuing that mastery changes inside. Indeed, such changes make the transcendent, salubrious environment of the dojo even more indispensable. To make sure this special place gives you all the nourishment you need, be sure to

   • *Treat it with respect.* Endow it with the properties of a shrine. Don't profane your sacred area with outside work, business meetings, social gatherings, or any activity unworthy of soul-making—its primary function.

   • *Tell your teacher about it.* Your *sensei* should understand the kind of environment you find most helpful to your quest. Often he or she can suggest ways to get the most out of the time you spend there, and suggest alternative locations if and when your favorite retreat is not available.

   • *Budget your dojo time wisely.* The line between retreat and recreation can be a fine one, especially when your special place is visually appealing and offers lots of collateral things to do. Relaxation is a vital part of renewal, but spirit-mending is a serious business and ample time and energy must be set aside for introspection, speculation, discussion, meditation, and other thought experiments.

From this very active (never passive!) reception of energy from the dojo and new ideas and feelings from our subconscious, conception begin—clarifications and insights that might never see the light of day had they confined their attempts at renewal to the bustling world of deadlines and obligations.

In short, the dojo is there to be used for what it is. If you try to make it something else, the spell will be broken: it will simply become another place. The person you were trying to put temporarily at arm's length—to see in a new perspective—catches up to you and the opportunity for insight passes, at least until another day.

3. *Practice a favorite ritual—or find a new one.* An evoking of the sacred goes hand in hand with dojos. Most leaders who use such retreats to cultivate spiritual awareness link them to the rituals, big and small, that they practice in other places.

   Alan Jones, dean of Grace Cathedral in San Francisco, a man on cordial terms with both spirituality and its manifestations in workaday life, thinks of Grace Cathedral as his dojo, a place where invigorating, uplifting rituals come naturally, even to those not professing the Episcopalian faith.

"A great cathedral is a gathering place for ritual," he says. "The original cathedrals were the center of community where art, music, birth, death, and marriages were ritualistically celebrated. We can make such celebrations of the spirit a connection with the universal and the sacred." The building itself is a physical expression of that spiritual sensibility—not just its soaring lines, but its deepest, most elemental structure: such as the floor plan that takes the shape of a cross, or the many visual references to the trinity—a reflection of one of mankind's most elemental views of nature. Yet the rituals Alan speaks of know no denomination. They do not require surplice and miter to connect each celebrant with his or her own sense of the eternal. As Jones writes in *Soul Making,* "We need rituals that speak to our experience of transitoriness. We need feasts and ceremonies that speak hopefully of the future that binds us together."[6] These are sentiments that transcend any liturgy or dogma—even theology. The explanation and justification for them lies in the simple fact that we are human.

One ritual that is uniquely American, and uniquely postindustrial as well, is the phenomenon of jogging. People who habitually walk, jog, run, or bike for the purpose of maintaining or improving their health are involved in a sacred undertaking, with spiritual as well as physical benefits. They are saying to themselves and their community, "My health and well-being matter." Their rewards—better health, compliments on their appearance, more energy for the things they want to do, even the so-called runner's high—are proof that this message has been heard. As joggers' wind and muscle tone improve and more miles slip beneath their sneakers, they expand that sense of flow to include a oneness with their surroundings.

This is just one example of an ordinary ritual you can use as a vehicle for crossing from one plane of perception and thinking to another. The better we get at rituals, and as long as they hold their meaning, the more harmoniously we fit into our surroundings, including that part of the environment that challenges us with change. Here are some ways to make the rituals in your life more meaningful and better vehicles for renewal:

• *Embrace the rituals that define your life.* If you believe you practice no rituals, think again. Ritualistic behavior is deeply ingrained in the human psyche, was put there for a reason. To spot your rituals, keep a log of each day for at least a week. Write down what you do, how long it takes, and why you think you do it. Even money says that by the end of a week you will have spotted several activities that seem to have no significant purpose—like dawdling with coffee over the morning paper or habitually taking the slower, more scenic drive home on Fridays—but which you wouldn't even dream of changing. Now analyze why these simple, habitual acts feel so meaningful: What do they tell you about yourself and your life situation? Do they make you appreciate your other tasks and relationships even more? Or is the ritual's main function to take your mind off of other things—to make what you don't like seem more endurable? Either function is valid, and both help us cope, appreciate, and stay in touch with the spirit that moves us in the world. That's the value of rituals; that's why we need them in our lives.

• *Discuss your rituals with your teacher.* Since rituals are vehicles for getting in touch with our deepest hopes and dreams—and since they are also inoculations against our fears—good teachers are good at reading them and may be able to suggest ways to make yours even more healthful, meaningful, and rewarding.

• *When a ritual begins to feel like boring, mindless work, discard it.* People dislike change even when change is beneficial, so we cling to familiar routines even when they no longer serve us—another sign of a spiritual crisis. If duty or inertia has replaced passion as the reason for your ritual, discard it and seek a new one. Your log of daily and weekly habits should provide you with abundant clues to where to look. Above all, keep your rituals simple, doable, joyful, and rewarding.

4. *Make a fresh start at an old endeavor—or find a new one.* Unless a task is very simple, most people start not once but many times, and they must keep at it until they succeed. We forget about all the beginnings we made—from diets and other self-

improvement projects to whole careers—that came to nothing or were aborted because we lacked commitment, confidence, encouragement, or resources. The fact is, human change is nothing but a collection of serial beginnings. Each thing—relationship, activity, belief—in our life is tied to another, so a new effort in one place necessarily requires adjustment elsewhere, just as a new job requires changes in your commuting patterns, work habits, social life, and so on. This new arrangement is achieved through a complex series of trade-offs—adding here and taking away there, but aikido-style leaders make sure that these exchanges are not mere compromises but an optimization of the new life they have in mind.

Suppose you feel the emotional bonds with your loved ones are weakening and you want to make a new start in both your home life and your career. This means finding or crafting a new position with equivalent job satisfactions and opportunities that will also yield more time for your family. This is a classic dilemma most leaders face at one time or another. It was the dilemma brought to me by two dynamic young leaders—let's call them Maryanne and Bill—who worked for the same advertising firm in Chicago and were married to each other. While I am not a marriage counselor by trade, much of the advice my clients seek involves reconciling the often conflicting goals of a lasting marriage and an enduring career, so this territory is familiar to me.

Maryanne was worried about Bill's health, which was starting to deteriorate from the strain of overwork. He was afraid his neglect would cause his desirable wife to wander. The diagnostic questionnaire they completed showed a perfect match between their goals. Both yearned for lasting career success, yet neither wanted to sacrifice the marriage to achieve it. Like many people in similar high-demand situations, they had simply been unable to find a way to make both work.

"I'm deathly afraid of losing her," Bill said candidly, and I believed him. "She's smart and attractive and really good at her job—and I'm not the only guy who sees it."

Maryanne's moist eyes belied her outward composure. "I know Bill worries a lot about that. I tell him I'm too busy to have an affair, even with my husband. The truth is, he's burning himself out, and I feel that I'm going to be the biggest loser. He's already got a bleeding ulcer and a briefcase full of medications. He's afraid I'm going to wake up one morning next to a strange man. I'm afraid I'm going to wake up one day next to a corpse!"

There was little posturing or blame-laying within the relationship. They seemed perfectly sincere, which made their anguish—and their inability to resolve their dilemma—even more disturbing. I asked them what adjustments they had made or were willing to make to achieve their goal of preserving their marriage as well as their careers.

"I could cut back my hours," Maryanne said immediately, "but we just can't afford it. You know the ad game—you're only as good as your last big success. And Chicago's an expensive town. If one of us gets downsized, the other's got to pick up the slack."

I asked Bill if that applied to him as well. "Absolutely," he said firmly. "If I tell these guys I can't come in on the weekend or I need a few days off to take Maryanne up north, they'll say, 'Great! Have a good time.' Then they'll give my projects to somebody else."

"So which is worse," I asked Bill, "being a one-income family or"—I looked back at Maryanne—"being a widow at thirty-five? It seems to me those are the only two choices."

"Well, not really." Bill squirmed uncomfortably in his chair. "I could quit the AE track and go back to Creative. Nobody hassles those guys about how they use their time. And there are other, smaller agencies who'd love to have a guy with my experience. We'd get by. It's just that—well, that's not what I've been working for."

Now we began to approach the real issue that was keeping these two talented and ambitious people apart. They had swallowed—hook, line, and sinker—the industrial-age myth that demanded one's soul in exchange for success. They simply could not envision a life that contained everything that was important to them. Of course, they weren't dummies. They knew you couldn't pour a gallon of milk into a quart jar. They just hadn't given themselves permission to think creatively about ways to accommodate the fullness of their lives.

After a bit of "awfulizing," they agreed that nothing so bad could happen to them that would not be made worse by the loss of each other. They decided that if they were really as clever, talented, and experienced as they believed, they should be able to fashion a life that was right for them both. Although finding these new ways to live—ways to realize the values they treasured while giving up only the burdens that weighed them down—would be financially risky, it offered more chances for happiness than they would have found in a hospital emergency room or in the cold halls of a Chicago divorce court.

Still, deciding to begin again is not the same as actually starting over. They needed a plan as flexible and expansive and open to improvisation as the task they had set for themselves.

To start this process, I told them they each had three valuable commodities to bring to this new effort. Two of these commodities were finite—there was only so much of them to go around. The third commodity, though, was inexhaustible. They could produce as much of it as they liked whenever they wanted. Best of all, while all three commodities were needed to make their plan work, any one commodity could be substituted for another. They leaped to it with a passion, and began applying it immediately to their lives. Here is the formula I showed them: Time + Resources + Spirit = Success.

Time is marked by the relentless ticking of the clock. The moment you have now must be used now because it will never come again. This reality sometimes causes people to forget the other aspects of a balanced life and focus entirely on gainful employment and wealth-building. Such people don't see that unless you use that precious, irreplaceable moment now to achieve, or begin to achieve, your other valuable goals, those goals will simply never come to pass.

Charles Handy says that when he was a college professor, he devoted about 20 percent of his time to research, including self-development. "Companies should manage at least 10 percent of work time for people to be free to grow and explore," he claims, even in cultures preoccupied with short-term results, like firms in the United States. If your company won't give you that time, Handy says, "Create it yourself. Find an assignment that means you have to learn a new skill."[7]

Your resources are your income, wealth, physical health,

training and experience, and so on. They are the basic productive engines that procure for you all the other things you value. They can even substitute for time: invested wealth, for example, can produce income that will allow you to divert your time to other uses or to hire people to expand your competencies and reach. Similarly, time can be exchanged for resources you presently don't have: if you can't afford something, you can often do it yourself, or save and invest until you can afford it. If your health is poor, you can consciously decide to use a larger portion of your time to make it better, and so on. Still, there's a cap on the number of resources available to you at any given moment, so resources are finite, like time.

Spirit, as you've guessed, is the only inexhaustible commodity in the formula. Used to augment time, it makes you more efficient and productive. Used to augment resources, it makes you more satisfied and effective. By itself, a healthy, well-centered spirit makes every aspect of your life better. Even if time is short and resources are low, a soaring spirit makes every aspect of your life worth living.

Of course, I offered Bill and Maryanne—as I'll offer now to you—a final word of caution. Although our power to change ourselves as individuals is almost unlimited, our power to change relationships is never quite as great. When another person is involved, our ultimate success depends also on that person's willingness and ability to change: to take risks, expand trust, fail and forgive, and try again. For leaders, this diminishing personal power deepens as the number of relationships—that is, the number of constituents you lead—increases. Therefore, while you can still look out for number one, establishing and maintaining spiritual health for a couple, family, group, or company will always be a communal affair.

The good news is that group synergy works both ways. While slow learners and those with wounded souls, alternative agendas, and surrogate issues to deal with can always hold the network back, the group can speed up personal growth and evolution by making its aggregate time, resources, and collective spirit available to the individual. This is not just an option in organizational renewal; it is its essence.

A Tool for Establishing Balance

Mystics and mathematicians alike consider the circle to be nature's most perfect shape. Aikidoists pattern their defensive techniques on circular, or spherical, motion. Ancient Hindus and Tibetan Buddhists chose the circle to represent the universe (the word "mandala" means "circle" in Sanskrit), within which they inscribed a square, each corner representing one deity in balance and opposition to the others. In time, the resulting symbolic diagram was used as a tool for self-discovery as well as religious thought.

Most of the time, our ego controls our thoughts—but ego is not the entire self. The mind is composed of conscious and unconscious elements that form our personal internal universe—a unified entity composed of many opposing forces that is modeled nicely by mandalas. When Carl Jung began to explore his own ego's relationship to the unconscious in the early twentieth century, he drew mandalas that contained symbolic representations of the oppositional and complementary forces he encountered.

Jung wrote: "The 'squaring of the circle' is one of the many archetypal motifs which form the basic patterns of our dreams and fantasies. . . . As is to be expected, individual mandalas display an enormous variety. . . . Their object is the self in contradistinction to the ego, which is only the point of reference for consciousness, whereas the self comprises the totality of the psyche altogether, i.e., conscious and unconscious. It is therefore not unusual for individual mandalas to display a division into a light and dark half."[8]

These light and dark halves, Jung thought, revealed not only conscious and subconscious forces but—and most usefully to leaders—our positive and negative evaluations of them, forces that, like the deities of the ancients, govern our lives. After years of drawing and analyzing his own and others' mandalas, Jung concluded that "A modern mandala is an involuntary confession of a peculiar mental condition. . . . The mandala symbolizes, by its central point, the ultimate unity of all archetypes as well as of the multiplicity of the phenomenal world."[9] This realization has profound implications for anyone interested in pursuing self-knowledge—as well as the practices of enduring leaders.

First, the mandala can help us to see that while opposing forces may never be completely united, they can be brought into balance—and inner harmony found—but only by adopting the perspective of the whole person. We can reconcile the opposing forces in our lives—career versus family needs, group versus individual interests, and so on—by adopting a holistic view of the self.

Second, it suggests that tools like mandalas, which tap both conscious and unconscious creativity and energy, ideas and experience, really do work as vehicles for self-understanding and growth.

In drawing a mandala, you literally create your own internal treasure map: a guide for increasing your knowledge about the hidden forces that trouble and energize you. To make and use a mandala, keep three things in mind:

- *Mandalas are about finding harmony amid opposition and conflict, not reinforcing a specific philosophical view or religious belief.* They work because they reflect the way our brains perceive and internalize the world. If you don't feel stimulated and energized while you are working with your mandala, you're probably doing it as work rather than art.

- *The squares, not the circle, are the essence of your mandala.* Novices often begin and end their mandalas by simply connecting two conflicting ideas, or forces, on opposite (light and dark) sides of the circle. They forget that nothing—in the universe or the human psyche—operates in total isolation, that everything exerts a bit of influence on everything else, even if that influence is unperceived. In the model of the internal universe you create with your mandala, any two opposing forces are always acted upon by the other pair of forces that complete their square, plus the other forces constituting other squares. Only by assessing this mutual interplay can you find the proper balance that represents your most harmonious psychic center.

- *Only you can interpret your own mandala.* The labels or symbols you make mean different things to different people, but your definition is the one that counts. The usefulness of your mandala is also proportional to the time and thought you put into it, generating the polar forces and perhaps choosing colors for the lines, the labels, and the areas they enclose. What ultimately counts most, though, is not the pretty picture you get but the feelings and insights you experience while putting it together.

In the sample leadership mandala here, the inner secret I tried to probe was "Where and how does stress turn into strength?" I began by listing the opposing forces that complicate leaders' lives, including mine: individual versus group needs, linear versus holistic thinking, the need to plan versus the need to act, and so forth. I next cut these forces into strips, or labels (you won't need scissors if you write on Post-it notes), and distributed them around a circle, making sure that the polar forces still opposed each other. I then drew a series of squares by connecting the forces at each quarter point on the circle with a line. Finally, I analyzed the mandala by looking at how the forces in opposition—that is, those on the diagonals of each square— were influenced by the other forces in their square. For example, I asked how holistic thinking, or scenario planning, can help bring into balance the tension between individual and group needs, and how clearer communications might help balance the need for action with the need for planning, and so on. Gradually, insights into my current leadership problems began to come into focus, as indeed they will do for you.

THE LEADERSHIP MANDALA: WHEN DOES OPPOSITIONAL STRESS TURN TO STRENGTH?

Here is a sample of opposites that can be resolved:

Control	Trust
Unity	Diversity
Clear Communications	Creative Ambiguity
Bias for Thought	Bias for Action
Linear Planning	Holistic (Scenario) Planning
Spiritual Needs	Material Needs
Community Needs	Shareholder Returns
Family Needs	Career Needs

The above list represents some of the opposing forces that cause stress in leaders' lives. Feel free to add to or modify this list as you wish; just make sure that the total number of pairs you end up with is a multiple of two. When you have completed your list, array the pairs evenly on the outer edges of a circle, making sure the opposing forces still face each other directly. (Feel free to connect these original pairs with a line or a string, if it helps you keep track of them.) If you like, place all the forces you feel good about on one half of the circle, with their polar opposites on the other. Some people even color-code the forces, using red for those that seem particularly threatening, blue for those that seem mysterious, yellow for those requiring extra caution, and green for those they feel most comfortable about.

Next, beginning anywhere you wish, draw straight lines between one force and its complementary forces—that is, those halfway around the circle in both directions; then draw a line from those forces to the force originally opposing your starting point. Repeat this process with the remaining forces until you have drawn a series of overlapping squares, one square for every two pairs of opposites.

Now think about how the forces in opposition—that is, those on the diagonals of your squares—are, or may be, influenced by the presence of the second pair of forces in that square. How might the forces in the other squares affect the first? If you originally divided your circle into light and dark halves or if you color-coded your labels, how did those distinctions affect your conclusions? Some people report that the colors lose their significance; others say that rational versus intuitive forces pop out in relief, making interpretation easier. Still, there's no right or wrong way to read your mandala. Only you are the final judge.

If you're like most people, what initially seemed to be a chaotic mass of conflicting demands will end up a decidedly friendlier place: a universe filled with unlimited possibilities where no single force is so strong that it can't be shaped to any objective.

The mandala is a powerful tool for finding the balance in your life. As you read and begin to incorporate the mastery practices of leadership in this book, come back to this chapter, and the tools in it, whenever you feel yourself slipping out of balance.

5. Master Practice #1
Cultivate Self-Knowledge

It is not enough to understand what we ought to be, unless we know what we are.

—T. S. Eliot

For the enduring leader and the aikido master, the superordinate practice must be the cultivation of a deep self-awareness. The aikidoist must be familiar with each inner enemy before going on the mat. The wise leader must know what aspects of self and the organization are not in harmony and therefore will not be prepared to make the timely response to sudden change. The mat and the marketplace are violent places where only intense preparation, training, and self-knowledge separate the survivor from the victim. After a flaw was suddenly discovered in the Pentium chip, Andy Grove, the Intel CEO, described the company's half-billion-dollar-loss experience by saying, "It is like sailing a boat when the wind shifts on you. You don't even sense the wind has changed until the boat suddenly heels over. What worked before doesn't work anymore. You have to get a feel of the new direction and the strength of the wind before you can hope to right the boat and set a new course."

In his book *Only the Paranoid Survive,* Grove goes on to name a major inner enemy of most leaders during stressful times of pulsing change. He identifies this enemy as denial, which stops the leader from embracing and navigating change. The leaders' capacity to look inside, to examine the emotional rudder, is inadequate and thus leads to a "resistance to facing a painful new world."[1]

The search for self-knowledge is not the kind of work most leaders talk about. Yet all of the enduring leaders I have studied have practiced various ways of gaining knowledge about their inner lives. In my capacity as president of the Center for Leadership Renewal and as the former president of the California School of Progressive Psychology, a four-campus graduate school, it has been my privilege to serve as a temporary *sensei* for countless men and women who come to my study for a day of personal and professional planning. They have taught me a great deal about this work of digging for self-knowledge.

The planning day is the first time that most of these bright, accomplished people have honored their inner lives in this way. Often they come to prepare for a major change in direction and they have deep and vexing questions to sort out. Frequently they need to mend some neglected aspect of themselves: a weary marriage, flat creativity, waning vitality, unclear career choices. In this chapter I will outline and then reveal some of the wisdom that flows from these planning sessions and look at eight roads that lead to self-knowledge.

Roy, the energetic former president of a global parts-manufacturing company, arrived for his planning day looking more like a man in his early forties than the sallow sixtyish guy I had seen a year earlier. When I asked him for the source of this obvious change in vitality, his answer was immediate: "Getting away from my previous position, especially from the chairman."

Although our task was to create a plan for his next career phase, we were also searching to find out what lack of self-perception had allowed him to stay so long in the wrong place. Describing his former boss as someone who could never feel satisfied, he suddenly announced, "You know that guy is really sick, so why would I stay with someone like that?" Then he added rhetorically, "I must have been sick also. Right?"

The more we dug into this rich insight, the happier and clearer Roy got. He found a pattern of being a suffering pleaser (his phrase) who "found" people who would spot and exploit that tendency. By the end of our planning session, he displayed another powerful piece of self-knowledge: "I know how to be a success, but now I need to discover how to grow in wisdom." Wisdom for Roy meant having a life with joy as a new dimension of success. He also wanted balance and harmony as substitutes for the obsessive work patterns that had been his inner enemies.

The wisdom Roy seeks is that knowledge we keep locked deep

within us. It is the source of the aikido master's *hara*—good stomach—and the enduring leader's creativity and productivity over time. When we put a twist in our emotional lives by not examining our feelings or by displacing them, we lose considerable power and creativity. But for the leader with self-knowledge, emotion is not a dangerous spark to be smothered; rather it is an ember from which other activities gain warmth, energy, and meaning. Self-knowledge is more than a basic practice of leadership aikido. It is the core practice from which others spring, the Big Bang that informs our character and creates an expanding universe of opportunities.

LONG-LASTING LEADERSHIP BEGINS FROM WITHIN

Fashioning new leaders takes time and experience and begins from within. Unfortunately, for most of Western history we have prized our leaders for their square jaws, tight lips, true grit, and quick success. We have judged them mostly by what they did, not by how they did it or by the moral side effects of their acts. We have confused leadership with motion, not always in a forward direction, sometimes with disastrous results. Albert Speer, Hitler's architect and confidant, made a virtual science of looking the other way when the facts about his boss's atrocities began to surface. Speer, a well-educated and civilized technocrat, became so enamored of position and power that he totally forwent the kind of introspection that usually gives creative work its meaning. To the end of his life, Speer insisted that he was nothing more than a craftsman and administrator doing his best for an employer. His rationalization, which won him a long prison term instead of the hangman's noose at the Nuremberg trials, was not the "good German" defense adopted by other Nazi henchmen: "I was just following orders." His argument was new and was based on a shrewder reading of the industrial-age mentality. Like contemporary managers who think their obligations begin and end with a balance sheet, Speer claimed that his very dedication to his profession prevented him from seeing the evil that lurked further up and down the chain of command.

Contrast Speer's bottom-line behavior with the habits of enduring leaders who cultivate their inner resources the way good gardeners prepare the soil. They develop the capacity to genuinely feel as well as to give an outward impression of strong feelings. They value creativity—individually, in groups, in larger organizations, and in the world-wide networks that link them—as the veritable engine of life. "He who knows others is learned," the great Tao philosopher, Lao-Tsu, reminds us, "but he who knows himself is wise."[2] Indeed, by prospecting our inner territory and making it familiar, we better enable ourselves to map the hearts and minds of others.

JOHN GARDNER, ROLE MODEL FOR ALL SEASONS

For more than twenty-five years I have been privileged to turn John Gardner for wise counsel and encouragement. Many people view him as a role model for a life of self-renewal. In 1989, at the age of seventy-seven, John changed careers for the seventh time. When I asked him why he had accepted a teaching post at the Stanford Business School, he replied, "It was a time to replenish myself. When I thought about our nation's leadership deficits, I concluded that the answer lies in part in getting young people to accept leadership roles in their communities. So that is what I will work on."

Gardner's résumé is not easily summarized, but some highlights reveal the diversity of his interests and talents and how centered he is in his values. His first leadership job was as an intelligence officer in World War II. Following the war, he put his Ph.D. in psychology and his experience to work as a young professor with a passion for writing. In the early 1960s he was recruited to head the Carnegie Corporation, and in that position he developed a national reputation as a philosopher and writer on the subjects of leadership and education.

In 1966, Lyndon Johnson drafted him to be secretary of Health, Education and Welfare. He led that department—at that time the largest bureaucracy ever assembled—with a strong ethical center and a collaborative style. He assembled such unlikely partners as big-city mayors, militant street organizers, and business and union leaders into the Urban Coalition in an effort to rescue the nation's battered and burned-out urban centers.

Self-knowledge helped John to move away from the immense power and the potential for personal corruption of high government positions. In 1969 he founded Common Cause, a leading citizens lobbying group for better government. Later he would co-found Independent Sector in an effort to harmonize the work of the disparate organizations from the not-for-profit and philanthropic worlds. In 1989 he left Washington to return to the Bay Area, where he had been a student at Stanford and U.C. Berkeley.

Throughout his career, John has continued to speak and write on subjects for which he has considerable passion. *Self-Renewal,* written in 1965, reveals his strong belief in cultivating the inner resources we all possess by practices that lead to self-knowledge. "The conventions and artificialities of life, to say nothing of habit, routine, and simple momentum, carry us so far from our interest and conviction that we all need a few primer lessons on how to get back in touch with our inner being." In 1990, his book, *On Leadership,* helped to confirm his position as a modern Jefferson, a Renaissance man whose adherence to his principles and devotion to country have influenced thousands and left an imprint on America's future.

There are multiple roads that lead to self-knowledge. Each of us must find our special avenue into the self. Few of us will have résumés like John Gardner's. But all of us can use self-knowledge to refine our choices, to avoid dismal detours, and to select the best route toward a satisfying career and a good life.

Virginia Woolf, whose body of writing reflects her introspection and insights, stated the benefits of the pursuit of self-knowledge: "The man who is aware of himself is hence-forward independent; and he is never bored, and life is only too short, and he is steeped through and through with a profound yet temperate happiness. He alone lives, while other people, slaves of ceremony, let life slip by them in a kind of dream."

FINDING THE WAY INTO THE SELF

To visit one's inner self is a completely natural process. As one does in practicing aikido, we use the forces that oppose us to accomplish the desired result: to restore harmony to a life that has become imbalanced because we have lost contact with ourselves. Ideally we would all have a *sensei* to guide us, to spot any tendency to let introspection slide into subversive self-absorption. Such teachers or collaborators would hold up an honest mirror for us to see our progress and correct our errors. With or without such a guide, however, the eight roads in this chapter can lead us along the path to self-knowledge.

There is, of course, a time and place for everything. Productive introspection can become subversive self-absorption if it's taken to extremes. Healthy people don't spend their days fussing before a mirror, even the mirror to the soul. Endless narcissistic preening is a sign of an obsessive mind, not a balanced one. Although you can always hire a therapist to guide you on your journey, a mature relative—a spouse, a parent, or an older child—a close friend, a sensitive boss, or an empathetic teacher or coach can make a good collaborator, too, if he or she possesses learning skills, goodwill, and interpersonal strengths you never suspected. Or, if you are so inclined, you might use the principles in *Leadership Aikido*.

Your co-explorer should be a treasure chest, not a doormat. Share what you think you've learned about yourself with your helper, but don't burden him or her with old complaints. A helper can provide a reality check for your conclusions. When you think you've got a critical mass of data about yourself—your attitudes, beliefs, values, or behaviors in a certain area—run it by your helper and see if it resembles you. If your helper's perceptions differ too much from your own, don't argue. Just say thanks for the feedback and do your homework again. Too often, people eager to improve themselves resort to trendy methods and fashionable remedies when a different approach might suit them better. A helper who knows you well can assist you in choosing the technique that suits you best.

EIGHT ROADS TO SELF-AWARENESS

We often use the term "learning experience" as a euphemism for "bad luck" or "the consequences of a bad decision"—and that's too bad. Genuine learning experiences—that is, those with a moral we understand and can use in similar situations—are worth their weight in gold. Usually, though, we're too preoccupied with changing a situation—solving a problem or achieving an objective—to pay much attention to how that situation may be changing us in a positive way.

That's why the habits of self-discovery practiced by enduring leaders, gained by trial and error, by luck, and occasionally by design, are so important.

The First Road: Use Creativity Creatively

Through genuinely creative acts—the more visceral and manual the better, (painting, sculpting, woodwork, needlepoint)—we can encounter that less verbal, less inhibited side of ourselves that perpetually yearns to break free, to grow, and to become. The creative arts have been used by harried leaders for centuries to keep in touch with an ever-changing psyche.

We recognize famous artists, composers, and writers by their work. A few characteristic brush strokes, bars of music, or paragraphs are all an expert needs to identify the creator of a painting, symphony, or novel. To a lesser degree this same principle of self-discovery through creation applies to the weekend painter, scratch musician, or amateur cabinetmaker. Here are the key aspects of the creative act that make it a main highway to self-knowledge for many lasting leaders:

- *Creativity is a hands-on affair.* Carl Jung recognized not only the therapeutic benefits of the creative act but its value as a self-learning tool as well. He believed that much of our confusion about life comes from the way we misinterpret symbols that arise from our complex culture—particularly as they are transmitted by language, our primary means for learning. Jung felt that we could make an end run around this verbal jungle by working creatively with our hands and feelings and, in doing so, get in closer touch with the primal forces that drive us. He asked his patients and students to express themselves through such hands-on mediums as finger paint, clay, and masonry, and the artistry of meal preparation.[3]

  Winston Churchill and Dwight Eisenhower both found insight in a paint box—cultivating the gentle and loving sides of their natures during harsh, unforgiving times. Business dynamo Gordon Sherman cultivated Zen-like patience by tying flies and growing orchids. Actor Jack Lord explored his feelings about humanity by painting poems and flowers on canvas. New York insurance executive Charles Ives, a passionate music student at Yale, became one of America's greatest composers as well as a commercial success at business.

These are not isolated examples. And you don't have to be an analyst to see the wisdom of Jung's approach. The vast majority of the successful leaders I've studied found both solace and self-knowledge through creative pursuits. Powerful people seeking relief from high-stress jobs often report that a creative outlet, undertaken at the insistence of a doctor or loved one, quickly became a staple in their lives, providing access to other parts of the soul where personal insights were abundant. Indeed, because of the great efficiency of the creative act in scouting out and delivering up these treasured insights, the busiest leaders are first to admit that they can least afford to miss them.

- *Creativity transfers itself from task to task.* Although personal growth is its own reward, creative activity pays practical dividends as well. Discoveries about your essential nature—your ability to improvise, appreciate, and visualize previously unseen possibilities—are carried over into your profession. People who are used to thinking creatively are simply more resourceful, more flexible, and more inspiring. This is especially true for leaders already working in creative fields such as advertising, design, and the performing arts. People who feel pressured to be brilliant every day often feel drained and sterile. They discover that regular creative exercise in a completely different field helps keep the machinery of invention well oiled.
- *Creativity is a lifelong endeavor.* Hands-on creative work helps to condition any leader for the marathon of life. Early in our careers, we are so busy discovering how the outside world works that we seldom take time to map our inner dimensions. We rely on the opinions of others—feedback from counselors, performance reviews, the criticism of friends and family—to form a picture of ourselves. While that is better than nothing, it inevitably leaves us hungry for a truth that only self-discovery can provide. As Jung aptly summed it up: "The first half of life is preparation for the second. And the second is to be the creative half."[4]

Your creative endeavor can be anything from tying flies for fishing to building houses, from painting to playing the piano to cooking—anything that helps you see and think in a new way. For the aikido leader, time spent seeking a new creative endeavor, or returning to one set aside long ago because it wasn't earning money or fame, is time well spent. Just start.

The Second Road: Falling in Love, Finding a Passion

If most people "lead lives of quiet desperation," as Thoreau said, it is because they fail to find, or have lost, that aspect of the human spirit that animates even the youngest child. From the tiniest spark of interest, a consuming passion can grow—a passion for collecting art, appreciating literature, helping others, growing flowers . . . you name it. And from these grand passions and the way we go about them, we can learn volumes about ourselves.

Sometimes a leader's creative outlet becomes a reigning passion. A software mogul I once coached decided to join a book group for recreation. He met with a half-dozen friends once a month to discuss books of common interest.

"Someone suggested we read M. F. K. Fisher's *How to Cook a Wolf,*" my client reported, "because it was supposed to be about food as a metaphor for life. Well, before you know it, we had invited a local celebrity chef to a meeting to teach us the secrets of Italian cooking. After that, I was hooked."[5]

He found himself devoting more and more of his spare time to learning about cookery—Italian and every other kind—even after the book group had moved on to other topics. He discovered not only a talent for the culinary arts but new social skills and an aesthetic sense—presentation is half the fun of gourmet cooking—he never dreamed he possessed. Best of all, he reported that he now spent less time "striving," as he put it, in his business and interfering with the creative processes of his employees. The frustrations that before he could never quite name—a sense of detachment from the final product, a feeling that he could somehow do his employees' jobs better than they could—somehow dissolved as he pursued his passion. "Cooking was precisely what I needed to balance my life," he said after a year or so. Improvements in both his disposition and productivity suggest that he was right.

Ruth, a senior executive of a managed health care company, was remodeling her apartment when she happened onto a magazine describing traditional Japanese interiors. Although she had no particular interest in Asian culture, the layouts' elegant simplicity and economical use of space, which was at a premium in her apartment, impressed her greatly. First she experimented with Japanese flower arrangements. Next she began studying the other aspects of Japanese design, and eventually she became particularly enamored of bonsai, the art of pruning and shaping miniature trees. Her designs soon began to appear in her office and apartment—and later in the homes and offices of friends. She constructed a small hothouse on her terrace, complete with workbench, shelves for Japanese ceramics, and racks of precision tools. Feeling relaxed and energized by her creative weekends, she became more productive at work. Having learned to see infinite possibilities in a few twigs and bits of pottery, she found more creative ways to combine tasks and personalities in her department, and she appreciated more fully the many small contributions made by others, which she had previously overlooked.

Ruth's passion for her hobby also inspired her to join a bonsai club that toured Japanese gardens around this country and eventually in Japan. On one trip she met Tom, another bonsai enthusiast who had begun cultivating his late wife's miniature garden as a kind of grief therapy several years before. What had started for Ruth as an exercise in design and for Tom as a temporary diversion had become for both a life passion, a common yardstick for measuring their growth as human beings and identifying kindred spirits. The last time I spoke with her, Ruth and Tom were engaged to be married, a true case of serendipity, where one passion moved in directions nobody could have known.

In all discoveries of a private passion—answering a call that transcends simple economics or a need for recognition—the key ingredient I've found is readiness. We must be willing to take the plunge when the right opportunity presents itself. We must be so eager to pursue our passion, in fact to enjoy the giddy exhilaration that comes from any infatuation, that we're willing to sacrifice to it a goodly share of all those other things we thought were indispensable: late nights at work, skipped vacations, a sense of our own invulnerability. Although we may have struggled all our lives to master a profession, accumulate power, achieve ambitious goals, we must be willing in an instant to suspend those comfortable and praise-winning activities to pursue a passion that may be a total crapshoot—to stare into the abyss of potentially unfulfilled—and perhaps unfulfillable—promise, not only with courage but with absolute delight.

If you are lucky enough to have a good teacher to guide and encourage you, to help you savor the tiny miracles—what I call the bright dew that accompanies the dawn of each new discovery—so much the better. But when passion charts your course, expert navigators are not necessary.

The Third Road: Learning from Pain

Diaper pins, hot stoves, and fickle lovers are among life's most eloquent teachers. Bad experience is an eloquent teacher. Sadly, the lessons we sometimes learn from divorce, serious illness, the death of a loved one, or the loss of a job are not always the ones we need to make sense of the next dark time. For some, the lessons we learn from physical or emotional pain are all the wrong ones: to hate technology, mistrust the opposite sex, spurn politics, or otherwise despise whatever has hurt us. We all know people who habitually blame others for their own misfortune or who blame themselves too harshly when anything goes wrong. These people suffer from a form of hubris, a kind of spiritual blindness. Whether we blame others or ourselves, what we're essentially saying is that there's no changing, no learning, to be gained from this experience. Either attitude leaves life's most important lessons unseen and unfelt, and therefore unlearned.

John Gardner wrote that "The world is an incomparable classroom, and life is a memorable teacher for those who aren't afraid." Pain teaches the wise person a universal lesson about vulnerability, empathy, and compassion. It also presents us with a unique chance to learn more and better skills for coping in a challenging world.

Pain may lead us into deeper levels of self-awareness if we experiment and work on our methods. Let's look quickly at two:

- *By listing painful times in our lives we can see patterns of behavior that lead to our discomfort.* Often we lock in on certain behavior that no longer serves us. One senior marketing executive revealed a pattern of illness—migraine headaches—following angry confrontations with his associates: "Once I saw how my anger was really killing me, I started to try different ways to manage my work crises. It worked! Six months of no headaches!"

- *Pain is frequently associated with patterns of time (and purpose) management.* If we examine our schedules, we may see how we can avoid stress-related illnesses. A woman who left her law practice to have a child told me, "It was almost miraculous how my chronic back pain vanished when I changed my work schedule. It was partly carrying that heavy, damn briefcase, but my constant time anxiety was really the culprit. Now that I am on flextime, my back rarely gives me trouble."

Pain can certainly have more profound effects and bring to the surface deep issues for which the resolution can be life-changing. It sounds strange but this happened to me when my father died.

Although I had suffered my share of bruises in life, my first experience with real pain—the kind of crushing, dislocating blow that can close the book on future growth—occurred after I lost both my parents. I discovered that anxiety about my own death was at the root of my great pain. With help, I gradually came to understand, on a deep and personal level, that life and death are two sides of the same coin, the day and night of existence. I learned to be more vulnerable, more familiar with repressed emotions. I began to see that my stoic male grit-it-out way of coping was not working well for me. With that new self-knowledge, I could begin to change my behavior, attitude, and style.

We don't have to wait for painful lessons to begin learning from our pain. I suspect there's not a person alive who hasn't had some painful experience from which he or she might learn something new that might eventually be transformed into self-knowledge that would be useful in a variety of leadership situations. More likely you might have something like chronic back pain or headaches. Perhaps it's time to explore what your body is trying to tell you to do. Exercise more? Work less? Work differently? Note patterns. Seek help if the pain persists.

The Fourth Road: Taking Time Out

From coffee breaks to vacations, working people know that down-shifting gears and changing scenery can sometimes accomplish miracles. But beware: not all time-outs are alike. While a momentary change can distract us from our troubles, those troubles are often waiting when we get back. Unless the quality of that time off—from a few quiet minutes a day to a year-long sabbatical—somehow fortifies and renews us, we will be just as vulnerable to stress and error as we were before. Because of this, the vast majority of the enduring leaders I've studied employ some kind of regular reflective practice—long walks or fly casting or meditation—to recharge their batteries.

Leaders traditionally waited until the pain of a disaster showed them the wisdom of the therapeutic break. Today many leaders use some form of personal time out as a tool for keeping employees, and occasionally themselves, resilient. What both often overlook, though, is the potential of such mini-sabbaticals not only to refresh and rejuvenate but also to teach us more about ourselves.

The techniques for doing this on a brief or extended basis are more numerous, and certainly more potent, than most people think:

- *Harnessing the power of prayer.* One of a humankind's oldest forms of time out—simple prayer—is back in vogue, even among many who do not profess a specific religion. Throughout history, leaders took respite from battle—or from the stressful preparation for one, or the enormous psychological letdown that followed one—to pray. Whether you attribute its salutary effects to divine power or to human psychology, prayer has accomplished a lot for a lot of people.

  Prayer is a way of listening to our innermost selves while affirming our relationship with a higher being, a universal spirit. It has been explored and revered by cultures all over the globe and shows no sign of diminishing at the dawn of the twenty-first century.

- *Mastering meditation.* Experience shows that regular meditation, as it has evolved from many traditions, is yet another reliable path to inner knowledge, one whose potential and results only increase the more it is practiced.

  To know what meditation is, however, you must first learn what it is not. It is not a panacea for social ills or a way to levitate and bend spoons. Like centering and *hara,* it is simply another manifestation of the natural mind-body connection that people have known about for centuries and that we in the West are only now beginning to appreciate. In fact, scientific investigators have already documented meditation's usefulness in reducing stress, lowering blood pressure, and strengthening the immune system, to name only a few of its many benefits.

But even if meditation is healthful and relaxing, you may ask how it can teach us about ourselves. To answer that, let's take a closer look at where our thoughts, including self-knowledge, come from.

Most psychologists agree that thoughts originate in both the conscious and the unconscious mind. When we meditate, we relieve our conscious mind of everyday chatter and open it to the unconscious component of our thoughts—the place where our greatest creativity and deepest feelings reside. Near the end of a meditating session, when we allow conscious thoughts to ease back into the mind, we sometimes find that they've been enhanced by this close encounter with the unconscious. Stale ideas may have taken a creative turn, or we may suddenly possess some valuable new perspective. At minimum, our post-meditative state of alert relaxation will stay with us for hours and allow us to perform at a higher level.

Meditation comes in two forms: concentration and relaxation, with many variations of each. Which type you choose depends on your temperament and goals, though my own observations suggest that relaxation techniques suit most Western leaders best. In their extraordinary book, *The Life We Are Given,* George Leonard and Michael Murphy define meditation as "the disciplined observation of thoughts, feelings, impulses, and sensations, as well as the spontaneous turning of heart and mind toward a Presence beyond the ordinary self." As a blend of "contemplative prayer" and conscious introspection, it offers a convenient, relaxing, and energizing way of packaging a daily mini-sabbatical into one or two fifteen- to twenty-minute voyages into the self.[6]

Whole books have been written on the physiology, psychology, benefits, and techniques of meditation, so I won't approach those areas here. Instead, I'll simply share with you my own technique for meditating in the modern leader's natural environment: airports, airplanes, meeting halls, or the back seats of cabs—wherever you can be comfortable for a few quiet moments during a busy day. Your meditation can be as brief as fifteen minutes or as long as an hour. I've found it best to start with a brief period and work up, over time, to a longer one. You can devise a simple way to finish your meditation in any setting: a brief stretch will do the job.

First, get as comfortable as the situation permits. Loosen your necktie or belt, and sit upright with your back supported. Don't slouch or recline. Your goal is not to go to sleep but to set your body comfortably aside while you make your inner journey.

Next, begin separating yourself mentally from the immediate environment. Close your eyes. If that's inappropriate, stare at the floor or at the seat back in front of you or across the room—just don't focus on anything in particular. If you have a headset, put it on, but keep the sound turned off. Soft earplugs are also a great aid for meditation, but with a little practice you'll be able to tune out all but the loudest noises.

Now begin breathing gently, from the diaphragm, allowing your abdomen to move in and out. After a few moments you'll feel yourself settling deeper into your chair as your muscles relax. This is an early sign of centering—the body's way of telling you that it knows you're trying to harmonize your mental and physical states, and it feels great! To help this process along, I sometimes relax my muscles, one group at a time, from the top of my head to the tips of my toes. Rotate a stiff joint or loosen a tight muscle with a friendly self-massage. But don't get too active: you're settling down, not warming up.

When your breathing is easy and your body feels relaxed, become aware of the thoughts that currently occupy your mind. These may be problems you're try-ing to solve, troubles you'd like to forget, details of a presentation you're about to give, plans you're making for the weekend—just about anything. Your goal now is to let go of these thoughts—something more easily said than done.

If you find yourself unable to stop thinking, simply acknowledge the thought—for instance, "I have to be in Cleveland tomorrow"—and go back to letting go. Alternatively you might choose a mantra, a meaningless word or phrase, to repeat silently to yourself so that your thoughts do not take over. Eventually the mantra itself will disappear, and at that instant, your mind will be clear of all thoughts. At this stage, the benefits of deep relaxation begin so continue the process, and if you happen to doze off, that's fine. Enjoy your rest.

- *Quiet reflection and introspection.* Despite their power, meditation and prayer are not for everyone. Organized religion turns some people off, and others compare meditating to working with the lights off. They prefer to sift through their thoughts, feelings, and ideas more rationally and conventionally, the way they tackle such problems at work. Indeed, scientists and philosophers from Isaac Newton and Albert Einstein to Bertrand Russell and Ludwig Wittgenstein based theories—even whole careers—on elaborate "thought experiments" that pointed the way to great discoveries.

If this method appeals to you, you'll want to observe a few commonsense rules developed by these great thinkers:

  - *The best place for reflection is where there are fewest distractions—but not a place where relaxation is your main goal.* Busy offices and quiet bedrooms are two of the worst places for serious introspection. (A quiet bedroom and an active mind are the formula for insomnia, not productive contemplation.) Low-demand, noncompetitive, and repetitive pastimes like fly fishing, house painting, knitting, and hiking—but not in heavy traffic or in bear country—gardening, and swimming are best because they keep the body occupied while the mind is otherwise engaged.

  - *Stay aboard one train of thought at a time—don't let your mind jump the tracks.* Even if a mental excursion feels more satisfying, don't let your thoughts devolve into lazy, repetitive cycles, or endlessly loop through past ideas and feelings—don't resort to daydreaming, in other words, instead of thinking. Let one thought lead to another, but keep track of where you've been and be mindful of where you're going. After all, your goal is to explore new territory, not wander around in circles.

• *Give your mind some roughage—grist for the creative, analytical mill.* Gain perspective and take your intellectual bearings by surveying beforehand a bit of what other thinkers have written or said about your subject. This research shouldn't become a substitute for original thought, but if you haven't given yourself the benefit of insights derived by other smart people who have wrestled with similar questions, you'll very likely plow old ground.

Whatever you choose as a regular time-out—prayer, meditation, quiet reflection, walking, fly fishing, or whatever—you'll benefit even more if you periodically review how the practice is affecting your daily life. For instance, no program of introspective time-outs will be complete until you get some closure on your problem, even if it's only a tentative conclusion. Some people find it helpful to keep a small notebook for jotting down new insights and ideas at the end of each time-out session.

The Fifth Road:
Launching Self-Knowledge Ventures

While any activity can become a learning experience, the best ones start out that way. These are activities designed from the outset to achieve certain self-discovery goals, leaving you, not fate, in the driver's seat. Enduring leaders go out of their way to create such experiences, often using some form of informal learning contract that identifies both the knowledge they seek and the way it will be acquired.

Suppose you've spent most of your adult life pursuing professional goals—making money and accumulating power—and you now feel that it's time to put something back into the community beyond the tangible goods and services you've produced and for which you have been justly rewarded. You might write a few extra checks to your favorite charity, as many people do. But that wouldn't teach you much about yourself. What you need now is a new learning venture tailored to fill in those gaps in your self-understanding: a more complete specification of the person you'd like to be.

An example of this self-knowledge venture was offered to me by a highly successful real estate executive who was preparing for her retirement. Sarah went back into her painful past as a way of discovering a healthy new avocation. She devised her plan around her competence, interest, and outcomes as follows:

- As a result of a painful teenage rebellion, I have learned to be a good listener. Nobody would listen to me. And I think I may have some latent talent as a counselor for young women, and I care about helping them.
- I will need training to achieve the skills and temperament required.
- Once I have lined up my skills and attitudes I will find a suitable place to test my new career.

Based on this statement, Sarah was in a better position to find a specific volunteer program, counseling service, or community group to take advantage of her skills and motivation without wasting her time and their resources on false starts, misguided assignments, and demoralizing mistakes.

This approach can be adapted to any new learning project you decide to undertake. Once you find that specific program, class, or plan of self-study, and once you schedule your time, you will be prepared to pursue the venture you have in mind. Here are some important steps to take as you embark on this venture:

- *Set a specific learning objective.* You may discover you have less tolerance and empathy for troubled teens than you originally thought, a discovery that gives you plenty of reasons to grow. You may even realize that this particular form of community service just isn't right for you, in which case you can try something else.
- *Design your learning venture around your objective.* If you want to help troubled teens and explore your feelings about them, don't volunteer to be an adviser for the Junior Achievers or the church choir, where you are more apt to run into well-adjusted, highly motivated youngsters than those with behavior problems.
- *Include some way of showing that the desired learning has taken place.* People are great at deceiving themselves. Since you've taken the trouble to plan your learning venture, follow it up with

some evidence that you've accomplished what you set out to do. In our example, you might keep a diary of your counseling sessions showing how your thoughts and feelings have changed and recording the impact you have had on your clients.

The Sixth Road: Heeding Your Dreams

Throughout history, dreams have been a potent source of information that is simply unavailable elsewhere. In ancient and medieval times, dreams were often viewed as premonitions or messages from heaven borne on the wings of angels. Originating in the unconscious—that omnivorous maw into which a lifetime of experience, and perhaps even genetic memory, has been swept and stored—dreams show us not just what we are but what we aspire to be: they are the wishes made by the soul. With new discoveries made almost daily in sleep research, scientists are beginning to document what self-aware leaders have known for centuries: that dreams count and that we ignore them at our peril.

Although most of us spend a quarter to a third of our lives asleep, we seldom tap the self-discovery potential of this elusive and intriguing mental state, perhaps because dreams—those fragments of half-forgotten memories and impressions, hopes and fears, wishes and pleasures—are among nature's most perishable goods. Unless you write down the content and feeling of a dream immediately upon waking, chances are you'll recall just the high points, at most, and lose a unique opportunity for self-discovery.

Dreams are a combination of holdover business from the conscious mind and literal or symbolic messages from the unconscious. Far from being the "random firing of neurons," as some earlier researchers claimed, they contain their own internal logic and are surprisingly accessible to both memory and interpretation. Some people even attain competence in so-called lucid dreaming, wherein the sleeper, realizing a dream is in progress, actually takes control of the action—the original virtual reality!

Much of what has been written about the sleep state is conjecture. But most experienced observers agree that there is no one right or wrong way to analyze dreams. Indeed, the best and most useful interpretations invariably come from the dreamer, and the more time you spend reflecting on your dreams, the easier you will find it to remember and decode them.

Years ago two adventurous friends, John Levy and Frances Vaughn, who are highly trained in psychology, decided to take fuller advantage of these nightly peeks into the soul. Upon rising each morning, they jotted down their dreams, then got together on weekends over hot coffee and fresh muffins to compare notes. Before long, they discovered recurring patterns and isolated events that made their dream worlds seem less like terra incognita.

Here are some of the dream-interpretation techniques I have learned from many experts, including John and Frances, complemented by my own experience:

- *A dream symbol represents itself.* People get needlessly confused about imagery in their dreams. They assume that only a psychoanalyst can tell them what a horse or a waterfall "means." While many people do ascribe similar interpretations to certain dream objects—a large body of water, for example, often symbolizes the subconscious—these interpretations are accepted only because specific dreamers have linked them to those specific functions. Your symbol of the subconscious may be a cellar, a large closet, or one of a dozen other images that suggest to you personally something hidden and a bit mysterious. In these cases, lakes and closets still function as lakes and closets. They become linked to the subconscious only by what you find inside them and the feelings those discoveries evoke.

- *Dream messages deal mostly with situations and emotions.* Although it would be nice if dreams were like newspapers, filled with useful data, all they do reliably is convey our own suppressed feelings about relationships and situations: the raw material of life. Take, for example, one middle-aged man, an athlete in his youth, who had recurring dreams about playing football. He would suit up, warm up, then spend the whole game watching from the sidelines. This dream disturbed him greatly, since he had loved sports in high school and had seldom warmed the bench. He decoded the dream when he finally realized he was going through a dry period in his career, finding few opportunities and little recognition at work—in other words, never really getting into the game. Amazingly, after coming to terms with these feelings, his dream changed and he was back running and passing and scoring touchdowns—a big psychic reward for a minor bit of self-discovery.

- *Dreamers can control many dreams.* A lucid dream is one you become aware that you are dreaming and, without waking, interact with objects in the dream and even influence its course. This gives a sleeper great power to use dreams as self-learning tools, to become an active rather than a passive or after-the-fact explorer in the world of the subconscious. For example, lucid dreamers can ask dream objects directly what they mean. They can also make an active choice to go this way or that, open a door or go down a staircase. They can even create new dream scenarios peopled by characters and objects that can literally do anything. After all, what's impossible in a dream?

Here are some concrete steps that have helped active leaders put their dreams to work:

- *Learn to capture your dreams.* Give yourself a simple reminder before you fall asleep by saying, "I want to remember my dreams." Also keep a notepad next to your bed so you can quickly jot down key words or images to help you remember your dreams.
- *Find a book that explains the symbolic content that others have observed, or enlist a teacher or knowledgeable friend for regular sessions of dream-sharing.*
- *Pay special attention to what C. G. Jung called big dreams, the images that are powerfully disturbing or exciting.* These can be especially revealing during times of transition. At one time, before making a career change, my dreams were filled with images of slipping and falling, sliding into dark places, losing my way. Once I'd made the change, these dreams simply went away. Anticipating change is often more disturbing than the actual move.

In a sense, all self-learners are lucid dreamers: people who are eager to take control of the self-discovery process and illuminate past experiences, thoughts, and feelings. By examining dreams thoughtfully and making their wisdom part of our lives, we can become much more than we were.

The Seventh Road: Beginning Something New

While repetition may be the mother of learning, it is the enemy of discovery. The more familiar we are with something—a task, a job, a relationship—the less it has to teach us; and when learning slows, boredom strikes. That's when we make mistakes or, even worse, lose the joy of living. Lasting leaders inject everyday tasks with fresh learning without forgetting or negating valuable lessons from the past.

Everyone talks about the learning curve, but few people really know what it is, let alone how to use it as a tool for self-discovery. Essentially, a learning curve shows how a task gets easier each time you do it. The more you practice, the better you get. If it takes you ten hours to make the first wooden birdhouse but only nine hours to make the second, you have experienced a 90 percent learning curve for that particular task—that is, as the number of units doubled, you saved 10 percent on the previous effort.

As so often happens when people and math get together, however, nature throws us a curve—in this case, quite literally. If you make a lot of birdhouses and plot the number of units produced versus the hours it took to make them (a good measure of learning), you quickly see that this relationship is not linear, but takes the form of a curve: steep at first, then flattening out. This happens because your learning factor—a 10 percent saving each time your experience doubles—is applied to progressively smaller numbers: 10 percent of ten hours, or one hour, is larger than 10 percent of nine hours, or nine-tenths of an hour. A steep learning curve means that learning is taking place at a high rate. A shallow curve means that learning is slower.

What does all this have to do with self-knowledge?

Plenty—because it proves that the longer we pursue a task, the flatter our learning curve gets, even if it started out quite steep. If we stick with the same task long enough, we all but exhaust its potential as a learning vehicle. This is a real problem for leaders who have worked at one job for a long time or have led constituents who deal with repetitive functions. That's why I advise leaders facing this dilemma to shift periodically from a job or task where the learning curve has flattened to one where it is steeper, so that the corresponding potential for self-discovery and growth will be greater.

Let's say, for example, that you've always felt uncomfortable dealing with people face-to-face on sensitive matters like personnel actions and conflicting opinions. In these areas you prefer to use memos, E-mail, and other written communications to get your views across. After a while, your learning curve as an ace memo writer will undoubtedly flatten out. Boredom and complacency will eventually infiltrate your prose. You'll start relying on habit and formula rather than fresh insights to express your ideas, actually decreasing your effectiveness as a communicator and isolating you from your own emotions.

To break that downward spiral and reacquaint yourself with your feelings in these areas, try communicating about these topics in a different way—by phone, on voice mail, and especially in person. By having to focus on a new, less familiar medium, you will sharpen your mental reflexes and expose yourself to a whole new battery of communication tools such as vocal inflection, reading, and body language. Your learning curve here will be much steeper than it was for letters and memos, so you'll make progress fast—an exhilarating and energizing experience that will only increase your desire to grow in other areas.

Here is a quick way to spot complacency and identify your unused potential. Take time to write down your answers to the following questions:

- What do people say I do well?
- Where are my areas of greatest management or professional competency?
- Which of my skills or traits can I deploy with ease?
- When I take on a new problem, what are my first steps or questions?

Your answers should reveal those areas where you have developed skills and competence. Chances are, you will tend to overuse those skills and not develop new ones. Now identify those skills you rarely if ever employ. Look for those that you feel awkward using or that cause you to revert to the tried and true approaches. Herein lie your new learning curves.

For example, if you are gifted at delivering casual off-the-cuff talks and people give you high marks in this area, try presenting a highly structured talk replete with graphs, charts, and bulleted lists. Try it. You may feel awkward and stiff at first, but try again. You are on a new learning curve.

The Eighth Road: Changing One Small Thing

If we can change one problem-causing behavior pattern, even in a small way, the positive repercussions will show up elsewhere in the system, often greatly magnified. Twelve-step programs, such as the one used in Alcoholics Anonymous, employ similar principles, as do the techniques of brief therapy, now a staple in psychotherapy. These methods work because they increase self-knowledge in a specific, controllable problem area and, in doing so, help people improve other aspects of their lives. Few of us, after all, can change everything all at once. Almost anyone, however, can modify one behavior pattern and make it stick.

It is possible to achieve big changes in personal behavior and relationships by finding one or a few small things that, when changed, can affect all the others. For leaders, self-discovery means sorting through values, attitudes, and habits a few at a time until those that are instrumental to the "systems" upon which they depend come into clearer focus.

Here are the guidelines many enduring leaders use to begin change processes:

- *Begin with habitual problems, not a onetime crisis.* Systems become systems because they recur and we get used to them—which is why they exert such a powerful influence in our lives. Only chronic problems contain the feedback loop needed to make the small-change strategy work.
- *The new behavior you substitute is less important than interrupting the old habit.* A person who reacts angrily to recurring situations regularly pumps negative energy into the system. Defusing that angry reaction is more important to improving the system than finding a perfect new response.
- *Be patient—let the system find a new equilibrium before you make further changes.* Changing one small thing won't make things perfect, only better. This in turn creates new behavior, new feedback, and new avenues for learning—the object of the self-discovery game.

Here's my favorite small-step story. A high-powered Manhattan couple came to spend a planning day focused on their highly visible fast-track careers. Fairly soon it was evident to them that their careers were soaring at the expense of their personal lives. At the end of the day they had created plans for making some key adjustments and one or two larger changes to put their lives back into balance. But something was missing.

Aikidoists know that details really matter. Ceremonies and rituals are critically important in helping to focus and calm the mind. Both Robert and Allie (not their real names) suddenly realized that they needed new patterns for relating to each other. They finally agreed to go on an old-fashioned date once a week as a small beginning. That first step was auspicious, since it allowed them to spend more time together and a proper place to begin building a new relationship. This time was both an occasion and a restatement of commitment to make the changes necessary to renew their marriage, a proper first step for them.

Remember when you select your small step, it may open up a grand staircase of possibilities. So step out.

THE ROAD TO SELF-KNOWLEDGE BEGINS WITH SELF

For each of us there are open roads to the interior self. Finding the ones that feel right, that fit you like your favorite jacket, is the first task. There's an old saying: If you don't know where you are going, any road will take you there. Perhaps I can make my point clearer by saying that if you know where you are going—that is, to find and cultivate self-knowledge—there are at least eight well-trodden roads to take you there.

What matters most is choosing one and beginning your journey. Aikido leaders rely on more than their heads, or their rational thought processes. They learn to respond to their environment, sometimes in new and surprising ways. They rely on their bodies and spirits as well as their minds. As you read this chapter, perhaps one road seemed more challenging than the others. Or perhaps you had a gut response, a sort of flop of the stomach, that said, "Not me, no way!" In fact, that might be the road to start with.

Pick one, and enjoy the journey!

6. Master Practice #2

Practice the Paradoxical Art of Planning

> In a minute there is time
> For decisions and revisions which a minute will
> reverse.
>
> —T. S. Eliot

*Planning, like aikido, is a paradoxical art. In aikido the finest com-*petitors are in firm control of their basic movements and their emotions and yet are relaxed and loose in their adaptations in responding to attacks. In business, on the one hand tight control and disciplined execution are critical in the production, distribution, finance, and accounting functions. And on the other, only a freewheeling, open-ended spirit will yield product innovation, advanced process breakthroughs, and fresh marketing and venture approaches.

As we will explore in this chapter, enduring leaders have always understood and dealt with the planning paradox. To begin, let's look at some contemporary examples of planning-leading. If Silicon Valley software developers and Japanese electronic-device makers are harbingers of the pace and style of future planning, then all leaders are in for a fast ride. The launch of a new software product causes both the imitator and the competitors to begin planning at least two generations ahead for adaptations or new models. According to *Wired* magazine, the average life of a software product is less than eighteen months. Japanese firms are extremely good at moving their electronic devices and appliances onto the market with multiple styles and upgrades layered one on top of another.

Most experts would agree, however, that for the best overall model of future planning and execution in the Midwest, the U.S. firm

3M is approaching mastery. Their record of product innovation and delivery is astonishing, and their performance overall shows it. James C. Collins and Jerry I. Porras, in their book *Built to Last,* rated them at the top of visionary companies.[1]

Part of 3M's success arises from the company's creation of a culture that fosters mutations. Mutations cannot be controlled; they just happen. But they happen more happily and often in an environment where people are allowed to take chances. Here are some 3M leadership doctrines that reveal the attitudes that support innovation, as reported by Collins and Porras:

- "Listen to anyone with an original idea, no matter how absurd it may sound at first."
- "Encourage, don't nit-pick. Let people run with an idea."
- "Hire good people and leave them alone."
- "If you put fences around people, you get sheep. Give people the room they need."

Lest we treat 3M as a mutant company or a paragon apart, let's get some historical perspective. To aikido-style leaders, planning is second in importance only to self-awareness. General George Marshall, U.S. Army chief of staff in World War II and a true long-distance leader, said, "Plans are nothing, planning is everything."[2] As a statesman leading the effort to rebuild Europe, his Marshall Plan reconstructed the war-torn Allied states and helped make former enemies like Germany and Italy the economic marvels we know today—an aikido-style solution if there ever was one. During this period Marshall had to battle foreign foes like the Soviet Union, which saw Europe's postwar suffering as fertile ground for the spread of communism, as well as strong resistance from the America First crowd who believed Europe's problems were, and ought to be, its own.

The Marshall Plan was less a plan than a long series of planning activities—a set of well-reasoned beliefs—each of which had to take into account new variables, new limits, and practical choices among equally desirable (or noxious) alternatives, all the while holding firm to a few key principles. Peter Drucker took Marshall's idea a step further then he defined strategic planning as a continuous process of moving from the here and now toward the then and there: a never-ending tug-of-war between opportunities and constraints.

Julie Packard, daughter of Hewlett-Packard founder David Packard and a director of that company describes her family's brand of planning as the ability to "move forward and change direction without getting lost."[3] Princeton professor Michael Wood, writing about contemporary America, might as well have been describing the future of the planning function in the twenty-first century when he said (about America) "a deferred, endlessly self-correcting idea, always looking for its own best sense."[4]

Many industrial-age companies have a yearly ritual, lasting anywhere from a few weeks to a couple of months, called the annual planning exercise, during which the strategic vision of the top executives and board gets translated into tangible goals for the rank and file, along with operating plans to achieve them. For some firms this annual exercise is a top-down affair. Underlings are rewarded for how well they turn someone else's goals into reality, following orders faithfully even if those orders run the company into the ground. Some firms have taken a more participative approach, making sure that goals set by one management level dovetail with those of the next level, through joint decision-making and negotiation on the use of resources. What both systems have in common—and the reason that both systems so often fail—is that the end result of each is "the plan": a sacrosanct document carved in stone. As one widely distributed bumper sticker says, "When God wants a good laugh, she reads our annual plan."

In contrast, the annual planning ritual in companies run by aikido-style leaders lasts 365 days a year. The data digging and interpretation, troubleshooting and problem-solving, haggling and negotiation, brainstorming and decision-making that go into all types of planning literally never stop. There is no "plan" as such, only planning. Goals tend to be qualitative and are aimed at preserving core values and developing healthy processes, not achieving a fixed end state. It's like holding a race or tournament where the participants truly are rewarded for how well they played the game rather than for their numerical order of finish. In this environment the organization's performance objective is to attain a level of agility and flexibility that the leaders know will produce desirable results, including those measured quantitatively by people outside the organization, such as earnings per share and market share. Companies like 3M, Hewlett-Packard, Advanta, Informix, Toyota, and Sony adhere to certain aikidolike principles:

- *Be the eye of the hurricane, not the wind.* In aikido, the defender is often compared to the center of a spinning top, using spherical rotation to absorb the energy of a threat and send it off in a new direction.
- *Be the water, not the rock.* Rain and waves can wear down the tallest mountain. Aikidoist leaders are concerned about defending themselves against someone who may be superior in size, strength, experience, or finances. While always expanding and perfecting technique, they also know that mental preparation, or planning, is just as crucial to success. Flexibility conquers rigidity, and aikido-style planners know that well.
- *Fashion values that guide and bind the planning process.* The system of anti-violence ethics that guides aikidoists also forms the philosophical basis for making good partnerships and strategic alliances.

In short, just as one mode of defense spells disaster in the martial arts, one plan—or even one mode of planning—spells doom for companies entering the Green Glass Age. A single plan numbs keen minds and quashes initiative under the weight of an intrusive hierarchy. It generally results in an exaggeration of the threat, inculcating an all-or-nothing attitude that just doesn't resemble real life. True believers—including many hardworking and ambitious but inexperienced employees—sacrifice their personal lives for the sake of achieving some conquest over a supposed threat only to learn that they were only gratifying the leader's ego-boosting arbitrary goals.

Postindustrial planners use a different vocabulary. They borrow the language of biology, psychology, telecommunications, and computer science—terms like "network," "organic," "amoeba," and "online"—to suggest to constituents how planning might be implemented as well as what might be accomplished. Gradually, the planning culture begins to reflect the positive processes and values behind these terms, just as traditional corporate cultures reflected both the strengths and weaknesses of their competitive, combative models.

Aikido style leaders view constituents as indispensable nodes in a vast web, like neurons in the brain's neural net, that give the corporate entity consciousness and make it what it is solely because they are there, doing their job, in harmony with other elements. To such thinking, top-down hierarchical planning is anathema and as illogical as whales playing the piano.

Today—and certainly tomorrow—leaders and constituents must defend their organizations from competitors with deeper pockets, more resources, and other advantages in order to succeed without using deceptive, illegal, or self-destructive tactics and in order to personally win at work without losing in other aspects of life.

THREE AIKIDO-STYLE LEADERS' PLANNING STYLES

Compare leaders to orchestra conductors and their plans to the musical score. What is left unsaid in this analogy is how those plans come into being, change, and mutate and contribute to achieving the organization's and the individuals' goals. In short, who makes the concert? The composer? The conductor? The musicians? The audience? Entertainers without audiences quickly find other work; firms without customers quickly make other plans.

The answer, of course, is all four. Someone has to start the ball rolling, so the composer puts notes on paper in response to an idea, often on commission. In my analogy, the composer takes the place of a planning specialist; but a score doesn't make a concert any more than data makes a plan. Next, the conductor, or leader, studies the score and gives it a personal stamp: editing a bit here, rearranging there, matching the acoustics of the concert hall, and taking advantage of the capabilities of the orchestra. The musicians then study their parts, often making corrections and suggestions on how to implement them more harmoniously. They have their personal needs and agendas, too: some are soloists or first chair leaders of their sections, and so feel responsible for showcasing their talents and the strengths of their group.

Gradually, all these ideas are tried out in rehearsal, and still more changes are made. Even after a performance or recording session, the search for perfection continues. Audience reaction is measured and music trimmed or modified to elicit a better response. In most cases the last performance on a tour, like the last take in the studio—or a new product entering a market—is very different from what was originally planned.

Everywhere I go, I find aikido-style leaders using some form of a process of successive approximation that seamlessly blends planning with doing. The glue that holds it all together is learning. Here are three dominant future organizational planning-doing-learning styles I've discovered:

1. *The amoeba-style planner.* Amoeba-style planners see the organization as organic, with each part visibly connected to the whole. They seek to achieve healthy mutation and are capable of splitting the organization into even smaller and more focused problem-solving groups *and* of rejoining into a more powerful whole when it serves to circle a problem or pursue an opportunity. In this way they behave not unlike the single-cell organism, the amoeba for which they are named. Amoeba-style organizations are very sensitive to their environment. They sniff out new opportunities, then surround and absorb them, making whatever is necessary to succeed in that area an immediate part of their culture. Most favored by leaders who are grounded in science and best reflected in research laboratories, the organizations basically blend planning and action as they move.

   Sir James Black's infusion of "doing while planning" makes his research labs highly productive models of amoeba-style learning. The labs have also made his partner, the Johnson & Johnson Company, some excellent products and good profits. Black's term begins by focusing on an unusual problem or a ripe opportunity that, when solved or exploited, will have widespread application. It was this method that resulted in such breakthroughs as beta blockers and Tagamet.

   Black explained his job this way, "The only tasks I have as a leader are to help assemble good people and get them onto the right problem. They take it from there and organize themselves into the right teams to match the way the problems evolve. It is rather like an amoeba, always splitting into new configurations depending on what the organization confronts."

   One key to making this style work, Sir James—or Jim Black, as he likes to be called—says with his distinctive Scottish burr, is finding "the right people to fit our way of doing things." There are no stars in his organization, "just good, hardworking scientists who love the chase." From time to time, Black stops by to "cheer them up," especially when his team runs into rough patches. "They are young," he says with a gleam in his eye, "and haven't had much practice with failure." Trust—in the top leader and in each other—is the glue that keeps the amoeba together, the spark that keeps it alive.

How does one lead such "leaderless" groups? If Sir James is your *sensei,* you will

- *Lead by teaching.* Black uses the Socratic method of guided dialogue to help team members get the drop on prickly problems.

- *Lead by nurture.* Black knows that research, while specific in some areas, is open-ended in others. He evaluates plans for their dynamic, malleable, flexible qualities, not for slam-dunk efficiency. He knows creativity can't be programmed, but can be nurtured; that's the environment he creates and the example he sets.

- *Lead by humility.* Stars on any team, while radiating energy, have a way of outshining those around them while sucking in resources, leaving less for everyone else. Productivity and quality eventually suffer. Although Black rewards achievement, he believes the needs of the team come first. This helps keep a culture of accomplishment from becoming a cult of arrogance.

- *Lead from calm.* Emotions are the energy that fuels the intellect or deflates the spirit. Setbacks affect not only the plan but also the planners. If egos can be distanced from success, they can and should be distanced from failure, too. Thus the team's emotional energy is saved for the long haul and not wasted in costly sprints—to add extra gloss to an already shining victory, for example, or to make a setback seem less significant than it is.[5]

2. *The value-center planner.* Value-center planners combine a tightly focused, rapid response with a customer-oriented culture. Sensitive to any blip in their market, they're conditioned by their mentoring leaders to instantly deploy a wide range of problem-solving and opportunity-exploiting skills, techniques, and procedures. Far from waiting for new developments in their markets, value-center planners proactively seek ways to enhance their position even

when things are quiet—especially when things are quiet—by test-marketing new products and services, developing innovative technology, honing individual skills, and improving group processes. They can move rapidly because they operate from a solid value platform.

Marriott Hotels, Mary Kay Cosmetics, and Wal-Mart all employ some version of value-center planning, projecting the top leader's customer-centered philosophy on every strategic and tactical decision, then revising those decisions regularly as conditions change. Perhaps a look at Mary Kay and its style of value-centered leadership will illuminate how such planning-leading works.

Dick Bartlett is a soft-spoken, gracious leader of one of the largest direct-selling organizations in the world, with over 250,000 representatives and annual sales over a billion dollars. He is an active environmentalist and gumbo cooker. If Bartlett is your *sensei* you'll

- *Lead by using your base values.* Bartlett compares leading a value-centered organization to making a good gumbo: "Like any soup or stew, the key to gumbo, a Cajun dish, is in the stock. If you start with a rich base you can vary the spices and ingredients and it will still turn out well. Mary Kay Ash, our founder, set down three key values that are still the foundation of our culture: to be preeminent in personal-care products; to provide the sales force with the opportunity for financial independence, career achievement, and personal fulfillment; and to achieve total customer satisfaction."

- *Lead by passing along those values.* Mentors lead by example and close interaction, especially with new people. Bartlett says, "Part of my job is to be a mentor to new representatives and staff in passing on those rich values."[6]

- *Lead by relationship.* Bartlett's job as chief mentor compares favorably with the loving, compassionate kindness of the Tao mentoring process according to Chungliang Al-Huang and Jerry Lynch in their book *Mentoring,* in which they say that the process "creates mutual understanding and cooperative relationships." Mentoring "commands what is good in them and forgives their ignorance."[7]

3. *The holistic planners.* Big organizations that have successfully made, or are beginning to make, the leap from industrial-age to Green Glass Age thinking combine the best of both worlds—the highly rational, quantitative planning demanded by traditionalists and the more intuitive, flexible scenario planning demanded by the future. In a way, this new breed of corporate animal is the organizational equivalent of the "whole brain" thinker, blending left hemisphere (linear, step-by-step, logical, and quantitative) methods with the intuitional-global faculties of the right hemisphere. In a sense, the holistic planning style represents the highest evolution of the traditional quantitative approach, which—among its better practitioners, anyway—never pretended that numbers were better than people for setting goals, choosing options, and assessing human nature.

The best examples of holistic planning are currently found in comparatively low-tech, process-flow companies like Coca-Cola, Noah's Bagels, and Office Depot, where the triple whammy of high plant costs, expensive marketing campaigns, and a complex distribution system makes even small changes risky and expensive. In this environment, intuition about evolving customer taste supported with numerical analysis and even dynamic simulations gives leaders a better understanding of options that in the old days would have been expensive gambles at best, and at worst, disasters—like the new Coke.

When Coca-Cola decided to abandon their classic old bottle and logo in favor of a market-researched up-to-date new Coke, they discovered how emotionally attached their customers were to the familiar product they had grown up with. It was a classic dumb move of the kind that always happens when numbers drive discussions and when intuition and common sense are momentarily abandoned. Coke's top management rescued the mess by giving a rebirth to the old familiar soft drink and telling their customers that Classic Coke was back. The very smart, meta-message was even better: we listen and we care.

If you would be a holistic planner, you will

• *Lead by pulling together disparate elements.* Holistic planner-leaders recognize the complex nature of decision-making, timing, and getting the story right. They know that so-called facts always need careful mental massaging.

- *Lead with emotional intelligence.* Holistic leaders know that information always suffers some loss, emotional distortion, or missed interpretation in the transmission. Daniel Goleman writes in his book, *Emotional Intelligence,* that "when emotionally upset, people cannot remember, attend, learn or make decisions clearly." He defines emotional intelligence as "self-awareness, impulse control, persistence, zeal and self-motivation, empathy, and social deftness," and he describes the application of emotional intelligence (EQ) in organizational life as "being able to air differences as helpful critiques; creating an atmosphere in which diversity is valued rather than a source of friction; and networking effectively."[8]

- *Lead by direct, clear communication of goals and expectations.* Brian Clark, president of South Africa Telkom, invited me to help his top team think through their leadership challenge as the largest employer seeking privatization to support the nation's new mission and become a significant player in the global economy. Clark would certainly agree with Goleman's EQ applications as his new team of seasoned telephone executives combined with leaders from different backgrounds, sexes, genders, and races learn to work in a holistic planning-doing fashion. After struggling with core values, vision, and political and social realities during an intense retreat, he summed up: "We must lead from our diverse strength, collective wisdom, and creativity. We must be as smart as possible in delivering good service and as feeling as possible in our human responsibilities. We can do all of this as we learn to trust and listen to each other and to really care for each other."[9] Clark is clearly a leader for the future who believes in and exemplifies the holistic approach.

What do the three basic styles have in common? First is the way they accept, and do not try to fight, inevitable change. Like aikido masters, they use their own particular gifts and strengths to restore harmony—and advantage—in an otherwise unsettled environment.

Second, their planning process is inclusive, not exclusive. It is evaluated on the basis of how many people are involved and in the know, not how many are kept in the dark.

Third, their leaders are regarded as catalysts and coaches, not popes and emperors. Sometimes those coaches get into the game themselves, but more often they do best by providing and coordinating resources and teaching.

Finally, the constant tension between overarching, guiding values and expediency is encouraged and kept constantly in view, not ignored or swept under the rug.

Obviously, no organization uses any one style to the exclusion of all the others, and the best adapted, like the 3M Corporation and Hewlett-Packard, use a bit of each, along with plenty of fresh thinking and a lasting commitment to their core values, depending on the situation and the people involved, and that's exactly as it should be. Understanding how each style works and how well it suits a leader's personal style can go a long way toward making the relationship between organization and leader enduring, satisfying, and rich.

Finding the leadership planning style that fits you takes time and effort. Depending on your job or situation, once you start to know yourself and incorporate aikido-style leadership into your everyday life, you may decide, on the one hand, to make a radical change, even shifting from one style to another. Or you may choose to work in an amoeba organization because that's where you feel most comfortable. More likely, though, such a radical shift is not what you'll need.

Take time out to think of the last big project you planned for in your organization. Which of the three—amoeba, value-centered, or holistic—does it look most like? What worked? What didn't work? What were you most comfortable with? What were the people in your group or organization most comfortable with? Keep experimenting until you find a style that feels both challenging and healthy to you and your associates.

TWO LESSONS IN GOOD PLANNING

To aikido-style leaders, there is no such thing as a good or bad plan, only good or bad planning. The planning style will obviously change, depending on the maturity and competitive position of the organization.

- *Good planning leaves room for surprises.* Hyperrational, highly quantitative planning tries to take everything relevant into account, but life is full of surprises. Plans that try to eliminate—rather than exploit—surprises are worse than faulty; they're actually dangerous because of the false confidence they instill and the opportunities they overlook. If you still believe that more numbers are better, here are three cases that may help you change your mind.

Although I played quite different roles on each occasion, I had a front-row seat at the downfall of three organizational giants—IBM, AT&T, and the Soviet Union—each of which suffered from what I call planning hubris.

At the end of the Cold War, a highly respected Soviet behavioral scientist named Valery Venda came to California to talk to me about learning curves. This was not our first visit. Years before, the State Department had arranged a brief meeting, but my guest's KGB "interpreter" (read "monitor") made any real exchange impossible. Finally, in 1991, my colleague was able to speak for himself in surprisingly clear English about his country's long, hard fall.

"We pushed our machine-driven answers too far," he said. "Our leaders made planning and control into a pathetic religion."[10] Even Soviet reformers like Khrushchev and Gorbachev knew more about the outcomes they wanted to achieve than practical ways of getting there. They didn't know, or couldn't believe, that good planning involved trusting people as well as the statistics.

Switch channels now to the late 1960s. The scene is AT&T headquarters in New York, where we on the executive team are biting our cheeks with envy at IBM's command-and-control structure. (After all, we never succeeded even in getting our managers and salespeople to wear white shirts!) Although the freewheeling Age of Aquarius was dawning everywhere else in America, at AT&T we thought of little more than increasing our control over just about everything. All phones should be black, we reasoned, because it simplified inventory control and accelerated our customer response—both worthy goals, even today, but what about customer choice?

You can understand our trepidation about the threats to break up AT&T—then the world's largest legal monopoly. How could we exercise adequate quality control or grow our network according to plan or fulfill our other obligations as a quasi-public utility when that control and that planning would be blasted apart and scattered over regional companies?

These concerns—the arguments AT&T subsequently presented along with reams of computerized studies, plans, and data in court—were not just intellectual abstractions or rationales for a cozy status quo but the heartfelt beliefs of the leaders involved. The same hyperrational quantitative methods that had helped make us the biggest telecommunications company in the world were substantiating our worse fears. Who could ignore evidence like that?

Well, the presiding federal judge at the AT&T divestiture trial was not convinced by AT&T's facts and arguments. Was the judge wrong? Let's look at the evidence. Competition for long-distance service and telecommunications hardware has not destroyed AT&T or its spin-offs. In fact, they're getting ready to compete with cable TV and computer internet providers for a whole list of new services. The post-divestiture parent, AT&T, eventually realized that less is more, and in 1995 it voluntarily decided that it would be good business to divide itself again—like Caesar's Gaul—into three parts, each leaner and better able to compete in rapidly changing and rapidly globalizing markets. Thus decentralization—once thought to be anathema to efficiency and effectiveness—is now seen as virtually the only way to plan new hardware development, reduce time from R&D to the showroom, and cultivate creative new partnerships at every stage of design, manufacturing, and distribution. The lessons learned from what looked like a dreadful defeat at the judge's hands became the basis for good planning.

And what happened to IBM, the object of AT&T's admiring glances back in the 1960s? Although the waters get murkier here, the big picture and the lessons about corporate planning remain quite clear. Caught unawares by the desktop computer revolution of the early 1980s, IBM fought the upstarts in Silicon Valley with one hand while battling the Justice Department's frequent antitrust threats with the other. This, in part, prevented them from bringing the full weight of their enormous economies of scale to bear in the personal computer market. IBM nonetheless managed to recover after a decade to use their DOS-based platform along with their fortuitous alliance with Microsoft to put, at this writing, Apple's corporate future in doubt. This turnaround was not a triumph for IBM's "Soviet-style" planning. It results from the aikido-style moves of good planner-leaders.

- *Good planning requires nimbleness.* Giganticism by itself is grounds to suspect bad planning. Some of the ills that can come from size alone include slow response to changes in markets and other outside forces—it simply takes longer for an impulse to travel along the corporate nervous system, register, then travel back again, sparking a response. Big creatures, like baleen whales, also get dependent on one diet—long-distance business calls, for example, or mainframe computers—and tend to forget that there are other creatures in the sea, some of which are hungrier and equipped with sharper teeth.

  Fast-growing companies must work in the zone of tension between the entrepreneurial spirit that got them to the party and the discipline required to plot a favorable course and navigate it well. An excellent example of this planning stress is Kinko's. Founder Paul Orfolea started a small copying service while he was a surfer-student at U.C. Santa Barbara in 1968. In 1984 he set up a corporate service corporation for the growing franchise holders and owners. Now there are well over 800 locations that are owned by 130 separate corporation-franchise holders.

  When I was asked to design and deliver a workshop on leadership to Kinko's key leaders, I asked Paul what he felt were the most important issues to address.[11] Without hesitation, he answered, "The trouble good people doing good work have in maintaining their balance during the stressful times of rapid growth and relentless competition."

  Orfolea was right on target. Many of his associates had become very successful, but the pressure got greater, not less. Staffing for round-the-clock service is stressful enough, but then add one new service after another and meet the attacks of other office-service suppliers, then watch the tension grow.

  Each store leader must be aikidolike in staying centered and focused while meeting local customers' needs, creating the right inventory levels, hiring, training service-minded people, and conforming to national service standards. Good planning at Kinko's and for any upstart organization must be nimble. Note the way these operating and leadership requirements fight with each other:

- Stay loose and be entrepreneurial.
- Adhere to tightly focused service standards.
- Be ready to meet national advertising expectations.
- Remain local and customer-friendly.
- Use mass buying potential.
- Run your store as your own.
- Finally, have a healthy, learning life outside the business.

FIVE STRATEGIES FOR SUCCESSFUL PLANNING

Adapting yourself to the planning style of an organization, and vice versa, is a matter not just of success, but of survival. This is especially true for new leaders at the far ends of the organization who, like a transplanted vital organ, can either save or kill the host—or be killed by it. When that leader is an alumnus of the traditional command-control school of planning, where one quantitative solution is assumed to fix every problem, this transition can be even harder. As one ex–IBM planner, now looking for his second new job after leaving Big Blue, told me, "I really feel uncomfortable in many newer, smaller companies. It's like being in a country where you can't speak the language."

Remember that successful planning is about setting realistic goals with currently available information for the benefits we hope to gain. By now it should be apparent that the benefits aikido-style leaders hope to gain are long-term and flexible. Here are some techniques individual leaders can use to help smooth out the rough edges when planning cultures clash:

1. *Make hidden agendas visible.* The aikido-style leader creates a culture of open planning where mistakes are quickly revealed and no stigma is attached to an error as long as it is not concealed. The leader must set the model of transparency and not allow the cult of secrecy and rumor to flourish in the shadows.

   It is the leader's job to inoculate each person against the disease of self-inflation. In all my years leading organizations, I made my most serious mistakes by not ferreting out and stopping those who developed a star complex. Once a person suffers from over-weening pride it is his or her natural tendency to bend every mirror to make the best impression, to puff up results, skim credit, undermine competitors.

I failed to stop one person from hiding his agendas and stealing credit, partly because I liked him and felt his talent could grow rapidly, and partly because I let him keep some small personal secrets. I also listened with a less than critical ear to his stories of battles won and how his comrades were not quite up to snuff. And, finally, I was not quite as open with him as I should have been. The result was that my hidden feelings and glossed-over evaluations set him up as an underground operator. He began to trade in gossip and take massive credit for work that was only partially his. Soon he became so inflated that he began to undercut my role. The story didn't end well. He finally had to be removed from his job and put where he could do less harm. He became bitter and withdrew and finally left the organization.

The lesson is very clear: leaders must be models of openness, clarity, and candor and must reward others who follow that example. To ignore this lesson is practically to guarantee that plans will be distorted from their inception throughout their implementation. Revealing hidden agendas is an ongoing process most likely to be problematic with new relationships or when leaders are new. Although they don't talk about such things at first, one party may love numbers and stacks of computer printouts while the other mistrusts any concept that, in the words of Wall Street's Peter Lynch, "you can't describe with a crayon." With these basically opposite instincts, neither is going to be happy when these latent tendencies come out—and they will.

2. *Avoid goals that create or reward guilt.* Guilt is the silent killer of leaders. Some years ago I worked with a closely held corporation whose founder had recently died. The new CEO, the founder's son, pushed himself relentlessly and at age forty-one had already increased the company's business fivefold, creating growing pains for the organization and chest pains for himself.

After his first heart attack, which took nobody by surprise, I listened to his quiet confession: "I guess I pushed myself too hard to prove why I deserved to have so much more than anyone else."

When I assured him no one begrudged him his ample salary, majority stock position, and other perks, since he was universally praised as the hardest worker in the firm, he replied, "No, that's not what I mean. You see, Dad built this business from scratch. I only inherited it. I was trying to prove myself to him."

Trying to prove himself to a dead man! That's a losing battle if there ever was one, and it's a sure sign that an inner enemy—in this case, guilt—was in full charge of the company.

Guilt is the ransom demanded by our inner enemies. Guilt silently but continuously overrides our other emotions and eventually leads us to do just about anything to quiet its shrill voice.

One obvious source of guilt is real or perceived failure; but winning, as in this case, can produce even greater guilt if we suspect our victory came at the expense of friends, family, or worthy, and perhaps more deserving, colleagues. Long before guilt takes its toll on our health, however, it shows up in our feelings, moods, and thoughts about the future. It colors how we interact with others, especially when we analyze options, set goals, and make plans. We unconsciously bias what we think we can do or want to do so that we can compensate for the guilt we've already suffered or avoid new guilt in the future. If you think about it, you can easily see how otherwise rational, satisfying goals can become wildly irrational and self-defeating in order to appease these personal monsters—and at a price that you and everyone around you is eventually forced to pay.

How can we separate guilt-producing goals from valid goals? First, we must stay fully aware of the consequences of each decision we make. One way to do this is to determine who really benefits and who really pays when a particular goal is accomplished. If unsold inventory is backing up and you raise your sales quotas by 20 percent, for example, you are really trying to motivate your sales force by giving them aggressive new targets, or are you hoping to assuage your own guilt for making a bad production decision? And if the sales force resents this new pressure, as they very well might, will you punish manufacturing next quarter by laying off the excess workers—creating even more new guilt?

A second way to avoid guilt-producing goals is to use terms to set goals so that everyone can feel the updraft of success when the goals are reached and share the parachute when the forecast fails.

A third method is to use goal-setting as a way to create harmony instead of destructive competition across work groups. Decisions about growth, downsizing, allocation of scarce resources and even scarcer rewards, and balancing group against individual needs are to guilt as swamps are to mosquitoes: dangerous breeding grounds for disease. At Hanna Anderson Clothing every group is invited to evaluate the plans before goals are set, and then all employees are told where the plans fell short or worked well. Rewards are based on plan achievement.

3. *Make managing anxiety part of your planning.* Good news is often as stressful as bad. New or seasoned leaders can feel anxious as well as proud when they set goals that will take an organization in new directions or through difficult times. Here's what happened to one hardworking executive in her middle forties, a veteran of fifteen years in the management trenches and an alumna of a well-known graduate business school, when she finally got her break and joined the "president's club," leading a successful New York–based home furnishings company.

Things started well. The chairman himself had been her mentor, and after her appointment, the board engaged a well-known consultant to coach and encourage her. She also made full use of her peers in the Young Presidents Organization for indispensable moral support. Within the company, she was popular with employees and an icon to women managers, who were proud of her achievements and eager to see her succeed.

She started her administration, as many new leaders do, with a goal-setting and strategic-planning exercise. Feeling anxious about her powers and determined to build as wide a base of support as possible with her senior staff, she hired another outside consultant to facilitate a series of participatory planning and team-building sessions. As sometimes happens in these freewheeling environments, things kind of got out of control—at least from the new president's perspective. Enjoying their collective power, the executive team went way beyond her mandate and began planning new ventures that exceeded both their experience and the company's immediate resources. This left the new president in a quandary. If she pulled rank and reined in her colleagues, she feared she'd be viewed as a hypocrite and lose the tightly knit team she hoped to have guarding her flanks. If she backed them in spite of her better judgment, she was afraid she'd be forced to espouse projects and programs in which she had little confidence. Fortunately or unfortunately, the consultant came to the rescue and promised to help fill-in the expertise gap, as required, using other specialists from his firm. This gave the new president no alternative, she thought, but to say yes to the team's ambitious agenda.

During her first presentation of the plan to the board of directors, raised eyebrows and polite questions soon turned to head-wagging and opposition. Despite several opportunities to compromise or to dissociate herself from the plan, the young president stuck by her guns—or rather the team's guns—and made the plan an all-or-nothing referendum on her leadership. This changed the level of discussion from a debate on the merits of the plan to a question of the president's judgment, and the chairman wisely adjourned.

After the meeting, he met privately with the president and quietly explained why the plan—and, more important, her approach to managing relations with the board—simply would not work. They parted amicably, agreeing to disagree, but their relationship was never the same. Business went on as usual, and after a few months of constant lobbying, one of the team's minor initiatives was reluctantly approved by the board, but only on a trial basis. With inadequate resources behind it, the project quickly ran aground and was scuttled. The president finally told the team that the rest of their plan wasn't going to fly either, at least with the current board. Disgruntled now, as well as disappointed, the management staff groused privately about her obvious "lack of advocacy" and made it known, through a variety of subtle ways, that her honeymoon with them was over. A few talked openly about leaving the firm. Productivity and morale sagged.

On the first anniversary of her appointment, with a gun-shy board in front of her and a disaffected, cynical team behind her, the young president resigned. (Although it would be cold comfort to the ex-president, and slightly humbling to the board, after some unrelated economic reverses hit the company, the board did indeed reverse itself and adopt one of her riskier projects, which became a resounding success.)

What can we learn about planning and leadership from this unsettling story?

First, we can reject the conventional wisdom that blamed the president's "inexperience" for the disaster. I know many more seasoned executives who, seeing a chance to revitalize and redirect a complacent company, would've done just what our first-timer did. Some of the staff blamed the president's "arrogance and ambition," though it was, in fact, their own pride and frustration, not hers, that got the ambitious plan in trouble. Interestingly, the chairman alone got it right: anxiety had "killed the cat." Anxiety is a potent force that became an instant inner enemy in an otherwise intelligent, talented, well-educated, and well-intended young president who, by any measure before or after her departure, was well qualified to lead the company.

4. *Put the brakes on pride and provincialism.* Let's look at the president of a different company. This one left his office under decidedly more auspicious—some say legendary—circumstances, though the company still managed to muck up what should have been a flawless and positive transition.

Max De Pree, president of the Herman Miller Corporation, made his reputation by hiring great furniture designers and giving them license to create distinctive, high-quality merchandise that sold like hotcakes in the premium furniture market. So highly was he regarded, in fact, that his 1989 book, *Leadership Is an Art,* became an instant classic not only in his industry but in many others as well. Leadership gurus wrote praiseful, pensive tracts about "the Herman Miller tradition" and its culture of success.[12] De Pree himself idolized the small-town virtues of Zeeland, Michigan, the company's headquarters, which permeated Miller's corporate culture. One Miller consultant told me that Max De Pree's influence was so pervasive, you could literally go to the furthest reaches of the Miller organization and, if you closed your eyes, you could "hear" Max himself speaking through the voices of his employees. When De Pree left, the board went through two new CEOs in rapid succession—nobody's feet, apparently, being big enough to fill the great Max's shoes. And therein lay the problem.

As one insider who wished to remain anonymous told me, "While the board was busy looking for a Max De Pree redux, hiring and firing and making employees and shareholders understandably jumpy, the furniture business was changing—and fast. A souring economy made high-end furnishing chancy while lower cost knock-offs began selling in record volumes. The time was right—and times demanded—not another Max De Pree but someone as closely in tune with the new circumstances as Max had been to his."

Still, the board hung on to its security blanket: the legend of Max De Pree. Anxious about a future that appeared "black and blank," and worried about losing their previous stature, they persisted in making plans as they had done for years, based on old assumptions and myths. While the board was looking for a Max redux the company slid into trouble, which it finally reversed. But, they lost valuable time in a tight, competitive race.

The trick, of course, is to separate justifiable pride from hubris, team confidence from provincialism—and all in the thick of battle, where plans and profits are made and lost.

5. *Use scenario-based planning.* One reason planning is so confusing is that we are confronted not by one possible future but by dozens of them. The problem is, even the twenty or thirty things that could influence our goals are enough to boggle the mind when we consider their mutual interaction. If you lead a firm that is a major government contractor, you may pick the winner of a key election—which can certainly affect your chances of acquiring government contracts—but you may overlook an important breakthrough in technology or a major change in relations with an allied nation or passage of new restrictive legislation in your industry, among many other potentially important factors. It's as if you'd need a separate plan just to react to all these developments, in their various likely combinations—and if that's what you've concluded, you're right.

Scenario planning is based on the fact that multiple futures are possible and that you only need to identify the likely interactions of a relatively small number of key factors in each—and have a general idea of how to handle them—to avoid disaster or position yourself for gain, provided you're ready to act when those scenarios develop. Two of the best-known practitioners of scenario planning, Peter Schwartz (former planner for Royal Dutch Shell) and Jay Ogilvy (working philosopher and former Yale professor), define scenarios as "alternative environments in which today's discussions may be played out." Those discussions, of course, are what's known as planning.

The scenario approach to planning oil production, which Shell still uses, makes a handy case in point. The scenario approach uses the same data base as other, more linear models, but it also takes into account chaos and catastrophe, branches of mathematics now being studied seriously by world planners as well as the gut feelings of experts, the consensus of workers and media observers, and even the creative ramblings of artists and visionaries who spend their waking lives thinking the unthinkable and imagining the results. For Shell planners, these imponderables include global warming, breakthroughs in cheap substitute fuels, and the shift away from petroleum-based products in general manufacturing. Out of this hodgepodge of input, certain "stories" start to emerge. These stories, or scenarios, gain their power because, while they cannot predict the magnitude and direction of key factors with great certainty, they can approximate the effect of these factors in all their interactions, and that's what matters most to leaders.

One key to making scenario planning work, Jay and Peter have found, is to use diverse people in the process. The world, after all, is a challenging, contrary, diverse place, and those differences should be reflected in your planning team. In fact one of the best things about scenario planning is that people throughout the organization can participate. It takes planning out of the hands of analytical experts and makes it a healthy culture-building exercise.

Best of all, scenario thinking liberates the leaders' mind. Like aikido, it requires multiple, flexible strategies, not the "master plan" or the "great leap forward" so beloved by, and destructive to, dictators. It promotes the ability to listen, question, and learn, and it weakens the all-too-human desire to pontificate, dominate, and control. In other words, it teaches humility.

To learn more about scenario-based planning, I heartily recommend Jay Ogilvy's excellent book *Living without a Goal,* an excellent eulogy to the now defunct practices of industrial-age planners and an excellent primer on scenario thinking.[13]

PLANNING AS YOU GO

For example, the Todd Company—the Kalamazoo-based, global family business that deals in essential oils and spices—has for generations articulated its leaders' strong commitment to customer service, fair dealing, and lasting relationships. This philosophy looks fine on paper but is severely tested when real-world developments strain the bottom line. One such upheaval hit Todd's business world in the 1980s as companies in every industry began insisting on just-in-time delivery of raw materials and goods earmarked for further processing. This transferred the pressure of close schedules and costs of inventory from the purchaser to the vendor of these materials, and most suppliers grumbled and resisted that change for as long as they could. The Todd Company, however, saw that such changes were inevitable, and—guided by their principle of proactive customer service—planned to implement such a program well before their customers began banging the table and demanding it. The cost of this initiative was considerable, but the results were gratifying. Todd's reputation as a company that anticipated customer needs grew, bringing in new business and expanding the customer base.

This habit of planning while in motion is typical of leaders who think of themselves as immersed in a network of customers, technology, and environmental and economic forces, where developments in one sector can reverberate throughout the web. Linear planning and step-by-step attacks on fixed objectives mean little; preparedness, flexibility, and adherence to a larger purpose while improvising mean a great deal. Such planners know they cannot control the world, only their reaction to it.

I recommend that you review your own planning styles and beliefs at this point. Below is part of the self-assessment I use with leaders seeking to import or re-instill these new values, to make planning, learning, and doing the one seamless act of creation that makes all of them work better:

1. *Support.* Do you have the personal and professional support you need to change your organization's planning style or to reinforce a healthy planning style and make it last? As therapists say, "It takes a heavy stick to break thick ice." Old habits are addictive, as are the narcotics of pride and nostalgia.

2. *Self-awareness.* Do you know what forces are pulling you in which directions? Are you in charge of the planning process or is an inner enemy in charge? How much time do you devote to thinking deeply and critically about your organization's possible alternate futures? Do you understand your own personal needs and desires for the future? Do you know which planning style suits you best?

3. *Learning.* Would you characterize yourself as a student or a teacher in your organization's planning process? If a student, do you have competent teachers available to help you learn? If a teacher, do you know when and how to let students be responsible for their own learning? Ideally, *sensei* relationships develop among leaders and constituents engrossed in continual planning: some teaching in certain situations, others teaching when the situation changes, but all learning all the time.

4. *Functions.* Does your planning model include the following:
   - Differences between your current and desired organizational culture?
   - Information on the current operating environment (constraints and opportunities)?
   - A specification for organizational readiness (understanding of its strengths and weaknesses and ways to employ or compensate for them when you act)?
   - The mission, vision, and overarching values and goals of your organization as they are understood and agreed to by everyone involved in planning?
   - Relevant details about the stories (scenarios) your competition is watching?
   - Relevant details about your customers' current and upcoming wants and needs?

If your answers reveal your aikidolike planning-leading style, this chapter may be considered a good review. But if your answers felt less than satisfying, you might wish to use this short assessment as an invitation to begin a learning venture into aikido-style planning.

7. Master Practice #3

Speak the Language of Mastery

> I will endeavor never to write more clearly than I think.
>
> —Niels Bohr

Leaders differ widely in skills and beliefs, but all face a common hurdle in going the distance: mastering communications. Phil White, CEO of Informix, puts the problem in practical terms: "We get talented, energetic, ambitious people who simply cannot make an effective presentation. It is not just technique they lack. They seem communications-challenged. They lack the basics. It's the biggest threat to developing the leaders we need."[1]

Aikido-style leaders continuously work at communicating and see the struggle to get it right as a master practice. In aikido the failure to listen and understand the *sensei* can result in injury. As black belt aikidoist Phillip Moffitt explains, "You must always blend with your opponent, first absorbing the attack energy and then blending with it, thus moving together. A failure to communicate at a visceral level is a very serious matter."

Enduring leaders practice finding and fashioning new metaphors and analogies, creating economic, clear, satisfying dialogue. They meet their competitors' attacks by first absorbing the energy and then bending it to a useful purpose, often with a good-humored quip. They avoid cheap, profane, and combative language that would rile the enemy and make the contact needlessly dangerous or rancorous. According to a September 1996 article in *Upside* magazine, a Microsoft executive dismissed a rival's plans as "a dorky idea." We all get the point when someone speaks to us like that. But what's the long-term cost to future dealings with that person?

Leaders seeking mastery, like students of aikido, are deeply respectful of silence as well as sound. They know how to relax into the void.

They understand that we must often seek understanding with action preceding words. In fact they may be properly suspicious of words, as Andy Grove says, "Words are cheap." This statement is surprising from an earnest teacher and writer of books on business leadership that are cogent, useful, and hardly cheap. Aikido leaders must have a bias for moving from action to reflection and vice versa. They work diligently to speak and write the language of mastery, the symbols, words, and phrases that move others to purposeful action.

Since leadership is a group activity—a communal, social effort— it can't take place without two-way communication. For enduring leaders, language is both a tool and the object on which that tool is used: the thing manipulated, shaped, and crafted. Even deconstructionists like Jacques Derrida, whose philosophy seeks to undermine the power of authors, do so only by promoting the power of words. As Plato showed us in his well-known Allegory of the Cave, where a lifelong subterranean dweller must generalize about the world by looking at shadows cast upon a wall, words can only give us the illusion of truth; they are signs standing in for other signs. In our logocentric Western culture, words often take the place of reality, a substitution that for most of us goes unnoticed because so much of our reality is imagined.[2]

In popular culture, as in depth psychology, symbols—meaningful images—have enormous power. They arise from leaders' subconscious minds, the source of our greatest creativity, to connect directly with constituents. Because they combine our rational and intuitive faculties, they are probably the most genuinely and thoroughly human form of communication we know.

Throughout history, language and its symbols have reflected and shaped society. In the industrial age, image words—"extracting," "forging," "producing," "selling," "taming," and "conquering"—were the language mirrors of the nineteenth and the first half of the twentieth centuries. They reflected a society obsessed with acquiring, exploiting, appropriating, and expropriating resources—often in connection with other emotion-laden words like "frontier," "territory," and "patriot." "Manifest Destiny," the "Wild West," the "New Frontier," "Winning is everything"—these became the catchphrases that industrial-age leaders used to marshal their constituents and expand their power. The value symbols behind these terms included words like "independence," "growth," "loyalty," "certainty," and "profit." We think, therefore we are. We speak, and we become. But who is speaking?

WHO DOES THE TALKING FOR YOU?

By this I do not mean who is the hired spokesperson you might rely on to spread the word about your organization. I mean what is motivating you to say—or not say—clearly what you mean. Too often one inner enemy or another puts words into our mouths. George Bush hurt his reelection bid by allowing his inner enemy of elitism (lack of empathy) to speak out at the wonders of scanning at a grocery checkout counter. Today's sound bite becomes tomorrow's blooper—the off-hand comment, the deadly quip, the angry retort—that reveals all too graphically the half-digested thoughts and feelings that churn inside us. To a leader, these self-inflicted wounds can be merely annoying or they can be deadly. They can delay or derail a fast-track career. They can kill a new business venture or product launch. They can cost time and money.

One inner enemy—intolerance, bias, or lack of empathy—will sometimes surface in conversation or a meeting or even a broadcast. In recent years, two sports announcers lost their jobs for making biased comments. One made statements about athletes' racial characteristics and the other about women golfers. These inner enemies of intolerance are surprising when issued by professionals. Yet we see in our own experience countless examples of problems the inner enemies deliver.

Phil White is not the only CEO who's concerned about the lack of good communications among leaders today. Weeks of a team's time are spent researching a client's needs and creating a solution that will meet those needs. Then maybe several key people fly across the country to the client's headquarters. The costs climb, and the opportunity costs are often higher. The client assembles another team to hear the recommendations. Too often the result is a wooden, unimaginative, poorly articulated presentation. The client is not getting your message.

It hurts to see that, and yet it happens in business meetings almost every day. To quote White, "It's a terrible waste."

Since politicians' effectiveness depends on their being able to get their message across, one might think they would set a good example. Not so. Watch the Anita Hill–Clarence Thomas tape and see how crude, inept, and disingenuous the senators sounded. In contrast both Hill and Thomas spoke clearly and cogently. One poor presentation by a politician can cause a career to crumble. In 1980, for example, the normally composed and articulate Ted Kennedy's groping, stammering, ill-at-ease response to NBC reporter Roger Mudd's question, "Why do you want to be president?" ended his hope of becoming president.[3] Why was this simple question so difficult for such an experienced leader to answer?

To observers familiar with leadership aikido, Kennedy's confusion and discomfort signified a soul uncentered. I am convinced that if Ted Kennedy had responded quickly and clearly with something like "I feel it is my personal and family duty to continue the political legacy of my older brothers," Americans—whether they ultimately voted for him or not—would at least have accepted the answer. As it was, Kennedy hemmed and hawed and finally muttered some platitudes linked to the Democratic platform. His response sounded utterly false to everyone who heard it. Four years later Kennedy announced that he had permanently given up his presidential aspirations "for family reasons." This time the public had no doubt that he spoke the truth.

Here, I think, was a clear case of a leader visibly torn between the image he wanted to convey and the self-image he carried in his heart—and his communications showed it. The man and the myth did not match.

When the message and the product really connect, however, it's a different story. Edward O. Welles wrote in the May 1996 issue of *Inc.* magazine about the beginnings of 3Com, a company that sells network linkages between computers. At the time the company started, others in the field had staked out their territories. But founder Bob Metcalf was on a pilgrimage to change the very nature of the game. At first his circuit board failed to attract investors. His technology crusade, as he called it, didn't connect until he began to sell "not a board, but a standard."

Venture capitalist Dick Kramlich saw in 3Com the prospects for a standard, felt the passion of the entrepreneur, and invested. He believed that "the idea has to change things in a big way, and the entrepreneur has to be evangelical about the idea." Today 3Com is heading toward a $2 billion business, and Kramlich's return on his investment is 141 times, or so it is estimated.

When a leader's utterances and the myths behind them match, the results can be astonishingly effective. Many millions of people have responded passionately and supportively to the words of leaders like Churchill, Lincoln, and Gorbachev; Gandhi, Mother Teresa, and Dr. Martin Luther King Jr.; Muhammad, Jesus, and Buddha; Homer, Maya Angelou, and Joseph Campbell—though they are all as different from one another in background and experience as the times and places in which they live, or lived. Enduring leaders like these use language that not only stirs us but changes us. We are moved by what they say: it somehow gets us going, and on our actions ride not just the success of our individual careers and organizations but the future of our civilization itself.

Who said words are cheap?

HOW CAN WE USE THE MEDIUM
TO MAKE THE MESSAGE?

How we say something can be as important as what we say. Recently I worked with the CEO of a venerable financial institution who asked me to come in to help senior management articulate a new statement of corporate values. As is often the case, there was more at stake here than simply presenting the new statement in a way the constituents could understand and respond to. There were problems with the medium and the message. What I found most telling in my work with this company was that none of the top managers talked straightforwardly and face-to-face about their concerns or their values. Why? Because the President-CEO felt ill at ease with large groups and disliked one-on-one discussion. He preferred top-down communications in formal staff meetings and handled everything else in writing. This had the effect of giving even a trivial letter the force of a papal bull (written messages are perceived as having more authority than spoken words) and elevating even his most offhand spoken remarks to signs of intimacy (What, he actually spoke to you? What did he say?). Neither of these effects is all bad, provided the leader in question knows that the medium often influences the message. Consequently, he enjoyed a considerable and justified reputation as a stickler for well-crafted prose. He spent hours composing his edicts and editing the directives and memos of his subordinates. The problem wasn't necessarily that he had bad or irrelevant ideas, but the fashion in which he was communicating them led to an atmosphere in which open discussion was actively discouraged. Once something is written down, for better or worse, it seems less open to discussion than when its spoken. And since the task was to create a new values statement that top management, and ultimately the whole institution, could live and work with, all constituents needed to participate in its creation. The medium—polished, written documents—didn't fit the message, which was simple: let's work together to create a value statement.

Sir James Black at work in his lab offers a stark contrast. His sessions vary from an all-hands-on-board seminar to one-on-one tutorials to impromptu problem-solving sessions. Questions fly and everyone's attention remains focused on the problem to be solved. Nobody wastes time making posturing speeches. All are expected to contribute, but people are also respected when they need solitude. In short, the lab is the site of ongoing deliberations where form and membership are a function of the query being pursued. Since the focus is always on the problem at hand and how to best approach it, there's a tight fit between the medium and the message.

How Can We Convey Both Sense and Sensibility

"Aesthetics" is a word that's seldom mentioned in organizations, unless the subject is advertising, architecture, or a logo's graphic appeal. That's too bad, because we all make aesthetic judgments every day about everything from the clothes we wear to the car we drive. We judge other people at least partly by their appearance, too, just as we evaluate organizations to a greater or lesser degree by their brochures, their physical facilities, and the way their employees look, speak, and behave. Savvy leaders can use aesthetic appeal to enhance a message and pack a gallon's worth of meaning into a pint-sized collection of words. Perhaps the simplest example of an aesthetic decision can be seen in the shift from industrial-age corporate towers to contemporary corporate headquarters being housed in open campus settings.

HOW CAN WORDS CHANGE THE WORLD?

Take, for example, a man universally acknowledged to be one of America's greatest and most eloquent leaders, Abraham Lincoln. In *Lincoln at Gettysburg,* probably the longest book ever written about the 272-word Gettysburg Address, historian Garry Wills credits Lincoln with essentially inventing modern political communication. In an age of flowery, lengthy, baroque oratory, Lincoln managed to "derive a new, a transcendental significance from this bloody episode." In that one brief speech, he was able to "win the whole Civil War in ideological terms . . . cleanse the Constitution. . . . Lincoln found the language, the imagery, the myths that are given their best and briefest embodiment at Gettysburg."[4]

Lincoln's problems were pretty clear. The country was at war with itself, torn apart. But he knew his audience. He reminded his listeners of their common background—the time when this nation was conceived and the purpose for which it was conceived. He told them the story, or myth, of their common background. Then he reminded them of the problem at hand and what several thousand brave soldiers had done to solve it. Next he reminded them of the work yet to be done, creating in the process, one of the most often-quoted and revered phrases in our cultural history, which is, after all, the story we tell about ourselves: "that government of the people, by the people, for the people, shall not perish from the earth."

I can't imagine any enduring business leader not wanting to communicate with such clarity and inspiration. In fact, "of the people, by the people, for the people" surely describes the kind of organizations many of us are trying to build. Lincoln's words alone did not change the course of the war. But they inspired and continue to inspire those who would work to give meaning and purpose to their lives and their work.

While few of us are going to go down in history for our eloquence, our words—both what we say and how we say it—can change the course of our lives and the lives of our constituents, the people who work for and with us, the people to whom we provide products and services.

The paradoxical aspect of eloquent communication is that it won't work if it is labored, contrived, out of time. The harder a leader strains for the big, sweeping, memorable phrase, the more hollow it's apt to sound. But let a simple, honorable person say what flows from the heart and it stops us in our tracks. Aaron M. Feurstein went from being an obscure textile-factory owner to a national hero when he declared after a fire that he would rebuild the factory and keep his employees on payroll while doing so. He repeatedly said he was doing what was right, what he was morally bound to do. His message was clear: "I feel I am a symbol against the movement of downsizing and layoffs." He was honored everywhere, and those simple words have been echoed around the world.

THE FOUR-POINT FORMULA

Over the years, in working with leaders from different sectors—from business to health care—I have found certain common characteristics reflected in their communications. Their words come from a centered place, reflecting their own self-knowledge. In that sense, they are as true to reality as they can be. They address the problems of constituents in a way that shows the possibility of solving or transforming those problems. They use words, concepts, and images that communicate the truth as they see it and that evoke meaning. It all adds up to a deceptively simple formula for leadership communications, aikido-style, which has worked—and has worked miracles—since the dawn of time:

1. Discover the myths that motivate or trouble your constituents.
2. Update or transform those disparate myths into one aspirational common story.
3. Find the most powerful, meaningful imagery in that new myth.
4. Express those images in everyday language, choosing phrases and terms that matter most to constituents today.

Let's look at each of these elements, with a few illustrative examples.

1. *Discover the myths that motivate or trouble your constituents.*
   Let's begin with what a myth is and is not. A myth is not a lie.
   Because of popular usage—in advertising, journalism, and elsewhere—some people think that a myth is a falsehood: a fantasy believed in only by simple-minded or poorly educated people. In reality, myths are stories that convey an inner truth that is less accessible to other forms of articulation. If most myths sound fantastic, as most ancient myths do, it's because their plots and characters are metaphors for the real subject of the story.

   Ancient myths of both the East and the West often deal with important universal subjects and concerns, like the creation of the world, how to become a man or woman, how to find a proper mate and behave in a marriage, how to face one's own mortality. These are questions everyone asks at one time or another. The wisest among us make up stories—myths and parables—to show how characters involved in these situations or dilemmas act when they encounter obstacles and temptations, and what happens to them afterward. From their example, we learn how to act when these things happen or when those same questions occur, to us—provided we understand the metaphor behind the myth.

   As Marina Warner writes in *Six Myths of Our Time,* myths still "tell stories which can give shape and substance to practical, social measures." Of the TV shows, action movies, and computer games that convey our "common stories" these days to young male leaders-in-the-making, she says, "slaying monsters, controlling women, still offers a warrant for the emerging hero's heroic character; this feeds the definition of him as a man. But this narrative . . . has come away from the studs that held it to the inner stuff of experience: warrior fantasies today offer a quick rush of compensatory power but pass on no survival skills—either for a working or a family life."[5]

   This attempt to satisfy our need to know, to understand things on the most profound level, is the foundation of all great leadership communication. If things are going well, if everything is on course and there are no new mountains to climb, deserts to cross, or seas to explore, we have no need for leaders. If things are not going well, if things are in a state of flux and if the myths we've inherited from our parents and teachers, from the media and the workplace, fail us, it's because the leaders we depend on have failed to refashion them to meet our changing needs.

We are fortunate to live in a time when exciting new myths are emerging and converging. First there's the compelling story of a digitally connected global community. Part of the power of this myth is the elimination of artificial boundaries that were drawn in earlier times to separate, contain, and control people and resources. Another aspect of this myth is the magical feeling of having personal access to minds, information, and culture that was impossible even to contemplate just a decade ago. Add to this the mythic global image of the Berlin Wall being destroyed rock by rock and the evil separation of apartheid being replaced by a flowering of constitutionally based human rights in South Africa. Later in this chapter, we will see how the power of the myth of digital connection made palpable by the power of Nelson Mandela's language has changed one enterprise. In another example, we'll look at how the potential of digital networks and the possibility of giving every child an electronic tutor is fueling one ambitious start-up. But these are just a few examples in a climate where great emergent myths embolden people's minds and wills and fuel the entrepreneurial spirit that has been dormant, awaiting the day when it can be free.

2. *Update or transform disparate myths into one aspirational common story.* Although they frequently take place in the past—sometimes the very distant past—all effective myths are about the future. A common story that takes place "long ago and far away" may be entertaining, but it is relevant only to the degree that it awakens us to new or forgotten possibilities and guides our future decisions. Leaders seeking to update, consolidate, or rejuvenate old myths to better serve the present should always keep this in mind. Transformative leadership means evoking a desired or longed-for future, even if part of that transformation means rediscovering old truths, or returning to old values, just as leaders during the Renaissance urged a rediscovery rather than a literal re-creation of classical ideals.

One of my favorite clients is a large research institute in South

Africa, C.S.I.R., headed by Geoff Garrett, that is completely changing itself to conform to both the living realities of the new democracy and the power of tribal ways of thinking and acting. The leadership team is attempting to blend together, aikido-style, the aims of its emerging myths with disparate bits of old mythology and the current reality into an aspirational common story.

The senior team invited me to join them in a retreat in the bush to reconsider and recalibrate their future. The team, still mostly white males, was also discovering the true power of diversity. The excitement was high. Together we developed new tools and strategies for the creation of a compelling new story for their mythic future. These six steps can guide you as they guided us.

- Look intensely at the immediate environment. In concrete language, list the real problems and possibilities it contains. Among our problems were limited funding sources and a need for new technology. Then look at the emerging global possibilities for new directions and opportunities for participation. These might include new customers and strategic alliances.

- Examine the shadows and problems that are part of your current reality and discover which ones are common to others and which are unique to your organization. For example, as a common reality, we were dealing with a long history of unequal opportunity based on race. More particular to our situation was the need for new educational initiatives to close the gaps left by apartheid, to cast lots of light on these shadows, and to examine them realistically and dispassionately without laying blame, casting aspersions, or offering defensive explanations.

- Discover the best practices of master leaders and then use them to test yourself, to set new benchmarks. What leaders do you admire? Why? How can you emulate their practices in your current situation? Our group was inspired by images of a free society, with rising optimism inspired by President Nelson Mandela.

- Express your highest ambitions and hopes for the future

in simple, concrete language. Our ambitions were to create jobs and eliminate poverty. Connect those to your ideal values and to the emerging myths.

• Create a powerful story of who you are by looking at your values. Our own included fair treatment and an equal opportunity for each person to grow within the organization and to discover where he or she fits into the new myth of freedom and fair play.

• Go back and test your story on your constituents. Invite them to participate, to make the story their own.

There was magic stirring in all of us in those intense, somewhat sleepless days and nights in the beautiful bush. We formed teams to write the best new mission statement, our story. Negotiations were serious as words were chosen, discussed, and discarded until the right ones emerged. People's individual myths were sorely tested until the common ones were found. Finally it came down to the words of a veteran executive who, as someone said, "Spoke from the heart." This outwardly tough, streetwise veteran had great poetry in him and he was bold. He began his statement by saying the firm's first task was to eliminate the crippling poverty in South Africa. Then his language was more concrete and focused on such things as learning from others, including both developing and developed nations. As we listened to our new collective myth, our common story of the future, we were all deeply moved and grateful to have been a part of its invention.

3. *Find the most powerful, meaningful imagery in that new myth.* In addition to articulating new myths, the enduring aikido-style leader must sift through the myths and symbols we've inherited from the past, find their latent truths, and restate them today in a way that will still be meaningful tomorrow. Leadership words of the industrial age are already giving way to a Green Glass Age vocabulary. Aikido-style leaders regularly use words like "cyberspace," "random access," "webs," "data warehouse," and "online." These new words, and the forward-looking myths they convey, speak as much to constituents' inner needs as they do an outward reality. They describe a society and organizational culture concerned with developing, becoming, transforming, optimizing,

facilitating, participating, and sharing. The goals they aspire to are described by words like "healthy," "virtual," and "fair."

Appreciating the power of myth is one thing: doing something about it is another. Here is an excerpt from a speech given by a man widely regarded as an enduring twentieth-century leader, South African President Nelson Mandela:

> Our deepest fear is not that we are inadequate. Our deepest fear is that we are powerful beyond measure. It is our light, not our darkness, that most frightens us. We ask ourselves, who am I to be brilliant, gorgeous, talented and fabulous? Actually, who are you not to be? You are a child of God. Your playing small doesn't serve the world. There's nothing enlightened about shrinking so that other people won't feel insecure around you. We were born to manifest the glory of God that is within us. It's not just in some of us; it's in everyone. And as we let our own light shine, we unconsciously give other people permission to do the same. As we are liberated from our own fear, our presence automatically liberates others.

By updating a few major myths and expressing them with imagery appropriate to both the old era and the new, Mandela is able to present it convincingly in a single moving paragraph. He addresses his black African constituents, who for so long suffered under and struggled against apartheid, by contradicting in an unusual way the old white South African myth that blacks are inferior. He does not deny the emotional reality behind the myth: to be black in South Africa was to feel economically and politically inferior; the system made it so. By acknowledging this reality, Mandela increases the power of his subsequent point: that black Africans are anxious about using their new power wisely, a concern shared by the white minority. Although distinctions between blacks and whites remain, Mandela has consciously blurred that boundary.

Mandella also mentions light and darkness. Both Christianity and the ancient Mazdean religion depict the struggle between good and evil as a contest between light and dark, an image rooted deep in the Western psyche. Superficially, the struggle over apartheid took place, and continues to take place, in terms of light and dark skin. But Mandela reverses the myth. He begins by saying that black Africans aren't afraid of being inadequate, they are afraid that they are to be too powerful. That is a masterfully empowering statement. In the third sentence, though, Mandela calls up yet another mythical image: that light equals good and dark equals bad. Thus to be black in South Africa is not to be inadequate, weak, and evil; rather it is to be powerful and good. Some factional leaders might have stopped there, but Mandela's goal is to throw his rhetorical net around the entire population and bring all of the people closer together. He affirms that God is within everyone, not just an anointed few: light can indeed shine in whites as well as blacks. As the speech progresses, we see a new South African myth unfolding before our eyes—one that consolidates rather than separates, and elevates instead of belittles, the individual. We all share the essential trait of being human, Mandela reminds us. Be proud of yourself, he says, because if you are, you give others permission to feel pride, too, and only self-esteem can vanquish fear and hate. Don't fear your neighbor, black or white. Your self-love will be repaid in trust.

Donald Padwa, an erudite mountain-climbing sixty-five-year-old entrepreneur, looked at the new myth of digital connectedness and found his own powerful, meaningful imagery. Padwa veered into business after graduating from Columbia Law School by starting a company called Basic Systems. The concept of the company—now called Xerox Learning—was to bring good training to lots of people in a cost-effective manner.

Next he worked from the myth of bioengineering to form a new company that would combine seed propagation and the scientific talent to improve agricultural production in places where the need for food was greater. Once the company was flourishing, however, he made a graceful exit. "I don't do well actually running things," he said.

Today Padwa is pursuing a personal dream to extract from the current mythology of a global, digital community the reality of a new form and style of education that allows all students to participate fully in the intellectual and cultural niches the world possesses. His new company, Agent Based Curricula (ABC Corp.) provides software that will revolutionize the worlds of software development and educational reform. As a climber and also as a serious student of science, he is both pragmatic—one toehold at a time—and bursting with visions of profound change. His language shows it: "Why can't each child have a friendly, powerful electronic tutor? Why should only the wealthy have access to knowledge and culture? We have the technical know-how to change these things. What we need is a powerful movement, a real agreement about changing our minds, how we think about these things. In five years' time, each child should have the educational access that can set that child free."[6]

4. *Express those images in practical language.* In this fourth step, we circle back around to the first. Ideas must be cast in practical language—that is, in terms that are meaningful to constituents today. Look at the first point—discover the myths that motivate or trouble your constituents. Let's say they care about growing oranges. If you give them a story about this history of wheat agriculture, even if, in your mind, it really does address the problem, you're going to have to struggle to make them understand that you're really talking to them about their concerns. The most blatant example of an image that reveals a failure to understand constituents is Marie Antoinette's famous retort when she was informed that the peasants had no bread. "Let them eat cake," she is supposed to have said.

It's the specific words that really count in conveying an image. America Online (AOL) is a fascinating example of how some astute business and technical people took the big myth of connection and made a big business out of it. The proposition was grand: we will connect you to the virtual world. The proposition was simple: we will make your connection easy and quick. Very appealing stuff. AOL was a dominant force in the connecting realm until others decided to enter and either give away access tools (AT&T) or provide more stuff (Microsoft and Netscape). Then the whole language of myth changed, and AOL responded by offering a cheaper, open-ended service—$19.95 a month for unlimited use.

Then a problem arose: the new AOL access was so successful

that it created a wild demand, which the company was unable to fill. Result: massive traffic jams and many very angry customers. The CEO, seeing a crisis, responded to the problem by reinterpreting the easy-global-access myth they had started with. He articulated the new myth as a small-town problem that, for the time being, only constituents could solve. He likened the situation to the single pay telephone that several people needed to use and pleaded with customers to show common courtesy and not hog the line. It remains to be seen if his homely example will have an effect. Meanwhile AOL is rushing to put in new servers to manage the traffic its story created.[7]

Politics, business, and the arts are full of curious and instructive leadership models, such as humanitarians Mother Teresa and Norman Vincent Peale; and caste-breakers Mohandas Gandhi, Margaret Chase Smith, and Aaron Feurstein. These people tapped the myths that were important to their constituents, then substituted new, more useful images using powerful, evocative language. I saw this process work in a variety of startling ways during the State of the World Forum in San Francisco in 1995:

- *Mikhail Gorbachev.* He communicated like an image on a Soviet Mount Rushmore: a man well aware of his historic persona and given to long, rambling soliloquies.

- *Margaret Thatcher.* A warrior queen in her own right, she combines an elevated presence with neatly formed, pungent phrases worthy of any backbench politician.

- *Tich Nhat Hanh.* The soft, simple sweetness of this self-effacing Buddhist monk belies his stature as a great religious leader.

- *Carl Sagan.* His billions of fans—and I am one of them—applauded his lucid wit and flair for the dramatic. This communicator probably did more than anyone else to give twenty-first-century science and technology a human face.

- *Ted Turner.* Broadcasting's *novus homo* has turned his personal tastes into an electronic and publishing phenomenon. I sensed beneath the well-crafted, corporate spokesman an earnest, old fashionged American who is angry and impatient for his own mythology to emerge, for his ideas about the digital future to be preeminent.

All these people and more are living examples for the would-be leader-communicator. Study their lives, their styles, their speeches, and you'll see the myth-imagery cycle come to live.

When was the last time you left a corporate dog-and-pony slide show ready to scale Mount Everest—metaphorically, at least? How often have you waited in line to shake a speaker's hand and say how much his or her vision moved you? Did a corporate speaker ever keep you up all night thinking about the things you heard? Did such a person ever motivate you to do your own research into a topic, change your attitude toward a controversial issue, or experiment with a new type of behavior?

If any of these things happened, the speaker was probably not an active corporate executive, an organizational leader, or a politician. More likely, this was a paid motivational speaker, perhaps a business consultant, a former sports star, a famous entertainer, a best-selling author, a cable TV "infotainment" guru, or an evangelist. Why are these speakers better or more successful than practicing leaders at influencing an audience? Is it simply a matter of native talent and practice or is something else involved? Although many of these people are public speakers, the principles that make them a success also apply to written communication, meetings of all sorts, and other media, including videos. Here are the things these high-priced pros seem to have in common with the uncommon leader-communicators I've worked with and observed:

• *Good speakers mirror the thoughts and feelings of their audience.* A mirror merely reflects what's put before it. A speaker who would use words to change an audience first must understand what needs to be changed—and that's usually an outdated belief or unsettling emotion. Gandhi's speeches in support of Indian independence wouldn't have been half as effective had he not traveled the length and breadth of that land for years learning about the hopes and fears of its people. As one well-known Silicon Valley executive told me, a speech is successful if the audience "arrives worried but leaves hopeful." That sounds like a modest objective until you realize how often the reverse is true.

To change an old idea, you must offer a new one. To change an emotion, you must stir a better one in its place.

Lincoln and Mandela did both these things in the speeches we examined earlier. You can do it, too, if you tap into the myths that trouble an audience and replace them with vivid images of the place to which you want to lead them.

• *Effective speakers bind their audience to the culture.* Back in the days of mass illiteracy, poor transportation, and no mass communications, it was easy for a speaker to sway a crowd. People knew only what was around them, and leaders could use those existing bonds to manipulate feelings and opinions. Fortunately, those days are gone for good— although their absence makes the leader's job much tougher. Multiculturalism and mass communication offer us a whole smorgasbord of options. To knit that often disparate collection of people into a cohesive team, a leader must create a culture of unity, drawing together complementary bits and pieces from a variety of beliefs and traditions. Still, that overarching vision—the one that provides the catalyst for self-directed learning—must come from the leader first.

Know who you are speaking to. Choose examples that will speak to them. Those examples may seem obvious.

The next step is crucial: to bind the audience to your vision, you must translate their symbols. For example, Lincoln chose a battlefield that had become a mass grave site to talk about higher values, aspirations for a democratic experiment, and sacrifice.

George Russell has grown the firm his grandfather founded, Frank Russell Company, from a two-person brokerage and mutual fund business to a global enterprise with 1,200 employees and $700 billion in assets under management. In spite of all this success, he continues to work at maintaining the values of a small, family-owned business in Tacoma, Washington.

There is a natural grace and humility about George and his life and business partner, Jane, which employees recognize as the source of the healthy values and culture that set the company apart from its sleek, and often slick and arrogant, competitors in financial-center towers.

To reinforce the homegrown value system, the Russells

join all of their associates in a local theater for an annual review. Powerful symbols are brought into play. One year each person received a replica of Mount Rainier, the beautiful and imposing nearby mountain, mounted on a wood base inscribed with the company values. The symbolic importance of this daunting mountain is that George, at age fifty, and nineteen of his associates climbed it together to plant the Russell flag on top. Mount Rainier symbolizes teamwork and achievements reached through good planning and reliable people. George and Jane are gifted at welding symbols and values into a powerful, sustainable culture.

The Russells' success is based on integrity, doing the right thing, being creative, hiring people who are smarter than they are, hard work, sharing the credit, transition planning, recognizing luck, taking risks, and having fun. Jane and George, who try to live their lives as value models, have appointed a successor, CEO Mike Phillips, so that they are now free to scale some new mountains.[8]

• *The best speakers use their personal presence, along with overarching ideas and values, to create unity.* A common language implies a common heritage and a similar worldview. In the Green Glass Age, where languages and heritages are diverse, something else must provide that unity. In a speech, this connection is provided by the leader: the personal relationship each person feels with the speaker. Later, as the leader's ideas are discussed and mutual feelings expressed, personal bonds begin to form independent of the speaker's presence. From the dozens of myths the audience originally brought to the exchange, the new, overriding, affirmative images offered by the leader begin to take hold. Once these relationships get started, the role of the leader-speaker switches from catalyst to caretaker. Often I ask diverse groups to list their personal and career satisfactions and dissatisfactions. I then ask them to discuss one or two of these with others in small groups. Voilà! They discover how similar they are in their struggles.

• *Good speakers provide a hopeful vision of the future.* You already know that effective myths are about the future.

Although influential speakers may begin as naysayers and doom-criers, their speeches seldom end that way. Just as that Silicon Valley executive always tried to leave his audiences feeling hopeful, so do most successful leader-communicators deal in common aspirations, undiscovered treasure, and developing trends that—like the friendly conductor on a local trolley—invite constituents to step on board and enjoy the ride. The more closely the examples fit the real world of the audience, the stronger the effect will be. I often pull together three or four components of future success that I know are reachable, such as how they might connect to the digital network, set out on new ventures that will keep them interested, or improve their productivity so that they will spend less time in meetings.

• *Good speakers share information and never hoard it.* They don't try to enhance their position by trading in lies, half-truths, speculation, or innuedo. Even their most effective imagery is expressed in useful terms: words the audience can relate to, discuss, and use for future planning. In this way, trusted leaders empower constituents by keeping them informed.

The best leaders always deal with the hard news first. They cast light on secrets and shadows. They dispel their audience's anxiety, if they can. Then they proceed to build the presentation around the issues the audience needs to deal with.

USING THE LANGUAGE OF MASTERY: A CASE STUDY

I find myself irresistibly drawn to clients who face what is possibly the leader's worst nightmare: trying to restore an organization's morale and productivity after eviscerating staff cuts. Although most companies retain a core of seasoned leaders after a downsizing, too many organizations burden these survivors with unnecessary bureaucrats, meddlers, and placeholders who end up doing phony cheerleading designed to tell the remaining personnel do the same things the same way with fewer people.

Recently I was invited back to AT&T by a remarkable young leader, Waring Partridge, vice president for HomePlace Services. Waring is a true business hybrid: part consultant (he worked first for McKinsey, then started his own firm), part entrepreneur (he began a cellular phone company in the early days of that business), and part citizen-activist (he has testified many times on Capitol Hill and lobbies tirelessly for legislation he believes in). Raised as a navy brat, he crewed his way through Yale and served as a naval officer in Vietnam. Though he knows his numbers and is an excellent analyst, this vigorous, motorcycle-riding intellectual eschews the usual big-company M.B.A.-style posturing. In these and other respects, he is quite unlike most other leaders I had known in the Bell System before divestiture, although he shares their calm demeanor, quiet modesty, and earnest decency. In short, he is a man who means well and wants to do well, too.

We first met at the World Economic Forum in Davos, Switzerland, in 1994, where I heard him describe his dream of AT&T's new customer-focused, technology-enhanced network. I was impressed, but it wasn't until the following year, when he invited me to advise him and his associates on ways to implement their vision, that I came to realize his true talents and abilities, particularly as a leader-communicator.[9]

- *Discovering the myths that motivate or trouble your constituents.*
  Many old myths were shattered when Ma Bell broke up in the 1980s. Not least among them was the visceral belief at all levels that AT&T was special, that the rules of the marketplace somehow didn't, and couldn't, apply to AT&T.

  My first task was to discover which story Waring's constituents—particularly his two dozen or so key leaders—carried in their hearts. Did they still believe in the old myths? Or had a new postdivestiture mythology already taken its place? If so, how well did this internal script about "how things ought to be" fit Waring's vision of the future?

  I was impressed with the people Waring had, as he said, "negotiated for." Every last one seemed able, experienced, and willing. HomePlace was a polyglot organization drawn from all over AT&T—and that meant from all over the world. Their backgrounds, ages, and technical abilities were incredibly diverse—and therein lay our first challenge. Some had come from within AT&T or the Bell Labs. Others came from places like Wang, Newsweek, Phillips, and IBM and had brought bits of those cultures and myths on board with them. Once I began talking to them about their past—and how well they thought that experience fit in with the future they saw for AT&T—they began to use words like "fair," "decent," "open," "encouraging," and "intelligent": hope-filled words connoting commitment and an admirable business ethic. Some of these traits and values obviously came from direct experience with previous employers; but I was even more impressed with the people who said the lack of values in their old situation made them yearn for them even more in their new position.

- *Update or transform these disparate myths into one common story.* We had all the raw material we needed to begin formulating a new HomePlace myth—one that would retain the things constituents already valued while articulating the new things that made Waring's vision unique. Planting the seeds of this new myth was absolutely crucial, since planning teams had already been formed and a few rough edges—from different career perspectives, professional outlooks, personal goals, and corporate and social cultures—were beginning to appear. Our ally here was the organization's start-up character. People who choose to be a part of change are more open to new ways of thinking than those who believe themselves to be victims of change. We simply needed to express a few of these new ideas in a strong leadership context before the fledgling team devolved into factions, as groups of aggressive, intelligent, and goal-oriented people tend to do in the absence of a clear central vision.

Here are some examples of how we transformed the old myths into something new and exciting.

  - *Career aspirations:* Old AT&T hands, understandably, feared a lack of continuity. The big myth that AT&T was an exception had proved false, and so by inference (sometimes justified, sometimes not) did many of the other things AT&T stood for or had promised in the past: job security, guaranteed promotion paths, opportunities for advance technical education, and so on. People moving over from certain other companies like IBM shared these old myths too, but were one step closer to resolving them since they had already taken the initiative to join a different company. Curiously, while AT&T veterans felt their postdivestiture careers were less secure, those joining the company from other firms recently downsized felt more secure at AT&T. Here, obviously, was fertile ground for cross-talk, cross-pollination, and synthesis: the genesis of an important component of the HomePlace founding myth: together we will create an environment where careers can be at least more fulfilling.

• *Personal aspirations:* Waring had chosen people who were self-reliant and self-directing. The problem was that although each had already discovered the paradox of success—that is, the tendency for highly motivated corporate employees to sacrifice personal growth and development in the name of career advancement—in their old jobs, they weren't quite sure how to resolve that paradox in their new ones. This, again, gave us fertile common ground for an energizing component to our new common story: HomePlace must believe in the power and potential of the whole person, not just the part that draws the paycheck.

• *Business ethics and competition:* A few old-timers still believed that might makes right in the marketplace—that if your business clout is great enough, you have wide latitude for making your own rules. Many more, however, believed that economic power and social responsibility went hand in hand. In this respect, AT&T's trivestiture (breaking the company into three separate organizations) and the general climate of increased corporate social responsibility that came out of the 1980s served us well. People didn't need much convincing to see that there were clear limits to corporate power, even when it was exercised with good intentions. An important article in the new HomePlace myth, then, seemed to be: Big isn't automatically better; it's what you do with what you have that counts.

In a surprisingly short time, our list of mutating myths grew longer. Like iron filings taking shape around the magnet of shared beliefs, a clearer picture of what HomePlace actually was and what it wanted to become—based on the feelings of the constituents and the vision of the top leader—gradually took shape.

- *Find the most powerful imagery in the new myth.* The language people used to tell the stories of their old bosses, departments, and companies gave us important clues to the words that would best convey the new shared imagery of HomePlace. Those constituents whose experience had been negative used vivid terms like "back-stabbing," "Machiavellian," "dead bodies littered the floor," "running for the lifeboats" (when a downsizing was announced), and "looking out for number one." People whose experiences had been positive used much kinder, gentler images: "helping hands," "supportive family," "everybody pitched in" or "pulled together," "the welcome mat was out," and perhaps most important of all, "go with the flow."

The negative words connoted a cold, threatening, hostile, win-lose environment—war of all against all. The positive phrases suggested warmth, inclusion, and safety. It also became clear that something else had been gained from the bad experiences: a realistic perspective. Stress is a lens that warps our view of the world. When stress is great enough, entire organizations can lose their balance.

I had been studying aikido at the time I undertook this assignment, so I had some experience with introducing the concepts of balance and center. But the way some HomePlace key leaders took to the concepts made me sure we were on the right track. Consequently, I soon found myself using the imagery of aikido to express what HomePlace was all about, how its leaders and constituents wanted it to function, and where it wanted to go in the future. We talked about a "harmonious atmosphere," "genuineness," "using negative energy positively," "finding win-win solutions," and, when necessary after a setback, "rebalancing and finding a new center."

When it came to handling conflict—among constituents, between constituents and leaders, between HomePlace and its suppliers—we reminded ourselves that not every conflict must be turned into a contest. To best resolve most conflicts, we all agreed that HomePlacers would:

1. Use empathy to defuse an attack and keep it from becoming a destructive contest.
2. Control our own responses, which would open up new options.
3. Restore harmony as soon as practicable and commit ourselves to finding mutual agreeable solutions that would satisfy all sides, center the organization, and restore our personal sense of balance.

These were not revolutionary ideas or even particularly new ones, but it was the first time most constituents had heard them offered by a leader. Using images derived from aikido principles and tailored to the practical needs, outlooks, language, and background of the constituents, Waring was able to express in concise, vivid, and consistent terms the essence of the new HomePlace culture: its founding myth—the common story everyone wanted to agree to but just hadn't yet heard.

Another powerful aspect of learning aikido leadership is the preparation for surprise attacks. In organizations that were once stately ships that plied their waters with grace and power, the very idea of nimbleness, of sudden movements of any kind, is hard to fathom. But now the external and internal environments at AT&T were constantly under the siege of change. Some of the turmoil came from competitors, but the biggest surprises came from within, as disbelievers and capital competitors watched, worried, and attacked. At last report, Waring Partridge was still in the match, blending his energy with that of his attackers, telling his revised story for a new president, and acting as a *sensei* for his newest team members.

- *Cast the story in terms that matter most to constituents.* The fourth and final step in communication mastery is developing the top leader to be the organization's chief storyteller—the Homer for the group's collective odyssey. This translation of aspirational imagery into practical language is no simple task. It is the place, in fact, where thinking and planning become doing; it is the realm of action as well as words. Aikidoist Herman Kauz puts it this way: "Words are only the labels we attach to some part of our experience and are not the actual experience. They are meant to represent reality but can do so only in a limited way. In the kind of training found in martial arts, words are a poor substitute for direct experience."

Just as Lincoln compressed four score and seven years of American experience onto the back of an envelope, so must aikido-style leaders express their constituents' aspirational myths in the most concise and compelling terms possible—in words that will inspire action as well as new beliefs.

Fortunately, just as the Marquis de Lafayette inspired Thomas Jefferson and other American revolutionary leaders to win our freedom, so has another Frenchman, philosopher Jacques Derrida, the father of literary deconstruction, given contemporary American leaders a powerful tool through his "analogy of the postcard."

Consider the humble postcard, Derrida says. What a masterpiece of communication it is! First, it shows great economy of concept—who doesn't have time to read it? Second its meaning is irreducibly clear, specific, and unambiguous. If you write "It rained all day" or draw an arrow to a window in the picture on the front and say, "This is my room," who can doubt that's not precisely what you mean? Even more important, the postcard is an artifact that goes beyond words to tie itself directly to a specific culture—even to a particular mood, feeling, or aesthetic. The postmark certifies the time and place, while the picture on the front speaks volumes about the author's taste, aesthetic sense or sense of humor, and what locals think about themselves. The message on the back reveals the author's priorities and preoccupations: "Wish you were here" or "You would love this hotel" conveys an entirely different set of personality attributes than "I lost my luggage" and "I slept badly last night"—and the recipient can tell the difference.

All in all, these particularized symbols stand in for much broader, deeper concepts. Finding and expressing them is the essence of the master communicator's art. Here's how Waring Partridge put the postcard principle to work at HomePlace:

- *Economy of concept.* We remember the Gettysburg Address because it disassembled one myth and used the pieces to build another—all in the space of a two-minute speech. In the age of fax machines, E-mail, and MTV, constituents' attention spans have become shorter. As a leader you should do all you can to make the constituent's job—as contributor and collaborator—easier. What Partridge did was to reclaim an early AT&T slogan—"Anyplace, anytime, anywhere"—and give it a contemporary meaning.

• *Irreducible meaning.* Many people confuse metaphor and other types of imagery with ambiguity. They think that if you want to say, "John is fast," that's what you should say, not "John is a deer," which will only confuse people. Most of the time, this kind of clear, straightforward language serves leaders well.

But there are times when the clearest, briefest, and most convincing way to communicate a many-layered, complex idea is not through terse, plain language but with metaphor—images that connect through even the most selective listening. For example, there are many kinds of swiftness. John may be a linebacker who is fast in the way that a Mack truck is fast, but one would never confuse a truck—or a linebacker—with a deer. If grace and agility are as important as speed for a particular image—suppose John is a wide receiver—then our one brief metaphor speaks more concisely, accurately, and compellingly than a whole page of data and description.

This combination of simplicity and completeness is what I call *irreducible meaning.* Although a good metaphor can be elaborated upon indefinitely, such elaboration isn't necessary to convey the idea completely and convincingly. Partridge aimed for heartland simplicity and futuristic excitement with the word HomePlace. It is both an electronic mailbox and a sense of place: You can feel comfortable, at ease, at home, using AT&T. HomePlace is a powerful metaphor.

The late John Cage, a noted avant-garde twentieth-century composer, once offered the following list of word-images to anyone interested in better understanding and describing his work ("Words," he said, "are soaked with associations that arise through no one's intention"):

method
structure
intention

discipline
indeterminacy
interpretation
devotion
circumstance
nonunderstanding
contingency
inconsistency
performance

It would be hard to imagine a job description for a leader in the twenty-first century that does not include some of these words. Each reader might take one or two of these words and begin to fashion the first line of a new organizational or personal story. After all, good leaders are always good storytellers.

8. Master Practice #4
Let Values Drive Your Decisions

> The only true happiness comes from squandering ourselves for a purpose.
>
> —John Mason Brown

The calm core from which the aikido leader operates is formed around abiding values. Those core values allow us to operate in harmony. But if we lose sight of them or fail to adhere to them, we can become unbalanced, be forced to scramble, even become lost. Unfortunately, many of us either take our beliefs—and the values that drive them—for granted or impose them on others without debate. The worst offenders are those leaders who turn their backs on deep feelings, yet want to seem like paragons of strength and certainty. They engage in lengthy, sanitized, and ultimately wasteful exercises in "corporate decision-making"—which usually means decision-avoidance. They hide behind the bureaucratic process. Or they slam-dunk important questions that deserve more careful thought.

Even quick thinking, fast-acting cowboy entrepreneurs like Viacom chairman Sumner Redstone too often hide behind lawyers and PR flacks when their toughest, value-laden decisions are announced. Take Redstone's firing of Viacom president and CEO Frank Biondi, who first read about his termination in a press release. The fact that Biondi himself had used the same tactic to dismiss Simon & Schuster publisher Richard Snyder might be poetic justice, but that doesn't excuse the method. While sparing themselves the pain of emotional interaction, neither executive made survivors feel any more secure, committed, or trusting in the uneasy environment that often follows actions. As Biondi found out, such tactics may come back to haunt you.[1]

NEVER OVERLOOK GOOD BASIC VALUES

Positive, or aspirational, values are the things we seek to uphold, not just as whims or fancies but as good things in and of themselves—like life, liberty, and the pursuit of happiness, not to mention courage, self-reliance, and generosity; the list is practically endless. These are the things we hope to achieve in our lives, and our efforts to reach them fuels our other efforts. Negative values are the things we want to avoid, the things we fear.

Of course, talking about values is a lot easier than living them. That's the acid test for most leaders and the reason so many of them fail. As John Gardner writes in *Self-Renewal,* "The identifying of values is a light, preliminary exercise before the real and heroic task, which is to make the values live—first of all, in one's own mind and heart and behavior, second, in the customs, laws and institutions of one's society. We have a gift for professing much and delivering little."

Occasionally we see cases where very bright, well-trained leaders seem to come untethered from the values they purport to possess. As we will see in the following case the directors are often slow in catching dangerous drifts in values.

When Safecard's board of directors hired Paul Kahn as president and CEO in 1994, the corporation was making $150 million annually from its credit card registration and protection business, a service that spares subscribers the headaches of cataloging, canceling, and renewing stolen credit cards. The board had just jettisoned their litigious chairman, Peter Halmos, who had embroiled the company in a variety of legal battles that had hammered Safecard's stock. Rudderless, the board turned to a nationally known headhunting firm, which recommended Paul G. Kahn, a blazing star in the world of financial services and credit cards. A Mensa member who had graduated from high school at fifteen, Kahn logged his first corporate triumph by turning Wells Fargo's struggling credit card business into a moneymaker and launching AT&T's highly successful Universal credit card, in the process winning the prestigious Malcolm Baldridge National Quality Award.

At Safecard, Kahn relocated company headquarters from wind-swept Wyoming to Florida, brought on board high-priced talent and consultants he'd met on his old jobs, launched two new lines of business—a "lifestyle" credit card for golfers and a missing-child search service. He began a massive real estate development to house the hundreds of new employees his expanded operations required. He even renamed the company, calling it the Ideon Group to reflect a new era of big thinking.

Unfortunately, the executive search team seems not to have told the board about the equally well documented dark side of the man they had hired. A lengthy profile on Kahn published in the *New York Times* showed that Ideon's new leader had a long history of big spending. Wells Fargo had audited his expense account when questionable claims—one for a birthday party costing several thousand dollars—began showing up. He was fired by, then sued, his next employer, Capital Holding Corporation, when he fell out with his boss over management discipline and controls. After that, although he helped boost Mellon Bank's credit card profits, he also helped himself to company cash for lavish entertainment and travel. Even at AT&T, where his success was greatest, he spent hundreds of thousands of dollars on entertainment and spectacular company events and ran up so much personal debt that, even as fellow executives ceremonially issued him the first Universal credit card, they joked that he could never have qualified for his own card. He finally split with AT&T when they refused to fund his grandiose plans for a vast expansion of his division.

According to the *Times* profile, all this was complicated by serious lapses of moral judgment. At Safecard/Ideon, he gave lucrative consulting contracts to friends, one of whom was a convicted felon; hired his brother-in-law to run the new child search division, even though the man had no experience in this field; stocked the new corporate jet with Waterford crystal and $10,000 place mats; and hired several "personal assistants," including a food taster. Even worse, he earmarked corporate money for outside ventures that benefited insiders, like corporate directors, and failed to so inform the stockholders.

A year or so into his administration, both of Kahn's ambitious new divisions failed miserably. With soaring liabilities, little income, and Ideon's stock beginning to tumble—50 percent drop in two weeks— the board told Kahn to discontinue the new ventures, cancel the planned move to the new headquarters building, sell the corporate jet, and lay off the excess workers. The red ink continued to flow, however, and an investment banking firm, retained by the board to find a

savior, reported that nobody would touch the company as long as Paul
Kahn was at the helm. The next day Kahn was replaced by a director
as the acting CEO. A week later Kahn received this official termination notice. True to form, he contested the terms of his dismissal, not
for cause but because his contract permitted him to exercise his stock
options within thirty days of his termination. Since his formal notifi-
cation came a week after his oral firing, he argued that the board owed
him seven more days to cash in on the rally in Ideon stock caused by
the news of his removal.[2]

Alas, the Kahn saga is reported on a smaller scale every year in
dozens of lesser known companies. In this case, it's easy to blame the
executive search firm for not disclosing flaws in their candidate. When
your product is information, ignorance is no excuse. But did the board
ask the search experts to check on basic values?

The real villain seems to be the inordinately high value both parties place on "success," without ever agreeing on what that meant. To
Kahn, achieving success excused almost any personal foible, including
an irresponsible attitude toward other people's money and a lax moral
code. To the board, the quest for success justified uprooting and dis-
rupting innumerable lives—first in the move to a distant state, then by
massive layoffs. The other values we traditionally expect from our
leaders—prudence, farsightedness, integrity, consideration, compassion—were notable mostly by their absence. In the end, everyone lost.

LET YOUR ACTIONS REVEAL YOUR VALUES

Even if you don't consciously reflect your values and beliefs in daily
decisions, the actions resulting from those decisions reveal them all
the same. When those revealed values contradict the ones you adver-
tise, you become uncentered—your heart is at odds with your head,
throwing you off balance—a dangerous place to dwell. Václav Havel
writes that "our civilization has essentially globalized only the surface
of our lives. But our inner self continues to have a life of its own."[3]
Guiding that inner life, nourishing it, giving it a voice, and doing the
same for constituents is what Green Glass Age leadership is all about.

Industrial-age leaders often use values to exclude or silence people
who disagree with them. It never occurs to them that people with

diverse values might actually contribute to better organizational decisions. Instead we have taped conversation of Texaco executives disparaging African-Americans, revealing how little they value diversity.

Another industrial-age belief is that personal problems—that is, strongly held beliefs that are contrary to what the boss expects—don't belong at the office. If this is true, then so is its corollary: what happens at work doesn't affect you at home—a notion that leads to ulcers, heart attacks, and nervous breakdowns. Even values that the organization publicly embraces are often sanitized. Most corporate creeds are chosen not to inspire passion but to suppress it and to toss cold water on any embers of individuality or nonconformity. (If you think this is an exaggeration or that your organization is too hip and progressive to be guilty of political correctness, just think about how it treats—formally or informally—anyone who does not conform to the generally accepted image.)

Sadly, people who buy into a culture of self-denial—and by that I mean literally the denial of the self, not self-sacrifice—think there's no other way to live. Never mind that narrow beliefs and hypocrisies limit opportunities, force organizations to endlessly repeat old errors, and define successes to only those aspects that appeared to work in the past. Forget that decision-making and problem-solving processes remain task-oriented, hierarchical, and hypercompetitive—a Darwinian battle for scarce resources and even scarcer personal satisfaction. In these industrial-age organizations the top dogs impose on others their personal mythologies—idiosyncratic common stories, from which constituents are supposed to derive emotional nourishment or leave.

In this environment, decisions are all about assembling and manipulating data through endless processes. They are based on a narrow-belief value system in which there is only one way to do things and that one way can be determined by simply doing the numbers. Statistics are collected by a priestly accounting class and laid like bloody entrails on stone altars, to be picked over and pondered by soothsayers bearing arcane and mysterious titles. Abe Zaleznik, Harvard Business School professor emeritus, thinks the entire process of traditional corporate decision-making literally makes people sick. Endless fact-gathering and information processing—with only a hazy connection to the practical decisions people live with—leaves those involved feeling frustrated and incomplete—in other words, off center.

HOW AIKIDO-STYLE LEADERS USE VALUES

Aikido-style leaders know that values underlie our beliefs and that our actions reveal them. They know and live by what seems to others like a counterintuitive principle: if that value base is narrow, our options will be fewer; but if our values are broad-based, our field of choices gets wider and richer. To have a wide value base does not mean to be wishy-washy about principle. It means that one is open to new ideas and new ways to implement them. Take a sagging bottom line and the quite real need to change the company for its long-term survival. Operating from a narrow base would mean simply handing out pink slips wholesale, without looking at other options. Operating from a wider base might mean looking for other ways to solve a problem. It might mean top-level executives taking pay cuts so that more employees can work together toward turnaround. It might mean helping laid-off employees set up independent service organizations, then using those organizations and referring others to them. If one of your values is honoring all people, you might come up with thirty—or thirty thousand—different ways to enhance performance.

Three personal practices reflect the way aikido-style leaders use values leverage to find and stay in the whirling, harmonious center, balancing personal advancement with principled actions, short-term gains with long-term gains, financial return with growing future capability and new products.

1. *Aikido-style leaders provide access to creativity.* They engender creative ideas in themselves and consequently can reach, touch, and energize many more constituents and stakeholders.

    British poet David Whyte, for example, makes a good living teaching poetry to corporate employees—and the bosses who hire him happily pick up the tab. These leaders realize that even the best-designed jobs have their soul-deadening aspects, and lack of a creative outlet can, in the long run, extinguish the fire in any belly. "We simply spend too much time and have too much psychic and emotional energy invested in the workplace to declare it a spiritual desert," Whyte declares.

    The goal of these classes is not to produce great poets but to help people look at their world in new and creative ways, overcome their fear of the unknown, and learn to take joyful risks. "There is nothing more transforming to the American workplace than the thousands of daily decisions now being made that put soul life above the abstracts of organizational life,"[4] Whyte says, and more and more leaders are agreeing with him.

Mergers are not usually considered to be great opportunities to discover creativity at work, but if the values are in favor of openness and making creative fits, not carving out some small advantage or satisfying some predatory ego, merging can be a creative activity. That's one reason the Disney–Cap Cities/ABC merger of 1995 went so well and so quickly—four days from first query to final handshake. Key decision-makers already knew, liked, and respected each other's values. Nobody had a hidden agenda. With bedrock values demonstrated and acknowledged, it became a relatively easy task to specify obligations and liabilities and to creatively assess the compatibility of existing and upcoming products.

2. *Aikidoist leaders tend to correct, and not repeat, old errors and find new ways to succeed.* A well-known corporate leader whose company invests heavily in chemical production began to worry about global warming. For years he had parroted the company line, pooh-poohing scientific claims about the problems of carbon dioxide buildup—the notorious greenhouse effect. Then his son, a graduate student with a strong interest in the environment, gave him hard data on ozone depletion, water pollution, and other dangers, and he began to question his old assumptions. He looked for new ways to run the business so that bias against environmentalists wouldn't be a guiding value. He began to open up his value system to allow new thinking about products, and that began to change the core business. He didn't want to be the victim of the error of tight focus and narrow values.

3. *Aikido-style leaders value collaboration.* They want all of their constituents to participate according to their gifts, skills, and shared beliefs, not just by virtue of their position on a flow chart or table of organization. These leaders strive for common stories their constituents already recognize and believe in. They know that the power of common values, and the deeply felt beliefs we associate with them, can literally move mountains.

Collaboration is the secret behind Hanna Anderson, the company founded by Gun Denhart and her designer-artist husband, Tom. Ten years after starting a mail-order children's clothing business in her garage, she found herself on the covers of *Inc.* and *Business Ethics* magazines, and she won Forbes's 1994 Entrepreneur of the Year award. Her great success was neither accidental nor guaranteed, nor was it based solely on her superb retailing principles. It arose from an early decision to reflect her values in each strategic decision and one of her values was collaboration.

Denhart's first business plan was a model of targeted marketing and the open expression of values. She wanted to collaborate with consumers who thought as she did and to develop those consumers as a core customer base. So, based on their input, she designed sturdy, colorful, high-quality cotton clothes. She offered shoppers a 20 percent discount when they returned their offsprings' outgrown clothing to be passed on, through company channels, to needy children. Almost at once, the program was a huge success and propelled Denhart and her team to the front ranks of American retailers. Now, as the company grows, she continues her collaborative leadership style with employees and suppliers. As a result, she's had no lawsuits—a real achievement in today's business environment.[5]

If you practice creativity, correct mistakes instead of repeating them, and make decisions collaboratively, you're likely to find yourself building an organization that is pluralistic, trusting, optimizing, and pragmatic.

THE VALUES OF AIKIDO STYLE

"One reason I continue at the dojo," one black-belt aikidoist says, "is because of the harmonious atmosphere. I get to practice with various kinds of people, and there is no rivalry because no one wins or loses. This has affected my own attitude toward others. I try to work with others and listen more carefully to what they have to say."

Substitute the word "office" for "dojo" and this statement could be made by virtually any aikido-style leader or by the constituents who work for and with such a leader. The shared values of harmony, openness, mutuality, collaboration, and flexibility are the solder that holds the networks of aikidoist leaders together, even when those webs span continents and oceans, languages and cultures. Basing their decisions on these and other common values, and confident that the satellite beliefs which implement those values are also shared or at least accommodated within the organizational culture, these leaders are free to act quickly when conditions change, staying ahead of the competition.

Here are four key, overarching values I've seen at work every day in these leaders' private and professional lives. How many of them can you spot in your own?

- *Pluralism.* Fair play, egalitarianism, and inclusiveness are old themes in the American value system, although beliefs can differ considerably concerning how far these values can be pressed without restricting other important values such as the right to property and free choice. While traditional leaders have been taught to take sides and promote one belief at the expense of another, aikido-style leaders seek the "center of the mandala." They don't try to eliminate any particular viewpoint but rather to balance it with its complementary "other half." They seek harmony instead of domination.

  To me, this seeking of balance and harmony is the essence of true diversity—a word that's been hijacked by leaders at both ends of the political and cultural spectrum, pushed and pulled until its meaning has been all but lost. To some, the "call for diversity" means expanding opportunities and benefits for groups that have previously been excluded from cultural, political, and economic institutions. Others see it as a tool for entrenching unfair preferential policies.

  Saddest of all, turf battles are always transitory: even the greatest victories cannot last. Every action that seeks not to restore harmony but to advance one set of interests at the expense of another, inevitably draws a counterreaction. A 1995 poll by *U.S. News & World Report* reflected this gradual Balkanization of the American psyche. It showed that Americans by mid-decade had passed far beyond the usual categories of Republican and

Democrat, liberal and conservative. Shared values and beliefs, the researchers determined, are far more important today than the old considerations of race, region, sex, and political affiliation—news that came as something of a shock to special-interest advocates still operating on those old assumptions.[6]

Aikido-style leaders know that when one faction comes to power in a political, community, or private organization, usually with the help of a temporary coalition, and tries to impose its beliefs on the majority, the result is an angry counterreaction, a contest to regain and hold the reins of power, keeping the wheel of disharmony turning. The only way to end this perpetual, and perpetually troubling, cycle—the whipsawing from one extreme to the other in our institutions—is for a leader to make sure that all value-belief systems are not only included and heard from in subsequent decisions but are made an integral and indispensable part of the decision-making process.

This is a novel way of thinking for most Americans—indeed for most leaders anywhere in the world—but it's essential if decisions in times of seismic change are to have lasting value and coalitions are to become communities.

The late Dr. Jonas Salk, discoverer of the first polio vaccine and a lifelong student of the human condition, went even further. He saw the mutual influence of values and behavior as a key ingredient in human evolution. In his 1983 book *Anatomy of Reality,* Salk wrote, "If equal value is placed upon value to society and value to the individual, then, in time, we will be able to combine the two and eventually we will find that one feeds the other." In the long run, Salk said, the distinction between self-interest and communal interest is an illusion: they are really one and the same.[7]

Another humane and pragmatic thinker, Isaiah Berlin, coined a term for this new way of thinking, feeling, and doing: value pluralism. It means simply, and sensibly, that there are many definitions of good in the world and many paths (belief systems) for achieving it. Many, unfortunately, are incommensurate—that is, they are incompatible or mutually exclusive to such a degree that they can't even be measured by the same yardstick. Material wealth, prized by one system, for example, can mean perdition to another. This makes even more extraordinary Berlin's idea that the only way to achieve maximum good in the world is by allowing these different "roads to nirvana" to mix, mingle, blend, arrange, and rearrange themselves in the marketplace of ideas using the bonding agent of mutual consent, tolerance, patience, experimentation, observation, and trial and error. To preempt any one system absolutely and arbitrarily would be to lose whatever good it contained and increase the world's ration of ill will, frustration, and resentment—in other words, to reinforce the cycle of disharmony.

The bottom line, according to Berlin, is that leaders must sometimes make radical choices that are not based on the neat, orderly philosophical precepts derived from one accepted point of view; they must, instead, change the mix. These may not exactly qualify as leaps of faith, but they are leaps into the unknown, voyages as full of discovery as any sixteenth-century mariner's expedition or twentieth-century space voyage. The organizations such leaders cultivate are therefore like English gardens: a mixture of order and wildness, of the familiar juxtaposed with the unexpected. In this way, value-plural organizations evolve much as we grow and mature as individuals: sometimes quickly, by leaps and bounds; sometimes slowly, by effort and reflection. All experience is important; none of it is to be missed.

- *Trust.* Trust signifies the triumph of maturity over fear. Mistrustful leaders still let fear get the upper hand, even when they try to cloak their mistrust with code words like "empowerment"—which means bestowing on constituents the luster of participation while denying them its substance.

Beliefs that make trust work are respect for the right of others to govern themselves and faith in the process of human growth, which is always nonlinear and risky. Because mistakes often teach us as much or more than success, the delegation of decision-making power must be broad and deep enough to allow participants to really stretch, and that, too, takes trust. Mature leaders don't fear the twists and turns of fate by which we gain experience. In fact, they count on them.

In this regard, Janus—the two-faced Roman god of gates and doorways—has received a bum rap in modern culture. To us, "a Janus," or a "two-faced" person is deceitful, saying one thing but doing another. Originally, though, one of Janus' faces looked forward, toward the future, while the other looked back, on history and tradition—one reason the Romans prayed to Janus at the beginning of a new enterprise. This blend of gazing confidently ahead while not forgetting where you've come from or what you've learned—and knowing that you are capable of learning more—is for me the essence of aikido-style trust.

Quarterbacks who play the odds—never pass and always hang on to the ball—seldom wear Super Bowl rings. From this perspective, the magic we often talk about between a game-winning passer and receiver (Joe Montana and Jerry Rice, for example), a president and a general (Lincoln and Grant), male and female costars (Tracy and Hepburn), or business founders (Hewlitt and Packard) is nothing more than simple trust. If you doubt this, think of similar combinations where trust wasn't present, and consider the results.

- *Optimization.* It may seem odd to present optimization as a value, but optimization is at the very center of a scale often used, or at least talked about, in value-related decisions. How often have you tried to maximize one thing (such as the return on an investment) while minimizing another, like taxes? In noneconomic decisions, you probably try to maximize your enjoyment at a party while minimizing the pain you'll endure the next day. In reality, you neither maximize nor minimize either of these things; none of us do, although we often pretend we do, and we may carry that pretense forward in our sales presentations, political speeches, and advice to colleagues, friends, and family. To truly minimize taxes, for example, you'd have to invest in tax-exempt securities, which always pay less than their taxable counterparts, so there goes your maximized return. To make sure you felt great after that party, you'd have to sip a glass of water and go home early—pleasant, perhaps, but hardly a prescription for maximum fun.

Aikido-style leaders forgo all these word-games—little hypocrisies that devalue life—and make all their decisions on an optimal basis, balancing one good against another so that gains are made on every front. Decision theorist Herbert Simon called this brand of thinking "satisficing," since far-thinking leaders faced with multiple, conflicting, and often irreconcilable choices generally opt for satisfactory results, not some self-defeating, lop-sided victory that, while promising short-term rewards in one area, would bring disproportionate penalties in another.

This concept isn't nearly as exciting as the uncompromising "quest for excellence" that some leaders call for, and will certainly disappoint people who value success at any price, but I've found it's much closer to the way enduring leaders really think and behave—and aikido-style leaders aren't ashamed to admit it. Indeed, they all readily confess to

- *Building multilevel relationships with many customers.* Profit maximizers, such as firms that sign many agreements but service only the biggest accounts, or those that use temporary shortages to price-gouge consumers, can't understand why it makes sense to treat all of their customers as if they were the most important. In the short term, they aren't; but over the long haul they are.

- *Investing without the prospect of immediate payback.* Basic research infrastructure expansion, technology development, and employee education all contribute to tomorrow's profits, but they do little to pay their way today. Profit maximizers and cost minimizers prefer to let competitors take these risks, even though those competitors often end by leading the field. To leaders who value optimal results, success is seen as an ongoing process, not a quarter-by-quarter score. This is especially true when it comes to trading off the expenses of new technology against its gains. Closing outdated plants, using robots on the production line, laying off thousands of workers whose only crime was to faithfully do what they'd been told, turns many stakeholders into neo-Luddites—technology haters who see only the diseconomies, not the gains. Enduring leaders keep people in the center of all their equations, at the core of the enterprise, not on the periphery. They ask, "What great things can we do with this technology and our people?" And they don't pit one against the other.

- *Collaborating with employees, shareholders, customers, and suppliers.* The many myths surrounding free market competition deserve a book of their own. Leaders may say they value competition and then do everything they can to stop it—through gradual monopoly-building, industry cartels, discriminatory pricing, insider deals, captive vendors, special-interest regulations, and so on. This may maximize profit and minimize costs in the short run, but in the long run everyone loses—including the chief offenders—when markets, including capital markets, and government agencies react.

- *Pragmatism.* Naturalist E. O. Wilson, the father of sociobiology, describes a new form of group decision-making that is tailor-made for the Green Glass Age. Instead of relying on hierarchy, which is based on vertical levels of ever-increasing authority, he suggests we try heterarchy—that is, making and acting on choices based upon our individual skills, talents, preferences, and needs. He uses an analogy, interestingly enough, from the highly successful society of ants, which have optimally wedded individual responsibility to communal capability without relying on a superior-subordinate relationship—such as the alpha male, or pack leader, phenomenon—that we "higher orders" find indispensable.

Under heterarchy, anyone who detects a problem or opportunity can make it available for communal action. The group—really a network of subgroups that perform both independent and cooperative tasks—then "swarms" to attack the problem or exploit the opportunity, using each individual's strengths, availability, and capability to optimal effect. Strictly speaking, there are no leaders in a heterarchy (more accurately, everyone leads at one time or in one capacity or another), just individuals who serve as focal points for generating and disseminating useful information, coordinating resources, and generating ideas. All discipline is self-discipline or sanctions imposed by the outside world—useful feedback on the quality of work and its goodness-of-fit to the situation.[8]

Of course, neither Wilson nor other fans of heterarchy suppose, or advocate, that humans should behave like ants. They simply point out that it now seems possible, in an era of instantaneous communications, computers, and widespread literacy, to replace our somewhat medieval dependence on hierarchy and find a mode of decision-making that promotes individual freedom and personal choice while offering the prospect of effective and efficient action.

It's not surprising, either, that this insight comes from the modern scientific community. Research organizations for years have "swarmed" to solve sticky problems and pursue unlikely solutions. Sir James Black's wonderfully productive laboratory is ample proof of that. Unlike the old saw mentioned earlier, "If you don't know where you're going, any road will take you there," their creed seems to be, "Even if you know where you are going, try to find a better road!"

Whatever organizational forms predominate in the Green Glass Age, though, I like to think that the main value underlying all of them is pragmatism. One of these practical new leaders, Phillip Moffitt, says that, under the old ground rules, "By the time you get through a long, what-if planning process, it's too late." Like Waring Partridge at AT&T and Jack Welsch of General Electric, Moffitt has committed himself to teaching people how to "swarm" into action, eschewing dependence on the old command-control structures in favor of loose ad hoc work groups forming and re-forming in pursuit of fast-moving mutual targets. Winship Todd—former CEO and currently a director of the Todd Company, a family held firm that has survived and thrived for five generations using network-oriented strategies—says, "We always look at every opportunity to act on behalf of our customers. We look ahead with them for new ways to sever quality, reliability, cost, even new product development. Ideally, everyone in the company thinks and acts in that manner."[9]

And so they do. Todd is notable for the way it swarms after opportunities—often in joint ventures that anticipate customer needs—creating many more options in the process. Ian Blair, Todd's vice president of European operations, says, "Our whole business is about long-term relationships and service. We have fifth-generation cousins as buyers and growers." Win Todd adds, "Our mistakes [occur] when we wander off from our central business, our core philosophy. When that happens, we move to get back on course. We grow by decades and generations, not by some quick, exploitive new activity."

Craig Barrett—a man more easily taken for a Montana rancher, which he is, than president and COO of a major high-tech firm—leads Intel, another company famous for being prepared and moving fast when markets become a horse race. Intel's new computer chips are almost always technology leaders, the product not of a sudden catch-up frenzy but of years of R&D that also took into account cost-efficiency and producibility.

"Our sense of direction is pretty much set by our estimates of our customers' future needs," Barrett says. "We make very large capital investments in R&D and production to keep technology and applications ahead of current needs."[10] From this perspective, Intel's widely publicized 1994 Pentium chip problem was more than an exercise in successful public relations; it was, in Barrett's words, a very valuable corporate learning and team-building experience.

Creating a heterarchical culture is not easy—remember, it must develop from experience, learning, and practice, not from a top-down mandate—but it is eminently *practical,* a label most of these new leaders prefer over "visionary," which it also certainly is. They prefer to think optimally, in harmony with their place, with their time, and with the future, and so should you.

MAKING OUR VALUES TRANSPARENT TO OURSELVES

Whether we base our actions on positive or negative values, we need to be aware of our inner enemies, the unconscious impulses and unstated imperatives we carry around.

Over the years I've identified the Big Three Inner Enemies that work against aikido-style leadership in organizations by subverting our best intentions, distorting our values, or turning them into negatives:

1. *Self-deceit.* This is the unconscious at work. Often self-deceit comes from unexamined early success. What we've done impairs our ability to see ourselves and our values and our goals clearly. When we're lying to ourselves it becomes nearly impossible to separate what we want from what we fear and to act from a balanced stance to implement our true values. When we rely on a

fixed picture of ourselves and our values, we tend to ignore or try to kill the messenger who brings us anything that doesn't fit in. We're out to protect our image of ourselves at all costs, so our driving force becomes a lust to avenge all real or imagined hurts.

2. *Fixed values driven by unshakable doctrinaire beliefs.* A single idea—sometimes a wild idea—often formulated in our formative years may overshadow everything else. In the face of new evidence, we fall back on this old idea. Our impulse is to try to shove diverse life experience into a one-size-fits-all straitjacket. It's really an impulse to try to control the uncontrollable. From this stance, our impulse often is to right wrongs—real or imagined—by crushing anyone who presents any evidence that the world is not as we see it. When we lead from this stance, we get at best suppressed associates and at worst a form of tyranny.

3. *Giving over values to a rigid system.* We're still looking for control, for one right answer. We know it doesn't exist in ourselves, but we're quite sure someone out there has the right system for us to live by. When leaders succumb to these beliefs they leave themselves vulnerable to cults or doctrinaire belief systems. In looking for a powerful fix for problems of lethargy and inflexibility, leaders sometimes wind up with cultlike behavior patterns that are worse.

From the aikidoist's perspective, the Achilles' heel of all such attempts is the narrow range of options it creates. Each arbitrary decision hems people in a little tighter. They are required to judge each new choice not by its merits but against a growing backlog of precedents that cannot be overturned. Thus, people who begin as strong, principled leaders eventually become tyrants, marginalized in their industries, their organizations, and even their families. The world changes, but they are left behind.

HOW THE BIG THREE GOT APPLE COMPUTER

Apple was the prototype American Dream company. Started in 1976 by two college dropouts, Stephen Wozniak and Steve Jobs, in a Santa Clara garage, the firm by 1980, the year its stock went public, had virtually cornered the market in home computers. Just as important, it had developed a strong base of loyal supporters and a reputation as a hip, visionary company whose well-paid shirtsleeved-and-sandaled employees enjoyed a quality of work life that was the secret envy of its bigger competitor, IBM. Within five years, however, both founders were gone and the shine was off the Apple. Ten years later grave doubts would exist on both Wall Street and Main Street about the firm's survivability. How could things have gone so wrong?

Some observers think that Apple began to sour in 1985 when President Jobs was replaced by John Sculley, whom Jobs had hand-picked as his successor. My interest in this theory was piqued because many of these observers, enduring leaders in other fields, have no connection to computers, feel no special love for Jobs, and have no ax to grind with Sculley. After all, Jobs had shown himself to be anything but infallible after the Apple III and Lisa debacles, and Sculley was universally praised for twenty years of brilliant marketing at PepsiCo. No, their theory of the "fallen Apple" was based solely on the interplay of strong leaders and the impersonal yet powerful forces of a growing, dynamic system—a morality tale of mismatched values and conflicting beliefs.

Here's how it went: The directors began to engage in self-deceit. Their early success blinded them and twisted their values. This brought about a discrepancy between core values and beliefs about how to achieve them—in other words, imbalance. Here are some of the new factors that now seemed to be in play:

- *Outside recognition versus self-direction.* Some directors wanted to thrust Apple into the big-league world of global data processing way before its time. They were tired of taking media hits and being the butt of private jokes about Apple's unorthodox methods, flaky California culture, and eccentric boy president. Curiously, Jobs—the flaky boy president himself—had more reasonable ideas about maturing the company than the graybeards he reported to. Those ideas included insistence on fidelity to the values Apple personified and the common stories its employees believed in. In one form or another, these concepts became a bone of contention.

- *Image versus substance.* Some directors agree with Jobs's vision for Apple—to provide exciting alternatives to standard computing options, giving real power to the people—but yearned for a smooth "corporate type" to lead the team. This faction believed that the way to achieve this was through increased corporate accountability, more self-discipline, and a commitment to helping existing Apple owners realize an enhanced return on their investment—virtuous, if uninspiring, goals.

- *Ambition versus fair play.* Still another faction was enthralled with Sculley's reputation as a marketing genius—a complementary skill that Jobs apparently lacked. They thought that if anyone could make Apple's existing products crack the lucrative business market—so long the province of IBM—Sculley was the man. Nobody seemed to worry about what would happen when the founder—the charismatic leader who still personified the common story that nourished Apple's employees—was effectively removed from day-to-day operations. They would soon find out.

Part of Apple's culture was an unshakable belief that their Mac platform was so superior that everyone would have to migrate to it. This arrogant myth caused persistent problems for them. The overhyped Mac—at least in its first incarnation—was underpowered and short on growth. Under Sculley's focused, though less inspiring, regime, Apple hunkered down and worked out some of Mac's problems, eventually fulfilling its technical promise, making the product a hit by anyone's yardstick. Sculley now played to the board's ultimate fantasy—to make Apple a global computing powerhouse. The company pushed aggressively into the corporate market and established operations around the globe.

By the early 1990s, though, Apple's products were perceived as overpriced—and still underpowered. Its clever, aggressive team had metamorphosed into the usual corporate talent lineup: a few gutsy innovators surrounded by too many indifferent, overpaid clockwatchers, many in the executive suite. Technical innovation had largely been conceded to the Microsoft-IBM consortium, which was quietly conquering the PC world. DOS-based clones proliferated, putting the IBM platform on more desks than ever before. Intel increased its chips' capacity and dropped their prices—more fuel for the IBM fire—while Motorola, Apple's captive chip maker, struggled to keep up with even the modest demand for Macs. The Apple

PowerBook, Newton, bombed and added clown makeup to the egg on directors' faces. Even to outsiders, "the Sculley choice" began to look like not only a bad decision but a disaster. From the symbol of all the board's hopes and dreams, Sculley became a pariah, the scapegoat for everything it had failed to accomplish, as well as everything that had been lost. In 1993, after the company suffered an 84 percent drop in earnings, he was replaced by Michael Spindler. The board was simply hoping to restore the Apple culture (or cult), thus abrogating values to a system.

In 1996, after a belated attempt to enter the clone market, an inexcusable failure to deliver on strong sales of the surprisingly popular Power Mac, and steadily increasing losses, layoffs, and bad press, Apple acquired yet another CEO, Gilbert Amelio, a turnaround specialist from National Semiconductor, who came on board specifically to trim the deadwood.

To me, the problems of Apple start with the board: first they engaged in self-deceit, then they locked into the values they believed had brought them early success, and then they handed leadership over to a system.

The one fact we can be certain of is that all stakeholders in a company, Apple included, have a vested interest in seeing that the values and beliefs upon which their common stories are founded are reexamined and restocked from time to time. The surest formula for failure is to consciously withhold what is needed to succeed in the hope that luck, or random chance, will save us from ourselves.[11]

BROADENING YOUR VALUES

Values, like leaders, have their own language, and you must learn to speak the vernacular. While changing language alone won't change actions, it's a start. The following diagnostic tool will help you spot values problems and solve them:

Symptom #1: Wishy-Washy Words

Sentences like "Surveys tell us our customers want . . ." and "The executive search firm recommends . . ." signify that the buck is being passed from human beings to "the system." When a decision-maker says, "The data made us do it," you can be sure that any number of important values were deliberately ignored. Sometimes this decision to abrogate responsibility for a decision allows leaders to put distance between themselves and an onerous choice, the way some leaders blame "bad economic indicators" or "adverse market trends" for lay-offs made necessary by their own bad decisions.

I once facilitated a strategic planning session for a name-brand consumer-products firm, and I waited three days for someone to use the word "customer." When this key term was finally mentioned and I had the temerity to point it out, everyone seemed genuinely surprised, then got very defensive. "Our surveys told us our customers were happy," one executive said testily. But will they be tomorrow?

Cure #1: Get Clear

Clear is when we eliminate the filters and distractions and say what we believe. Clear is when a CEO says we need many more creative solutions and therefore everyone has 20 percent free time to pursue them. This very policy produced fabulous results for Doug Shears, founder of an agricultural empire in Australia. When you hear cloudy words, always ask yourself: "Who gains by following the numbers? Who loses if we do something else? Is our competition doing this, too? What will our customers think—and do—after they hear the news?" So far Shear's great success indicates he is right. He has built one of the largest, fully integrated farming operations in the world.

Symptom #2: Committeespeak

"The corporation recommends . . ." and "The industry seems headed . . ." are part of a large, illustrious family of phrases that attempt to throw the cloak of corporate wisdom over the narrow shoulders of personal preference. One top executive I advised kept complaining that his senior managers were spread too thin and were always stressed-out and tired despite a supportive, collegial working environment that should have resulted in more, not less, discretionary management time. To understand the problem better, I followed a couple of key executives around for several days and examined the appointment books of the others. I discovered that these very responsible, experienced people spent over half their time in committee meetings—interdisciplinary gatherings that were designed to expedite solutions, not create more problems. It was clear that these executives knew each other well, had confidence in each other's ability, and functioned admirably as a team. They had become addicted, though, to the system that had initially created that bond: permanent and ad hoc work groups.

Cure #2: Get Honest

Find out what's really taking up time. To wean them of this meeting dependency, I proposed a shocking experiment: a six-month moratorium on committee meetings, cutting the number of committees by half, and shortening their meeting time by a quarter, arbitrarily, across the board. The executive team resisted, but the CEO persuaded them to try it. Two good things happened almost immediately. First, lots of productive, problem-solving time suddenly materialized. The atmosphere around the organization became less tense, nagging problems melted away, and a few of the top managers actually began to see what their families looked like in sunlight. Second, the terminology of decision-making discourse began to change. Instead of "The quality committee feels this way" and "The interdepartmental council says that . . ." people began to personalize and take ownership of their own emotions and beliefs. The lingua franca of success became "Bob and I decided . . ." and "Claire and I felt we just couldn't support . . ."

At the end of our experiment, nobody wanted to go back to the old way of doing things. Two committees out of a dozen were retained, the others were consolidated or dropped. I sat down with the CEO and hashed over what we had learned:

- Forcing the committees to be more productive made them recognize and then voluntarily reduce the "flab and blab" that had crept into their decision-making process. The desire for efficiency is a strong, deeply ingrained organizational value. In this case, we made it work for constituents rather than against them.
- With fewer fixed demands on their time, team members felt more powerful, more secure, more trusted, and therefore more trusting. They delegated more authority to their subordinates, multiplying

the decision-making capacity of the organization. As more decisions got made, nagging problems began to disappear, increasing the company's energy and optimism.

- Finally, the process of winnowing out the unnecessary is also a process of identifying what's important. To know what we can let go of, we must decide what we hold dear. Important problems finally got the attention and resources they deserved while the small stuff was set aside, not to be sweated over. Like well-centered aikidoists, the individuals in the group felt more balanced, giving the organization better balance, too.

Symptom #3: Warning Words

"The shareholders threaten to . . ." and "The government will never permit . . ." are typical phrases some leaders use to intimidate or manipulate constituent opinion. Except in cases of extreme malfeasance or misconduct, shareholders rarely "threaten" to do anything; they simply do it, usually by selling their shares. These references to nebulous but powerful third parties are almost always an attempt to exploit common values. They represent an abuse of a leader's responsibility, and they arise from that leader's fear of losing his or her power or reputation. The leader is saying, "Look, I know you won't go along with me because of the weakness of my argument or because my personal prestige is low, so I'll threaten you with a psychic atomic bomb: something disastrous that, even though I can't articulate it or realistically expect it, will sound too awful to ignore."

I've heard these threats used most often when the decision is related to executive compensation, stock options, and bonuses. The sums involved are often enormous enough to tempt a saint, so it's no wonder people try to avoid personalizing such decisions by invoking wrathful third parties, whose vengeance almost never materializes.

One board I am familiar with had voted for six straight pay increases for senior managers over a period of time when stock prices had dropped 8 percent. They listened endlessly to the CEO's claim that "management will never stand for this" and a board member's counterclaim that "shareholders won't sit still for that" but in the end, they voted their individual choices, which, after the majority had spoken, meant keeping the present management fat and sassy. The majority of board members were reluctant to rock the boat because they had been recruited by the same CEO!

Cure #3: The Calm Cure

I am about to share with you the most durable piece of business advice I ever received. Its beauty is in its simplicity. When you get a letter or call that makes you angry, take the following steps:

- Put the matter aside for a few hours and then write a response.
- Let the response sit in your top drawer until the following day, and then rewrite it without anger.
- Show your response to a colleague to see if it's measured and calm.
- Listen to your colleague's comments, and get calmer about the matter.
- When possible, calmly call the person and address only the issue, not your feelings or what caused them.

Following these steps is as calming as drinking a cup of chamomile tea, maybe even more restful.

Symptom #4: Wishful Words

"This should be a bottom-up decision." "We think unanimity is important here." "We believe the people feel empowered." These statements evoke the democratic values of participation, personal involvement, and civil virtue, but they are often used to describe how a leader wishes the culture was. This doesn't mean such leaders are hypocrites or liars; they're just people who want very much to claim something for their cause that other people value highly, and they hope you'll give them the benefit of the doubt.

One board I have known for many years included three senior executives, all thoughtful seasoned leaders who were well-intended and honest. The company was sound, but issues came up from time to time that prompted board members to seek the grassroots view. During site visits to discover what people were thinking, the directors were always escorted by one or all of the three executive directors. Their presence almost always stifled the grassroots input the directors set out to get. Conversations were influenced by the managers' relations with constituents. This problem was compounded by the fact that these executives really believed that these visits were open and unfettered. They wished it were so. But it wasn't. Here the value of responsibility clashed with the board's acute need to trust and be trusted—let the chips fall where they may.

Cure #4: Get Real

One of the great values of the new world of E-mail is that it allows leaders to get real-time feedback from customers, employees, and others. One executive I know has a three-hour weekly electronic "chat" with anyone who has a problem, a suggestion, or a wild idea. The whole senior team becomes part of this open forum wherever they are. It has provided senior management with many real moments, some headaches, and not a few solid ideas. At first they assumed people would mask their identity, but trust built very quickly and almost all of the electronic responses are signed with pride.

Symptom #5: Whining Words

"You've got the Republican Congress [or the marketing department] to thank for that." "Blame it on our Democratic president [or the chief engineer]." These statements mean just what they say: "The other guy did it. Don't blame me. It didn't happen on my watch." Such comments can be heard whenever leaders feel trapped between their own beliefs and the values of the group—a painful position. Society values leaders who dare to take the blame when things go wrong—like Harry Truman defiantly stating that "The buck stops here"—and who share the glory when things go right. Too often, however, leaders hire spin doctors when bad news comes. Or they spend more time finding scapegoats or whining about their lack of control than they do fixing the problems.

I was once asked to act as leadership adviser to the young president of a semiautonomous division whose operations were, for all intents and purposes, being held hostage by a sister division—really a mother division—whose in-house orders made up the vast majority of the smaller division's sales. Even worse, the parental division's power was enshrined in corporate rules that made it extremely difficult for the smaller division to break loose of the apron strings and prospect for outside business. In my initial interview with the president, I expected to hear the usual litany of complaints from a frustrated leader whose personal goals and values—independence, success, recognition—were being subordinated to the whims of others. Instead, my queries drew a curious answer:

"Actually, our way of operating feels quite comfortable," the president said. "If they have a good year, I have a good year. If things are bad for them, they're bad for us too, but we can always blame them. I don't do that because I can negotiate the kind of gross margin I need to keep things going—and keep my job." But everyone knows who gets the blame.

The more this genial young man talked, the more I felt myself seduced by the narcotic of benign symbiosis he described. Together these two divisions had achieved the perfect "welfare enterprise," the ultimate manifestation of the status quo–loving system. Risk of any kind was punished both administratively and monetarily. Here were leaders who not only reflected the system's values but were dominated by them—so much so that they could no longer see any alternatives. They could always blame the other division for whatever went wrong. They were hostages to each other.

After a few more visits and equally candid discussions, I went to the board chairman and told him, quite truthfully, that I could do nothing for his young protégé; he was already developing into the kind of leader the organization wanted and deserved—a bureaucrat with no profit and loss responsibilities.

Cure #5: Get Courage

Many people settle for comfort rather than finding their courage and using it. When the go-along-get-alongs become a critical mass, however, organizations can become stagnant. One large utility was the scene of so much whining that the new CEO took dramatic steps to stop it. He set firm targets for each division and put out the word: "Hit the targets or ask for a parachute." When I arrived, the atmosphere was bizarre. Instead of pulling up their socks and going to work, the executive team had cranked up their whining. I heard seven stories in a row about how everyone else was wrong. When I told the CEO that nobody believed his ultimatum, he took his top team to the woodshed and I went with him. Three of the nine management committee members agreed to move forward without questions. Four of them said they would try to learn, and two asked for parachutes. The CEO's resolute stance plus the two departures caused a quick shift in the culture.

TOWARD A CULTURE OF VALUE-GUIDED DECISIONS

Aikido-style leaders know that conflict is a natural part of life. They also know that all conflicts are not equally threatening. Such leaders value collaboration above domination and use only the minimum amount of power needed to restore harmony, since anything more could escalate the conflict into a contest which, if history is any guide, would only strengthen and renew the cycle of disharmony.

The organizations these leaders create are true communities grounded in common values—values that are inclusive, life-affirming, and full of creative joy. They fit their environment—be it industrial, governmental, community, business, scientific, or academic—as comfortably as any natural ecosystem: an interdependent yet individually evolving part of the whole. They endure not because they dominate but because they adapt, optimize, and satisfy. They draw constituents together like a net, porous yet secure, strong because it is flexible, enduring because it remains in balance. Its members make little distinction between work and play, since the boundaries of their jobs are wide-ranging, and their recreation energizes and renews them.

I want to end these reflections with a thought by aikido master Adele Westbrook—a benediction to the values we've discussed.

> It is a discipline of coordination that aikido has perhaps its widest field of application. In this dimension, the emphasis upon integration of mind and body, upon unity with the self, is expanded to include unity with a partner, with fellow men, and then that final flowering of unity of man and men with their universe. In this dimension, aikido moves from the particular and specialized to the general and universal. The improved physical and mental health, the deeper understanding and awareness of the problems facing every man, the essential unity and identification of all men, their integration with and necessity to one another, as well as a sense of "belonging" to their time and their world—this is the potential that the theory and practice of the art of aikido can offer all men, wherever they may be.[12]

9. Master Practice #5
Turn Failure into Success

> They have only stepped back in order to leap further.
>
> —Montaigne

Leadership, success, and failure have always been three corners of a triangle whose true dimensions become apparent only with the perspective of time. Real success and failure rarely have anything to do with the remarks of pundits, who usually have an agenda of their own. Fortunately, certain setbacks can turn out to be an aikido leader's "finest hour," to borrow Winston Churchill's fine phrase, much to the chagrin of critics. Still, such criticism is nothing compared to the torture most leaders put themselves through when things don't turn out as planned.

Sam Walton's expansion store failed, and he lost the lease on his first successful store. He had to start again. Upon reflection, he saw those stores as "painful experiments." But he never stopped experimenting because he learned so much from each trial. The result, of course, was Wal-Mart.[1] Andy Grove identifies the most serious failures as those where you miss a strategic inflection point—a moment in time when there are unexpected wholesale changes in the way business is done. Such a point for Intel occurred in the mid-1980s when the Japanese hit the market with lots of cheaper chips, surprising and scaring Intel. "We at Intel were fortunate to have gone through the terrible times of 1985 and '86," Grove said. "The fear of repeating [those years] has been an important ingredient in our success."[2]

Despite the lessons and examples we've all heard to the contrary, we continue to regard passing bouts with adversity as failures. And, if we're not mindful, we can let our errors and bad days lead us astray, subverting our hopes and dreams instead of informing us and making us stronger.

HOW FAILURE DEFINES OUR LIVES

Failure is not just a matter of perspective, colored by the lens through which we study it; it is also a state of mind. Our attitude toward failure and our reaction to it often have a more profound effect on our future than the unfortunate event itself. Consider the following people, who have in common only one thing—the uncommon degree to which failure dominated their lives:

- A West Point graduate failed so badly in his military career that he was obliged to leave the service, after which he failed even worse as a midwestern businessman.
- A would-be reformer suffered years of censure and public abuse for her radical ideas about the care and treatment of the sick.
- A self-educated inventor failed so many times in his most important experiment that he considered quitting and finding another line of work.
- A leading aviator spent a lifetime waiting for his chance to realize a boyhood dream—to fly in space—only to be grounded because of heart problems, a has-been at age forty.
- A journalist won early fame as a foreign correspondent only to be considered a failure when he assumed public office and disgraced himself both as a war leader and as a politician.

You have probably already identified at least a few of these characters, each of whom eventually overcame the stigma of great failure and became an enduring leader. Ulysses S. Grant, of course, left that midwestern business and rejoined the army when the Civil War began. He eventually rose to command the victorious Union forces and to win the presidency. Florence Nightingale pressed her unorthodox ideas about more compassionate, sanitary health care until they became the foundation for modern nursing. Thomas Edison persevered until he discovered a practical filament for the first incandescent lightbulb, then went on to become America's most prolific inventor. Mercury astronaut Deke Slayton, also beset by undeserved and unforeseen adversity, stuck with his NASA career until medication for his heart condition was discovered. He finally rocketed into space on the first Apollo-Soyuz mission of the 1970s. As for that flashy war correspondent who, as an admiralty lord in World War I masterminded the Allied catastrophe at Gallipoli, which cost his party control of Parliament, Winston Churchill went on to become in the 1940s arguably Britain's greatest wartime leader.

What enabled all these and many lesser known leaders to overcome seemingly insurmountable, career-stopping barriers and not only succeed but endure? Was it merely a matter of whopping good luck to match the bad? Or was there something in the "crucible of adversity," as today's motivational speakers like to call it, that forged a new dimension to their character? Did they succeed, in other words, because of their past failures or in spite of them?

After studying leaders like these for many years, I've concluded that the true culprit is the *idea* of failure, along with the emotional and mental baggage it carries. That idea is one of the major barriers, if not the prime obstacle, to lasting success for many people, whether great adversity ever touches their lives or not. Although the symptoms of this "failure syndrome" can take many forms, they all seem to flow from three sources:

1. *The pressure of staying ahead.* As the Australians say, "The tall poppy gets mowed down." Being a leader in anything makes you a target for anyone aspiring to that role. Oddly enough, the demands and challenges that must be met to attain a leadership position are insignificant compared to the mental and emotional drain of staying there. On our way up, we are energized by the thrill of the chase, the spur of ambition, the righteousness of our cause—you name the motivation and it will be there to support you and drive you on. As Bob Townsend, former CEO of Avis Rental Systems, said so aptly in his company's very successful ad campaign: "We're number two: we try harder!" And so does every contender. The sacrifices we make to become the champ seem like a small investment compared to the rewards we perceive at the end of the trail; so, like the Energizer Bunny, we just keep going and going and going—until we succeed.

   Once you've gained that position of leadership, though, the

calculus changes. You suddenly have much to lose, perhaps more than you have to gain. Indeed, many mature leaders feel greatly burdened by their accomplishments, and defending an empire is never as emotionally gratifying as building one. As John Gardner points out in *Self-Renewal,* "One of the reasons mature people are apt to learn less than young people is that they are willing to risk less. Learning is a risky business, and they do not like failure." By middle age, most of us are "once bitten, twice shy." We choose our battles so carefully that we often surrender before we start, then have the temerity to speak of our cowardice as "wisdom."

To be fair, this defensive, fatalistic attitude is attributable in part to the fact that none of us knows how long we'll have on earth to realize our dreams or our potential. We silently, even subconsciously, ask ourselves: "Is my current position as high as I am destined to rise? I have accomplished much. How can I be sure I am slated to accomplish more?" Life is like the poker game immortalized in a song some years back. How do we ever really know "When to hold 'em, when to fold 'em, when to walk away"? Or when to run?

These questions nagged one young leader, Trudy Desilets, whose story became a case study at the University of Pennsylvania's Wharton School.

Desilets was a fast-track sales rep who was raising an infant daughter while traveling constantly and whose combined work and family obligations left her an exhausted wreck at the end of every week. Desilets asked her boss for permission to enter a job-sharing arrangement with a co-worker. The boss turned her down flat. By the time her daughter was three, Desilets says, "I felt like I couldn't do anything right. I wasn't doing my job right. I wasn't doing my mothering right. I wasn't being a wife right." In other words, she felt like an abject failure.

Fear and doubt are lenses that distort everything they're focused upon. When we gaze through them, we call each disaster we've avoided a victory, another reason to celebrate. We steel ourselves for the worst possible outcome of a decision, then congratulate ourselves for escaping it, no matter how improbable our imagined outcome might have been. Slowly the world of opportunities made possible by normal, healthy risks begins to shrink around us.

Fortunately Desilets chose to expand that shrinking universe, to turn apparent failure into success. She established new priorities in her life and quit her job, opting instead for a career as a freelance marketing consultant. Finding that she could now juggle her schedule to accommodate both work and motherhood, she regained enough confidence to go back to school and complete her M.B.A.

This new accomplishment, though, like all successes, brought with it new chances to fail. Like many new M.B.A.'s, she was anxious to conquer the world and confidently accepted another high-paying, high-pressure corporate job. When her new employer demanded that she work through her family's most important religious holiday, she was knocked breathless with déjà vu. She felt sickened, pushed back to square one, as if all her hard-won gains had been snatched away from her. Was she doomed to be either a perpetually disgruntled employee or a marginally employed part-timer? Neither alternative was satisfactory; neither fit her image of herself.

Desilets cast her net again, but this time she was much more knowledgeable about what corporate values to look for. After a year or so she joined progressive retailer Eddie Bauer as manager of marketing systems, where the top leaders found flextime, job sharing, and other employee-friendly policies compatible with the button-down, customer-centered outlook she preferred. Desilets was happy; her family was happy; her new bosses were happy. All three consider her a success—and I do too—at least until the next success-induced crisis occurs. But of course the leader calling the shots in the future will be a much more experienced and failure-tolerant woman.

I once asked a spent and repentant executive—a man who had met his own definition of failure many times over and was immersed in litigation and very near to losing his family—why he remained on the board of directors when he felt himself to be the object of contempt and derision of a new CEO whose motives he mistrusted and whose methods he detested. He shrugged and gave a simple but eloquent answer: "I guess I don't want to give up those box seats at Giants games and those splendid semiannual golf trips."

Despairing, finally, of the substance of success, he had satisfied himself by grasping at its image, and in this self-deception he is far from alone. For too many battle-worn leaders, the ever-present prospect of failure becomes less a spur to new accomplishment than a ticking time bomb waiting to blow away everything they have won. They begin to think defensively, and they become more afraid of failing than of not succeeding—two very different motivations.

2. *The requirement to be consistent.* Even if we can defend our lead successfully in one instance, how do we know we can do it habitually—again and again and again? I've found the self-induced pressure to be consistent is the next most powerful barrier to handling failure successfully. Enduring, after all, means meeting not just the challenge that put you on top but all subsequent challenges to your continued success. In most walks of life, these challenges are seldom as visible as a heavyweight boxing match or a golfer rallying on the eighteenth hole. Usually the enemies of consistency are the hundreds of decisions we make every day that either fortify or erode our leadership position. While we all admire the long ball—the game-winning 90-yard pass or the miraculous hole in one—most championships are won in short-yardage situations: the many short putts that make masterful victories seem so easy and seductive, yet devilishly elusive.

One of the early warning signs of impending inconsistency is the way some leaders confuse their public persona with their private identity. They begin to believe their own press releases, confuse the group's accomplishments with their own, and think that, as one soon-to-be-unemployed French king said so pithily: *"L'état c'est moi!"* This danger is magnified when that public persona wins applause from every quarter—from environmentalists, say, as well as industry colleagues, Wall Street analysts, politicians, and employee groups. This "reality gap"—the notion that a leader can do no wrong—is a fertile breeding ground for failure, the breaking of even the most awesome winning streak. To witness its great power, we need look no further than the saga of former Chrysler chairman Lee Iacocca, whose decades-long rise to become capitalism's best-selling poster boy and rumored presidential candidate may be contrasted with his astonishingly quick fall into a quagmire of legal disputes, an abortive takeover bid for this old company, and name-calling—a decidedly ungraceful exit for a leader of quasi-mythological proportions.

Greg Norman is considered by many to be not just a great master of professional golf but one of its great artists. He has a *sensei's* natural warmth and great devotion to his calling as well as a desire to leave behind a legacy that will forever change the game. Unfortunately, part of that legacy is what commentators have come to refer to as "Norman's clutch." In the 1996 Masters Golf Classic, Norman led his opponents by a wide margin—until his closest rival caught up in the final round. As the margin of victory evaporated, the challenger got looser and Norman got tighter. He wiggled his left arm ritualistically before each putt, externalizing his great internal tension. But Greg Norman knows that his own tension is the greatest threat to his success and that the way to overcome that enemy is to meet it in true aikido fashion, with consistent focus and attention on his own game—not his competitors', not the weather conditions, not what the sportswriters are saying this week.

3. *The recurring need for courage.* When you combine the normal pressures of leadership with the self-induced need to consistently be at the top of your form, you begin to get a true sense of what the environment of enduring leadership is really like. The anxieties produced by not living up to expectations—your own and others—can eventually grind down even the most indomitable spirit. Facing this challenge takes courage: not just once or a few times in extraordinary circumstances, but day in and day out, every day of your life. It is natural, then, that most leaders eventually come to doubt their resilience, their ability to rebound and become preoccupied, distracted, and erratic. In short, they become afraid of fear itself—the potent enemy Franklin Roosevelt identified so accurately in his famous inaugural speech in 1933: "The only thing we have to fear is fear itself." Such fear remains a potent enemy today.

Perhaps the best way to describe the capacity to overcome fear is to call it the daily courage to keep on keeping on, the grit that pushes fear aside. Or we might call it founder's grit. Bill Hewlett and David Packard had it when they stumbled along with $500 in capital, inventing everything from electronic urinal flushers to a shock machine to help people lose weight just to keep going. Sam Walton says of his career, "It took twenty years to become an overnight success." Sony's founders survived several product failures before they had their first success. But all of them had the courage to look past the pain and confusion that failure brings.

HOW AIKIDOISTS HANDLE ADVERSITY

Adversity builds character *only if you survive it*. Knowing that, however, does little to show us how to integrate failure into our lives as a learning and growing experience. For this insight we turn to the teachings of aikido masters and the examples of leaders who employ those principles in daily decisions.

The first thing all aikido students learn is how to fall. This removes the fear of falling—a tangible barrier to learning. It also implants the important philosophical notion that success can rise from the ashes of failure: to know success you must experience failure and come to grips with your feelings about it. This, I believe, is the first line of defense against becoming adversity's victim. You must control the emotional response—be it fear, anger, or resentment—evoked by your failure and turn its energy to your advantage. Researchers Janelle Barlow and Claus Møller tap this aikidoesque idea in their fascinating study of management responses to marketing setbacks, aptly titled *A Complaint Is a Gift*:

> The aikido concept in martial arts works well with anger. It means to bend with the other person's energy so that it does not knock you over, and then channel that energy in the direction you want. Aikido masters do not resist the physical force of their opponents; rather, they turn with it and let it go right past them. If you approach anger this way, it keeps you out of your emotional side and lets you treat upset customers with detachment as you try to solve problems. Detachment, by the way, does not mean noninvolvement. In street language, it means not letting your buttons get pushed.[3]

Maintaining an even keel, a balanced temperament, is what I've previously referred to as centering. If you are continuously centered, with thoughts, feelings, and actions in harmony, adverse events—and the contemplation of adverse events—will have a much tougher time bowling you over. If your thoughts aren't scattered, you'll find it easier to focus on the problem at hand, and this focus may give you the mental and emotional resources to turn a looming failure into a mere setback.

This is one reason aikido masters insist that their students repeat a single move until it approaches perfection. For the same reason, golf masters like Greg Norman try to focus on their own stance and posture instead of on what their rivals are doing. It is not the outcome of the conflict that matters; too many things can intervene and rob us of control over that. It is our ability to control what we can control that counts, and in most cases, that's only ourselves. From this perspective, the old saying, "It's not whether you win or lose that counts, but how you play the game," takes on startlingly new importance. The aikido leader learns to return to the void, the calm center, and from there to work on the basics, restoring the harmony that failure disrupts. Norman can certainly do that.

Barlow and Møller take their aikido analogy one step further into practical suggestions for practicing leaders, particularly those faced with the consequences of other people's failures—dealing with customers and clients who complain, for example. They devised what they call the gift formula, which has applications far beyond the corporate complaint department. Certainly the service and legal affairs departments could use these ideas:

- *Say thank you and explain why you appreciate complaints.* You'd be surprised how disarming gratitude, as well as courtesy, can be. Failure, after all, is a potent form of feedback. Researchers estimate that less than 4 percent of service customers take the trouble to complain. This means that for every one who does, twenty-six others could, but don't! Be glad when someone takes the time to make this rare and valuable information available to you.
- *Apologize for the mistake.* Confession is good for the soul, and even if the failure was not your own, the customer will feel great for being the instrument of your absolution.
- *Promise to do something about it immediately, then correct the mistake promptly.* Good intentions are great, but results are even

better. Ask for any necessary information and offer your customers a deadline to have things resolved, even if they don't ask for one. Such "ticklers" are valuable for getting things started, and invaluable for seeing them through.

- *Check customer satisfaction.* This step has dual advantages. First, it shows the customers that you took their complaint seriously—that you and your organization are, indeed, quality-oriented and customer-centered. Second, everybody prefers to praise people rather than berate them. Following up this way gives customers a chance to stroke you in return—to make their most recent interaction with you or your organization a happy one.
- *Don't let it happen again.* Practice makes perfect, but you don't want to achieve perfection by continuously repairing old mistakes.

Barlow and Moller extend their gift formula into the area of personal criticism as well. The steps are essentially the same, with one addition:

- *Enlist the other person's help.* This is another very aikidolike idea: make your critic a partner in your remedial effort. At minimum, this forces the other person to assess how serious [he or she is] about the complaint. (It's easy to demand action if you're not part of the solution.) At best, if the critic takes you up on it, your problem-solving resources are increased and the relationship is deepened—perhaps to the point of friendship, a true win-win solution.[4]

In sum, the capacity to win flows directly from your ability to play the game; and your ability to play depends mostly on the way you react—to opportunities, to threats, to success, and to failure.

HOW AIKIDO-STYLE LEADERS BOUNCE BACK

I've discovered three practices that enduring leaders use most often when adversity rears its ugly head. In addition to being beneficial for coping with unbidden disaster, mitigating its effects and salvaging more than you may have thought possible, these tools are helpful reality checks for use while things are going right—a way to look around the corner and avoid the next sucker punch life may have in store.

Although the excitement of victory can fade quickly, failure's grip can linger for a lifetime, especially for conscientious and responsible people, the kind who make good leaders. To keep that from happening, aikido-style leaders greet each dawn as a new opportunity to move forward, to continue the work of learning. They know that occasional setbacks teach us the depth of our own resources and help us to maintain our compassion for others.

You will need all the help you can get to stay balanced, to focus on the here and now. Here's how some of the best leaders I know do exactly that:

1. *Find the "failure myth" inside each story of success.* Every tale of success carries within it implicit instructions about how to deal with failure. Your ability to find the hidden message can make the difference between rolling with a punch and being flattened by it.

   Y. H. Kwong, the leader of a far-flung family business selling everything from pharmaceuticals to earthmovers, delights in telling his family's story. A graduate of Cornell and Stanford, Y.H. and his gracious wife, Jean, felt at home just about anywhere in the world but especially enjoyed small gatherings of friends and relatives in their San Francisco condominium. There Y.H. would regale his guests for hours with hair-raising stories of his escapes from the Japanese Burma Road project during World War II and, later, from Mao Tse-tung's China, where capitalist entrepreneurs were anything but welcome. After further adventures in Southeast Asia, Y.H. settled in Hong Kong, where business began to flourish. Because he was an astute observer of customs and mores around the globe, Y.H.'s observations on both the new and old aspects of each culture were always insightful—and often breathtaking. "The basic story of our company and our family," he said with a wink, "is that we must be both dispersed and diverse."[5]

   I always enjoyed Y.H.'s stories—as, indeed, I enjoy collecting tales of successful leaders from all walks of life—but something about this leader's founder's myth, the values-laden common story his constituents find so appealing, made me stop and think. Like that of many other Asian family-owned companies, his firm's road to success had been seeded with land mines—personal dangers narrowly escaped, or not escaped; unjust expropriations of his assets by hostile powers; business mistakes; and an almost constant intervention by the forces of nature, politics, and bad luck—worthy of any Greek play. While these plot devices seem amusing in retrospect—how could they not, basking as they do in the glory of subsequent triumphs?—they must have seemed anything but amusing at the time. Indeed, I began to sense in Y.H.'s stories that these reverses, narrow escapes, and serious mistakes were not just colorful flourishes but the narrative's heart and soul: necessary ingredients for forging the character of a master leader and hidden lessons his constituents could turn to when they faced adversity.

I began to think about the other success mythologies I had heard from enduring leaders—the stories that appealed to me most. It occurred to me that every leader's myth has buried within it the shards of failure, without which the happy ending and the glorious sunset simply would not have happened or would have been less vivid. You must view a life in its full dimensions, filled with ups and downs as every life surely is, because that is the only perspective that yields the truth—at least as much of the truth as any of us will ever be privileged to know.

One of the best examples of a hidden myth within a myth can be found in the story of a world-class leader I admire very much: Václav Havel, the Czech playwright who became his country's first freely elected president after the demise of the Soviet Union. Havel's success story is understandably based on the contrast between his years of imprisonment and abuse by Communist authorities and his subsequent rise to power—but that's not where the failure message lies. One of his close friends and advisers explains:

> When Havel became a political figure, it was a great stage and an eager audience. The very idea of political self-determination for the Czech Republic was the stuff of great drama, and we had a heroic ex–political prisoner who was a playwright to lead us. It was very exciting. Then one day those of us who had been caught up in the melodrama began to realize that something was missing. Our leader was not interested in small things, the managerial aspects of leadership. He tried, but he couldn't find it in him to feign inter-

est in the details and meetings. He really loved the
drama of bold ideas, the philosophy of government
future, not the problem-solving and compromising
that queues up in daily life.[6]

Thus we have curious paradox: a poet-president who is so well
tuned to his people's humanity that they all rally around him as
the George Washington of their new nation, but who is incapable,
because of those very virtues, of executing some of leadership's
most basic functions. Fortunately, the good and capable colleagues around him have been able to take up the slack, but it's
hard to imagine anyone in such a position regarding this revelation—this unflattering self-discovery—as anything other than a
personal failure.

It occurred to me on hearing this that Havel's experience as a
failed administrator has undoubtedly caused him to rethink—and
refeel—his relationship with his constituents. He could have
toughed it out, pretended he was served by fools, and passed
blame where it didn't belong; but that was not his style. Instead,
he let the founder's myth—his constituents' common story—continue to develop, become more genuine, and speak for itself. By
tacit agreement, Havel has slipped away from the day-to-day
administrative functions for which he has little talent or appetite
and honed an even sharper role for himself as the soul of the
nation and the conscience of his country. Today he travels widely
and is an influential spokesman for rationality, calm, and putting
the human heart into international decisions. His countrymen—
and all of us—have gained from this recentering of the Havel
myth, and his reputation is even stronger.

An enduring leader must formulate a vision of an optimistic
future that is not only worth dying for but worth living for—every
day, day in and day out. That vision can move people, though, only
if it is anchored in reality, its light side tempered with shadow. If
the leader's success story does not possess this necessary balance,
constituents will add it before they claim it as their own—sometimes in a way that will come back to haunt the leader.

Mary Kay Cosmetics has been notably successful at adapting
its common story to the new people who join the system every

year. According to its charismatic founder, Mary Kay Ash, who learned her trade through brutal trial and error, "Nothing happens until someone makes a sale." That is an operational and moral imperative that offers more than a few ways to go wrong. The governors that keep this powerful engine from over-revving are the "failure-aware" common stories told by the current custodian of Mary Kay's culture, vice chair and CEO Dick Bartlett. "I see myself as a mentor, and my task is to pass on the culture," Bartlett says, "the values that make this a great organization. Ideally I would take each new member of our organization aside and explain how and why we do what we do. When they go out into their world, they need to know and feel what they are connected to, who is there for them, what support and quality is behind them." Being such a mentor—the resident truth-sayer—is the most satisfying aspect of Bartlett's job, he says, and in the long run it is probably the most crucial.[7]

Mentors and truth-sayers make the common story real, not a fabulist tale of remote gods on Mount Olympus. Such people breathe the necessary life, humor, energy, and insight into the corporate entity, shaping its soul to complement its leader's image. This is especially vital when developments are tragic, as in the case of massive layoffs. Here leaders and their truth-sayers must never insulate themselves from bad news; they must make it part of the common story, a tempering agent that can bond the survivors even closer together. Leaders who try to explain such developments as "a sacrifice today in order to enjoy a better tomorrow" are blowing smoke, and constituents know it. The people who are saved sacrifice little or nothing: it is the downsized people who pay full price for past mistakes, bad decisions, and bad luck. No future is guaranteed, and denying these facts just compounds the leader's failure.

Leaders who are disposed to separate themselves from their actions would do well to study the example of Aaron M. Feuerstein and his small textile factory in New England, which was closed temporarily after a disastrous fire. As you'll recall from Chapter 6, Feurstein wanted to stay in business and intended to rebuild, but instead of laying his workers off to cut costs, he kept them on salary with full benefits. Traditional industrial-age leaders criticized him as being "unable to make the hard decisions," but the enduring leaders I know admired him. By acting as he did, they say, Feurstein increased the loyalty of his constituents, multiplied their subsequent productivity, and bonded them permanently to the founder's myth—that good things can come from adversity—making his success story their story as well.[8]

When you tell your own story to yourself, what are your biggest failures? Your biggest successes? Explore how they led, directly or indirectly, to each other.

2. *Trust yourself to reliable partners.* Choose your partners carefully. Find a resilient team that will back you up when you're feeling low. Like the loser in musical chairs, nobody feels quite so alone as a leader in charge of a really stupendous screwup, even if that leader had little to do with the problem. In such cases the crew on hand can either help put out the fire or lead the charge for the lifeboats—and choosing that crew is something the leader can control.

Like most of the enduring leaders we've examined so far, more and more chief executives in both the public and private sectors are exerting their leadership not as solo stars or superheroes but as coaches who guide a team of creative problem-solvers. They are key nodes in a network of resourceful people, all of whom exert leadership in one form or another, at one time or another, relying on the failure-tolerant common stories they tell to boost them over the bumpiest parts of life's road. Here's an example of this new principle at work.

In Chapter 2, I recounted the amazing growth of Advanta. A year after my first consultation with them, I expected to find stress tearing the shared power arrangement apart. I expressed my fears bluntly to CEO Pete Hart.[9]

"How does this power-sharing really work?" I asked. "There are bound to be some sore toes around here."

He answered without hesitation, "It all starts with Dennis [Dennis Alder, Advanta's founder]. He is a great visionary guy who really trusts people and never seems to need the spotlight. He has a wonderful family and a healthy ego. The rest of us spend lots of time together, and we really like each other. Our jobs are well defined but give each of us lots of room. It's a great adventure, and we all work hard and enjoy it."

Pete's enthusiasm seemed to be shared by others on the team

and throughout the organization. Everything Advanta did was tied to a bold, exciting vision of growth based on a healthy respect for self-discipline—the kind of self-control needed to get through the travails of a typical business day without losing sight of the big picture. When things get tough and failure looms, they remind each other why they are there: to connect people, save them time, and help them find relationships that enhance their lives. They see the World Wide Web as a vast resource for solving problems and discovering new resources, a platform for unexpected connections; so the "failure modes" so common in other businesses in this fast-changing industry—distorted thinking, harsh feelings, panicky judgments—never have a chance to take hold.

Most important in keeping this system going are the dynamics among its three leaders. None of the three leaders are shrinking violets, afraid of their constituents or the media, but all are perfectly willing and, indeed, eager to present an accurate picture of how their system operates, why it succeeds, and how it responds to adversity.

At our last meeting Pete asked my opinion about a number of new ideas Advanta was working on. To be honest, not all of them sounded like sure winners, and a few seemed to require hard work, guts, and patience, so that's what I told Pete. He replied that that, too, was his conclusion—and didn't that make things exciting? Only then did I realize the true dimensions and power of the partnership they had formed. The idea of failure for this team was not the salty flood of tears that undermines resolve but the steel reinforcing bars that hold the whole edifice together.

In my view, Advanta and firms like it will succeed—at least in the foreseeable future—because they are so willing to fail. That kind of courage comes only from leaders who feel supported by a strong team when the winds of change are at their backs. As you consider your own partnerships, I encourage you to remember to look at partnership as an art form to be mastered as all things are mastered—through practice—not as another word for "helper," "supplier," or "employee."

3. *Learn to forgive failures.* Putting failure behind you means forgiving, not forgetting. One reason people are so quick to lay blame for a failure—aside from a natural desire to avoid part of the

blame themselves—is a laudable desire to learn, to profit from a mistake and move on. Lasting leaders know how to harness these opposing instincts: to forgive without forgetting.

No one is more critical of our failures than we ourselves are. Many leaders, in fact, openly apply a double standard: they are much harder on themselves than they would be on any constituent. This penchant for irrational self-blame may make you feel more worthy as a leader, but it's sure to animate that deadliest of inner enemies—a consuming sense of guilt, which you must exorcise if your leadership is to endure. That, of course, is easier said than done.

Not long ago I spoke at length with Nobel laureates Nadine Gordimer and Elie Wiesel on the subject of forgiveness. Gordimer is a South African writer, a friend and advocate of Nelson Mandela, whose cause she championed during the darkest hours of his imprisonment. The second is a noted professor, author, and Holocaust survivor, an ambassador for peace on a planet still dominated, in too many places, by intolerance. Both are extremely literate, sensitive, compassionate, and articulate people. Both have witnessed much that requires human forgiveness. Neither admits to having fully mastered that awesome task.[10]

"It is very difficult for any of us to get it right," Wiesel said earnestly, his only way of speaking. "If we forgive, we often forget. Monstrous acts must never be forgotten. We must remember what happened so that we can be alert to the same thing happening again. Yet we must not carry hatred around inside us and we must never forget our own capacity for doing the wrong thing."

Gordimer was also cautious but hopeful about prospects for forgiveness in her native land.

"It is Mandela's capacity to look beyond people's history and beliefs, to find ways to make common cause with people of different attitudes and values, that makes him a great leader," she says. She went on to describe Mandela's lengthy struggle, buttressed by a steely self-discipline, that eventually forged the forgiving soul he possesses. This is a prerequisite, she believes, for helping others heal. "Mandela is the most hardworking, disciplined man I know. The push-ups in prison were nothing compared to the mental and spiritual stamina he developed there."

According to Gordimer, Mandela developed several practices, or "drills," which led to a habit of forgiveness that is so powerful it works even on the self. Indeed forgiveness starts with self-forgiveness, and I don't know a single business leader who would not profit from Mandela's practices:

- *Celebrate each day as one filled with fresh prospects.* As the old saying goes, "Today is the first day of the rest of your life." If Mandela or anyone else dwelled solely in the past, the future would be literally unreachable. Each sunrise presents you with opportunities to write the songs that heal and stories that make you proud.

- *Find the sacred in every living thing.* This is not as esoteric, or as Zen, as it sounds. It doesn't have anything to do with religion, unless your beliefs already take you in that direction. By "sacred" Mandela simply means anything that is of transcendent value to you personally: life, beauty, family, health, compassion—whatever awes you and makes you feel you are part of something larger than yourself. From this perspective, no person or thing deserves contempt. Indeed, even the hand that beats you merits forgiveness, because it is driven by a fallible human heart just like your own.

- *Strive to achieve a constant state of grace.* Again, this has nothing to do with religion, nor is it something you receive from somebody else. Grace, as Mandela sees it, is living in harmony with yourself—body, mind, and spirit— even in times of rapid change and adversity. A desire for vengeance, for example, is a state of imbalance in which your hunger for retribution—your desire to even up moral accounts—temporarily overwhelms your desire for harmony. Unfortunately, vindictive people who eventually settle such scores seldom go on to live in grace. They continue to torture themselves with what they should have and would have done before or after their injury—the original vicious circle. They discover that the "hit contract" they placed on their enemy is actually a subliminal pact with the devil, a boomerang contract that, like all contracts, pays like for like.

This sophisticated bit of psychology was discovered by ancient philosophers, including the early Christians who advised skeptical converts to "turn the other cheek" when enemies abused them. Paradoxically, once you've achieved a measure of grace in your life, your ability to evoke that inner harmony actually increases as pressures build around you, a secret that allows many aikido-style leaders to focus on problems calmly even while those around them are losing their heads.

Elie Wiesel tells a similar story of grace, one related to him by Doug Huneke, a Presbyterian minister who interviewed some of the Christians who sheltered Jewish refugees from Hitler's vengeance even though they knew the Nazi penalty for such heroics was death.

One woman rescuer Huneke met had already lost her son and husband to Nazi retribution for sheltering Jews when, toward the end of the war, a terrified young German soldier, fleeing from the advancing Red Army, sought safety at her door. It would have been easy, Huneke supposed, for the woman simply to turn the young man away, and it would have been understandable if she had reported him to Soviet authorities. Yet these things, for her, would have been most difficult, even impossible, for she believed that living without grace in a world gone mad was the surest route to madness herself. Unhesitatingly, she gave the young man shelter and, in one small way at least, changed the world forever. Huneke considers her one of the most remarkable heroes of the war. Wiesel agrees, and I do, too.

Discussions on forgiveness with a variety of leaders in different walks of life yield other paths to grace—small daily practices that anyone can follow:

• *Greet someone you normally wouldn't—and smile!* We're all creatures of habit, and shutting ourselves off in our own little worlds where our feelings rule and our opinions are unquestioned is the most seductive habit of all. Opening yourself to others, then, even in this small way, will help cultivate a different habit and begin to appreciate our shared humanity.

I include with this practice the salutary habit of play. Some compulsive leaders feel they have failed if they don't devote every waking moment to gainful, purposive activity—in other words, work. This is an extremely arrogant, self-centered, and ultimately destructive process. The real hubris here is not thinking that you are so important that the world will be diminished if you take some time off (even God did that on the seventh day), but thinking that you know so much about the world that the only lessons it can teach you are those you select for yourself. Play, after all, is an act of discovery, and in discovery we learn.

Part of opening up, then, is the willingness to let yourself bloom. A lot of TV chef Julia Child's great charm is the unabashed delight—the sheer, uninhibited playfulness—with which she approaches her complex, sensuous tasks. She gleefully plops, drops, splashes, and spatters her way to glorious meals: her cookbooks and videos have sold millions and enriched the lives of multitudes. She knows a sauce or a soup or a stew is only as good as its ingredients; after that, almost any mistake we make can be absorbed. Each fallen soufflé is not a culinary failure, she tells us, but a little reminder that many of life's so-called big moments are full of nothing but hot air. If your soufflés fall flat, just call them pancakes. Your stomach will never know the difference.

One Saturday many years ago a friend of mine in Cambridge ran outside, along with everyone else on his block, to help a neighbor fight a fire in his house. Due to their quick response, the fire was put out. As the helpers headed for home, a substantial woman with a distinctive voice commanded them to come to her house for a celebratory snack, an informal feast giving thanks that a potential tragedy had been averted. Predictably, the impromptu gathering became a block party, and the neighborhood, a community. The neighbor, of course, was Julia Child. I am told that the snack, like the great lady herself, was unforgettable.

• *Look in the mirror while you scold yourself for past mistakes. Remember what you see, but don't forget to forgive yourself.* A walk through a museum of antiquities will show what our ancestors thought vengeful gods must look like. They were scowling, frightening, harshly parental faces designed to make worshipers feel like chastened children. Pick a prominent failure you really regret and silently—or even better, loudly—berate yourself with your harshest face in the mirror for what you did or didn't do. What you see will make you either laugh or cry. In any case, remember what that feeling looks like: it's how others see you when that emotion takes control of your life. Then, again, silently or out loud, as many times as it takes, repeat to yourself that you forgive yourself for your egregious mistake.

• *Call someone who owes you, but don't mention the debt.* By this I mean not just money but any moral obligation you feel has never been repaid. Such debts have a way of piling up, compounding, and dominating a relationship. As they become more powerful, they even begin to control our dialogue with these people. Subliminally, or sometimes openly and pointedly, we find ways to remind them of what they owe us, adding bad feelings like accruing interest on even the most modest obligation. Even when we say, "Oh, forget it—you don't owe me a thing!" we are evoking the memory of an unpaid debt and calling attention to the moral imbalance. The only way we can truly put such debts behind us is to forgive them in the most literal sense of the word: to remember them but choose consciously the path toward harmony, not retribution. After a while, that new debt-free response will become another graceful—and grace-filled—life-affirming habit.

• *Think about your worst enemy or your least favorite politician, and find something good to say about that person.* This is more than psycholinguistic programming. It's a literalization of your heart's fondest desire: that the person in question will somehow be made more likable and praiseworthy, making forgiveness easier. Just make sure what you say is not a left-handed compliment. My model for such compliments is Woody Allen's great line about the patron who complains that the food at a restaurant "is terrible, but at least the portions are large." Try to find the good in everyone and everything, especially the people and things you can't change.

• *Ask someone for help.* Ultimately, forgiveness is the supreme expression of trust: trust that you won't feel like a fool for doing it, trust that you won't be betrayed, trust that you'll be better off by forgiving than you would if you held a grudge. When we ask someone for help we are, in essence, writing a contract of trust with a codicil for forgiveness. If we succeed with their help, that's fine; everyone is happy. If we fail with their help, it's still okay because there is no one to blame. (We can't blame the person we asked to help because it was our choice.)

Employing all these little techniques can bring about big changes. Being more open, being more self-aware, canceling old debts, finding the good that hides in evil, putting a bit of ourselves in someone else's hands—all these things remind us that we are inexorably bound to a larger world. Resenting the adversity that world occasionally sends our way to test our mettle makes no more sense than cursing a rainy day.

TOWARD A MORE GRACE-FILLED CULTURE

The current rage in management performance evaluation is something called the 360-degree review. Maybe you've experienced it yourself. The idea behind it is to offer managers, or leaders, feedback on their actions, style, and decisions from constituents. Its goal is to make leaders stronger by exposing flaws they might not have known about. Typically this leads to a period of self-evaluation, or self-criticism, where leaders internalize the feedback and either modify their attitudes and behavior or stick to their guns. How well has the technique worked?

One chief executive who was fired after a 360-degree review claims his supervisors used the negative information to do him in. This allowed them not only to come up with "just cause" for a dismissal but also to blame the group for a decision that they themselves lacked the grounds and the courage to make. Needless to say, the executive drew different conclusions from the feedback than did his supervisors. One result neither party disputes is the fact that the disgruntled executive is now suing everyone in sight—and nobody knows how things will turn out.

This sad case highlights what for me is perhaps the most alarming aspect of failure: our unpredictable reaction to it. Anyone familiar with the scientific method knows that no experiment ever fails: it simply supports one hypothesis over another. Since so much of our behavior in this uncertain Green Glass Age is bound to be experimental, it is important to keep this fact in mind. Failures are the speed bumps on life's highway—the long, winding road to enduring success. Any evaluation, whether made by ourselves or others, is only one frame in a moving picture. Who can know how *Gone With the Wind* will turn out when they've seen only a couple of outtakes?

Without the occasional prod of failure to remind us of what's important and nudge us back onto the precipitous upward path we've chosen, we might well find ourselves wandering down the course of least resistance, following one easy success after another until we discover one day that we have ambled onto the vistaless plain of mediocrity. If we let core values guide our choices—even the riskiest ones—we may still choose wrong, but at least we will do so for the right reasons, taking much of the sting out of defeat. If we then have the courage to add these failures to our personal success story—the myth that engages our constituents—we will have enriched the base stock that flavors our lives, and we can say we have indeed turned failure into success.

But make no mistake about it: this positive perspective on failure is not a rationale for losing; it is a wake-up call for awareness. Failures are the cool, leafy valleys from which the stark peaks of success rise sharply into the sunshine. Without the benefit of their contrast, we feel no real joy in accomplishment, only a numbed, anesthetized existence that leaves us asking, in the end, if that is all there is.

Aikidoists learn from all experience—from the school of hard knocks as well as from a master's instruction. And what the mind often forgets, or represses, the body usually remembers, especially if the lesson was painful. Thus we are, all of us, much more than the sum of our memories, plans, and desires. We exclude these other valuable companions from our life's journey only at our peril.

I asked organizational expert, author, friend, and mentor Warren Bennis (at the time working busily on a book called *Organizing Genius*) for his thoughts about dealing with failure. Is it possible to base an entire corporate culture on grace? If so, would such a culture endure and be competitive in the Green Glass Age economy? Here are his answers as I have paraphrased them:

- *Shared adversity turns "me" into "we," and this is the aikidoist's idea of blending.* Leaders who respond dictatorially to adversity may gain certain short-run advantages such as cutting near-term costs, but they almost always establish a lifeboat mentality that infects the organization for years to come. Leaders who foster mutual concern, participation, and creative solutions, however, generate more than trust: they create a strong inner connectedness—a sense of transcendent harmony—which can be called a state of communal grace. Constituents who possess this connectedness become more than a team, more even than a family; they are a resilient, problem-devouring organism.

- *Shared adversity makes people feel exceptional.* The connectedness that comes from sharing and overcoming adversity makes the organization "feel" special to constituents—a feeling that may be unique in their experience. Combat veterans who have shared intense life-and-death experiences often report the same feelings, as do people who have undergone a transcendent religious experience. Such a group enjoys a special bond and sense of its own identity and destiny that outsiders can't comprehend unless they've had a similar experience of their own. Although this exceptional feeling is perishable, memories of it stick with constituents for years, fueling their desire to recapture it. Again, the best name for this beneficent condition is "a collective state of grace."[11]

How do these grace-filled groups function in a predominantly graceless world? Just fine, thank you, says Bennis. Indeed, his description of their efficiency and effectiveness closely matches the calm, collected responses of the trained aikidoist. The goal of both is to restore harmony after conflict, using a minimum of force. They know that no matter how committed your adversary is, and no matter how serious the apparent failure appears to be, the problems will be easier to handle if you remain centered and in balance.

10. Master Practice #6

Heed the Law of Unintended Consequences

> If you cry "Forward" you must make sure the direction. . . . If you fail to do that . . . a monk and a revolutionary will go in precisely opposite directions.
>
> —Anton Chekov

All leaders want to make a difference. They want to leave their mark on the world, and consequently they often have little patience with obstacles that might prevent them from doing so—including those obstacles they create for themselves. Old England's King Canute presaged many modern leaders when he commanded the flood to ebb. Leaders like these harbor secret (or sometimes openly declared) intentions to accomplish great things that require vastly more power, insight, knowledge, and resources than they or anyone else could ever possess.

But these leaders are often derailed in their efforts by what I call the law of unintended consequences. I assure you that this is something I've observed over years of watching leaders and life, and it's based on natural law.

In science, troublesome interactions where little decisions can have big consequences fall under the rubric of "complexity theory." One branch of complexity is known as "chaos." In brief, chaotic systems are rampantly nonlinear: their behavior is volatile and hard to predict. Unlike so many other things upon which we learn to base our rational expectations—from bouncing a ball to sharpening a pencil—chaotic systems are so complicated and sensitive to interactions among their elements that even minor changes in their initial conditions can radically alter the expected outcome, often in amazing ways.

The classic example of chaos is found the deceptively simple act of turning on a kitchen faucet. Left to trickle, the flow of water is quite linear and behaves predictably. Turned on full force, the flow becomes turbulent—chaotic—and can spray all over the room. Between these two extremes lies complexity—systems that are part linear and part nonlinear, part tame and part wild—the realm of human behavior. Thus complexity should be of great interest to leaders or to anyone else who hopes to influence what people do.

Nobel physicist Murray Gell-Mann, who has studied complexity for years, believes science has misled many political and industrial decision-makers who put too much faith in mathematical models. He says that, although science can explain a lot about the world, and that the long-awaited theory of everything (or grand unified theory predicted by Einstein) may be formulated and proven sooner than we think, it will be useful only in describing very simple structures like subatomic particles and the behavior of celestial bodies. We will still know very little about why some people lose their temper while others do not, or how this year's rainfall in Indonesia will affect the price of hats in New England. When unpredictable events affect our best-laid plans, we may call them unforeseen circumstances or outside factors, but that doesn't make them any less important in determining our fate.[1]

Physicians deal with unintended consequences all the time. They refer to the unintended consequences of their prescriptions and procedures as "side effects." They try to play these side effects down, focusing instead on the primary effects of the drug or the surgery— that is, the things the physician is trying to accomplish. In reality, such distinctions are purely semantic. Drugs and surgery have only one set of effects. We like some of these effects; we don't like others. "The operation was a success, but the patient died," is not just a dark joke told to make us feel better about our helplessness in the hands of powerful professionals. It's a cautionary tale for all constituents whose leaders try to control the uncontrollable, then placate them with semantic legerdemain.

Science and logic can help us see opportunities and avoid mistakes, but they can't guarantee success or inoculate us against failure. Unintended consequences will be with us as long as free will is loose upon the world. More important, and harder for many leaders to accept, is the fact that these sometimes terrifying side effects aren't always random; we often plant them like time bombs in our own plans.

This self-defeating aspect of control-oriented behavior led me to compose years ago O'Neil's law of unintended consequences: "Unintended consequences always follow, and often overshadow, any intentional act, their severity and adverse effect being directly proportional to the degree of control we try to exert over them."

The key to aikido-style leadership is not to try to avoid unintended consequences. It's to stay open, creative, and balanced in order to be able to respond to them and reap their benefits. You read that right: reap their benefits.

Like gravity, the law of unintended consequences takes effect whenever a critical mass—of ambition, arrogance, insecurity, stupidity, or brilliance—accumulates and implodes. Like most theorems, too, this one has corollaries:

1. A goal is never as valuable as the lessons we learn while achieving it.
2. A plan is no more durable than the assumptions behind it.
3. People change, and when they do, their goals and desires change too—and so should their plans.

The law of unintended consequences, like gravity, is always with us. Organizations encounter it whenever they undertake a project. It can be particularly obvious, though, when people willingly act in ways they know to be contrary to their own best interests, against their individual desires, and likely to result in outcomes that are the opposite of the goals they had in mind. Many corporate acquisitions have this remarkable outcome, like Sony getting into movie production and losing hundreds of millions of dollars. But virtually all grand plans, schemes, and designs stumble at some point if they go on long enough—that is, if they persist until their original goals become dim or obsolete—and receive enough organizational resources, management attention, and leadership commitment to keep the caravan moving. Such "commitment" is what turned Napoleon's long march into Russia into such a disaster; and is why the Vietnam War turned out the way it did.

Paradoxical outcomes don't have to be calamitous in order to demonstrate the law. The consequences of our plans and actions are never exactly what we intended, yet they can be positive as often as they are negative, especially if we are acting from an aikido place of balance and process and able to move gracefully with the changes as they occur.

This principle of action and equal-but-opposite reaction, so well known in physics, seems lost on many leaders. They fix their eyes on the bottom line, oblivious to the fact that of the thousands or millions of things that affect it, they can influence only a few. When their lucky winning streak runs long, they bow, take the credit for what others have accomplished, and pick up the fatter paychecks. When things go sour, as they inevitably do, they chop off every head but their own. When such a leader asks you to "stay the course," you should respond with a simple question: "Why?"

My point here is that the road to hell really is paved with good intentions, and the more single-minded those intentions get, the more atonement is bound to be required later.

GET OFF THE ROAD OF GOOD INTENTIONS

Not long ago I led a workshop where most of the executives involved felt dragooned into participating by their boss, a high-powered and opinionated individual who felt his team's spotty track record showed a lack of group initiative. It became clear to me at once, though, that the talented and well-educated members of this group were failing, not because they tried to accomplish too little but because they tried to *control* too much. As a result, the real world frustrated them enormously, which led to backbiting, finger-pointing, and endless petty disputes.

After hearing several war stories about how and why this or that plan had gone wrong—and which led to many good suggestions from the floor—I asked them for examples of unforeseen consequences that had arisen from their decisions. When no one would confess to any, I broadened the scope of my question: "Well, can anyone give me any example of an unintended consequence that occurred in any situation?"

After a moment, one gruff department head in bow tie and suspenders offered: "This conference!"

"How so?"

"Well, we were all told to come here, expecting it to be one thing, and now it turns out to be something else."

"What do you mean?"

"We came expecting you to give us some ideas about how to solve our problems."

"And have you gotten any good ideas?"

"Yeah, but mostly from each other." He waved a hand at the same colleagues with whom, just moments before, he had been engaged in passionate debate.

I could no longer hide my smile and said, "Well, there you go!"

It took a second for my meaning—and the irony of the situation—to sink in, but when it did, my interlocutor blushed red and joined the rest of the group in a sheepish smile and a lot of nervous laughter. Indeed, the truth seemed to dawn on all of them at once: not only had they demonstrated that the best answers usually come from the group itself; they had inadvertently proved that many of those good things are unintended consequences: something valuable flowing from something they originally feared or thought was useless.

The workshop concluded with an intriguing discussion about the "pseudoprecision" of the company's policies and procedures—a lesson every leader should learn. In this firm, the boss insisted on "double decimal place" accuracy—that is, very precise estimates with reams of supporting data. On the surface, this sounds like a fine management practice. But unfortunately the helter-skelter world we live in seldom allows that kind of accuracy. And, as we learned in the seminar, the best results are often the least predictable, especially when we are working on topics such as how people learn.

DEAL WITH CONSEQUENCES AIKIDO-STYLE

Aikido-style leaders have no aversion to double-, triple-, or even quadruple-digit data, provided that data makes sense, does not incorporate and proliferate false accuracy, and does not lose sight of the original problem. They keep such things from happening by:

- Changing their thought patterns as needed to fit the problem at hand
- Questioning the assumptions that underlie the facts
- Staying alert for—and open to—surprises

In short, they tap-dance where others trudge, skip to the tunes that others march to. When they hear such statements as "We must down-size by 2,550 jobs," they always ask: "Why would 1,200 be too few? Why would 2,600 be too many?" When they are told that the demand for a new widget is "3 million units over the next three years in all seven of our geographic regions," they reply: "Does that assume all our customers are the same? That their tastes and needs won't change over the next thirty-six months? That bankers in Hoboken will some-how think and feel the same way as farmers in Duluth?"

These questions aren't just pinpricks designed to deflate over-blown plans and egos—although they often have that effect. Indeed, consequences are unexpected only to those who are blinded by their own intentions. Without a willingness to be pleasantly surprised, with-out an openness to the serendipitous treasures lurking in unlikely places, Sir Alexander Fleming would never have discovered in that moldy piece of bread the first of our modern wonder drugs, penicillin.

Green Glass Age leaders must be ready to embrace the unex-pected consequence as there will be many of them. Here are some guidelines:

THE DESTINATION IS NEVER AS IMPORTANT AS THE JOURNEY

Arriving someplace new means leaving another place behind. A plan is nothing more than a road map to a destination that will leave you changed—a different person from the one who started the trip. This sort of change involves learning, and that's where tapping the hidden potential of all those unintended consequences comes in. How do aikido-style leaders facilitate this happy passage?

For many years, Eastman Kodak made so much money selling film that it could almost give cameras away—which it very nearly did. Relying on profits from film sales, Kodak let Japanese and German camera manufacturers gain increasingly large market shares until the name that originally meant "camera" to consumers eventually meant little more than "film."

Now, in industries that produce complementary goods—that is, where the success of one product, like cameras, guarantees the suc-cess of another, like film—symbiosis can be a trap. What would happen, Kodak's leaders wondered, if changes in technology, tastes, and preferences brought about a rapid decline in the popularity of cameras? How would a business so concentrated in its complementary product, film, expect to fare?

The answer they came up with—"poorly"—suggested that diversification was needed. That wasn't a novel solution, but it certainly revealed a very specific intention. Kodak leveraged its assets and bought businesses already established in such fields as health care, pharmaceuticals, chemicals, and home products. Only after the company had experienced this level of diversification for a while did its leaders begin to realize the unintended consequences of their purposeful decision:

- The management skills needed to run a film and camera business were not readily transferable to other industries, and the acquisitions disrupted the organizational cultures in the acquired firms.
- The cash flow required to service the enormous debt accrued in the leveraged buyouts left Kodak's core business, despite its profitability, sorely strapped for cash.
- While Kodak floundered, trying to decide what business it was in, its competitors concentrated their efforts in the film and camera markets and made even greater gains.

Was diversification a bad idea, or was it a good idea that was poorly implemented? Could or should Kodak have foreseen the resulting problems? More important, what should it do next?

The answer came in the form of a new leader, George Fisher, who left high-flying Motorola to head Kodak in 1993. At the time, observers couldn't imagine Fisher's motives for the move. Why would a proven leader in charge of a fast-growing, quality firm like Motorola stake his career and reputation on a tottering giant like Kodak? A hefty equity stake was one reason, but according to Fisher, new learning was his main incentive. A self-described techie—a Ph.D. mathematician with no formal business training—he saw in the Kodak experience a laboratory for testing his theories about building a business. At Kodak, which was in limbo between the old world of photochemical processing and the new frontier of electronics, all bets were open. The company could be saved—or ruined—by leaping in any direction.

Fisher began, in good aikido style, by using the strength of the forces opposing him to improve his position. He sold off Kodak's holdings in the unfamiliar and unfriendly worlds of health care, chemicals, and consumer products and used the cash to revitalize its core business, giving it a decidedly high-tech edge. His experience in other markets convinced him that the future lay in combining digital technology with the human passion for pictures. Gradually at first, then with increasing mastery, the company developed digital techniques for capturing, storing, and processing images without recourse to messy, costly film and chemicals. As the company's prospects improved, so did its balance sheet and stock price and, with those, the morale of its stakeholders.

Will the "Kodak miracle" continue? No one can say, least of all Fisher. He above all knows that each new decision brings with it an array of unintended but delightfully promising consequences—opportunities lurking amid the chaos of an ever-changing world. Instead of trying to bend such a world to his will, Fisher practices what he calls just-in-time learning. It began as a way for him to compensate for his lack of business training, then morphed into a formal strategy, a means of coping with complexity. The only intention that counts here is the intention to learn, because when waste goes down, profits go up. From this vantage, sporadic returns from a new venture are merely gusts from a gathering storm, failed products are probes launched into the unknown, and organizational mistakes are bonding experiences that build smarter, more savvy survivors. Like a planter who turns his eyes away from an acre of blighted crops to look at the marvelous countryside around it—forests bulging with lumber, fields dark with game, rivers teeming with fish, and hills rich in minerals—he focuses less on the failed product of his will than on the bounty that surrounds it. How can he not be pleased by what he sees?[2]

LEARNING TO ENJOY AND BENEFIT FROM THE JOURNEY

Here are two ways in which any leader can implement Fisher's ideas:

1. *Develop a wider field of vision.* Again, nature provides a good example of both the benefits and the drawbacks of focused intent.

Predators usually have binocular vision: eyes set close together on the front of the head, giving them improved depth perception when pursuing prey. Prey animals, on the other hand, are concerned about detecting threats from any quarter while they browse on vegetation, and so evolved eyes on the sides of the head so as to scan a wider view.

Leaders follow both models closely. Attack-oriented industrial-age leaders reward themselves and others for focusing completely on the goal, the mission, or the task ahead of them. They use words like "sideshows" for "peripheral issues" that "come out of left field" to distract them, which is why the unintended consequences of their highly focused acts so often take them by surprise.

Aikido-style leaders, though, know that with a superior defense, a strong offense is unnecessary. They scan the widest field possible, and therefore detect more opportunities, and threats, than do their competitors with tunnel vision. George Fisher's training in math and science allowed him to see much more of the world—its possibilities and its dangers—than could his predecessors who had taught themselves literally to see things in black-and-white. Further, his vulnerability as a business leader without a business background made him a superior learner, more open to new ideas than those whose prefabricated opinions and narrower worldviews allowed opportunities to pass—and problems to sneak up—undetected.

This need for leaders to keep all antennae out, to cover the widest possible field of vision, makes a strong case for diversity. Like animals with acutely different natural senses (sharp-eyed eagles, sharp-nosed bloodhounds, bats that hear their own ultrasonic vibrations), people from different cultures scan the same environment using different intellectual and emotional sensors. Those from high-context cultures like Asia and the Middle East are very sensitive to nuances in interpersonal communication: the telling gesture, the inflection in a voice, and so on. People from the science-loving West tend to have a talent for spotting trends and recognizing patterns. Of course, these are broad generalizations; it's our individual qualities and differences that count.

Perry Barnevik, president and CEO of Abbasea Brown Boveri Ltd., habitually assembles teams from Europe, Asia, the Pacific

Basin, and the Americas to evaluate and execute major electrical engineering projects in dozens of countries, including nations of the former Soviet Union.

"There are many opportunities and, more important, many highly skilled, intelligent people ready to work," Barnevik says. "We can quickly bring together talent for these efforts, and that makes all the difference." Not surprisingly his company has one of the lowest staff-to-line ratios of any major firm in the world. By distributing skills and decision-making throughout the organization, he finds he no longer needs layers of specialists to gather and interpret information for the elite, "focused" few.[3]

I often ask leaders of electronics firms how much they know about biology; I ask the leaders of manufacturing departments what they know about chemistry; and I ask managers of financial services about their knowledge of telecommunications. Matching the company to the discipline, however, is less important than merely asking the question. When forced to look beyond their immediate, parochial concerns, these leaders often see dimensions of their business they had previously overlooked—aspects that had not, perhaps, escaped the notice of their competitors. After thinking about their businesses in these terms, few go back to their blinkered ways.

2. *Give planning-and-doing room to breathe.* Aiko Morita, the legendary leader of Japan's Sony Corporation, describes how his company injects innovation into each strategic decision: "We work both the numerator and the denominator." This means Sony not only focuses on the big, distinguishing aspects of a problem or opportunity but on its nuances as well—the details in which, as Einstein affirmed, "God resides."

One tool that can give any plan more room to uncover these nuances is a leader's creative use of ambiguity. Ambiguity, after all, requires people to fill in the blanks of a partially expressed idea. By requiring this kind of imaginative participation, the leader helps constituents invest something of themselves in the idea's meaning or the plan's success. This makes them more committed stakeholders in its implementation.

Unfortunately, most industrial-age leaders have been taught to despise ambiguity. They believe that leaving any aspect of a plan, strategy, or policy unstated encourages "unauthorized thinking" by subordinates, creating a hash of individual opinions and autonomous actions. They are right, of course, but unauthorized thinking is just what you need during times of seismic change. Without the creative thought and individual initiative developed through active stake-building, a new consensus is hard to form. Without the hodgepodge of alternatives and bursts of energy released by this commitment, innovative solutions are often overlooked.

KEEP PACE WITH RAPIDLY CHANGING ASSUMPTIONS

In today's global environment, where players and capital move quickly into and out of markets, the half-life of most assumptions is very short. When we add to that the impact of technology and the power of diversity, the cycle of planning and doing becomes impossibly compressed. Aikido-style leaders therefore reverse this vicious cycle whenever possible. No better example of this can be found than in the way some Regional Bell Operating Companies, or Baby Bells, are responding to the fast-changing telecommunications market, at one time the very picture of stability and monolithic corporate control.

Early in 1996 I met the president of one large, regional Bell operating company for lunch. After the initial pleasantries, I smiled and asked him, "Well, what business are you in today?"

He groaned and rolled his eyes. "You're going to ruin my lunch with that question. Whatever I say today is going to change tomorrow!"

He went on to talk about the rapid expansion and cross-pollination of landline, broadcast, and digital data processing industries. "Every day something or someone new appears. Nobody stays in one place. Internet devices deliver telephone calls, cable operators switch from being competitors to being partners, long-distance companies go local. I used to be in the POTS [plain old telephone service] business. What am I now—an entertainment company? A wide-band distributor? An Internet-access provider? You tell me!"

He was, of course, a little bit of each—and he will be a lot more things tomorrow. AT&T's divestiture and deregulation of communications markets was intended simply to drive down consumer and business telephone costs. It resulted instead in the creation of whole new industries—products and services undreamed of in the days of

Ma Bell's monopoly, and only slowly, if ever, achievable under her tight control.

When infrastructure firms like telecommunications providers change quickly, the organizations that use their new products and services change even faster. Rajat Gupta, managing director of McKinsey Consulting, predicts that certain businesses will find their asset bases completely overhauled within the next five years, partly because the costs of accounting and communications will fall to practically zero.[4] Where that leaves firms like AT&T, the regional Bells, and their smaller competitors is anyone's guess, but you can imagine it will either be out in front, neck and neck with the Green Glass Age innovators, or choking on their dust.

If AT&T chairman Robert Allen has his way, it won't be the latter. After the giant firm's downsizing in 1995, the industry press jumped all over him for turning AT&T from stodgy to mean.[5] His largest single shareholder, former AT&T director Craig McCaw, is currently teaming with Bill Gates to provide a network of global long-distance satellites that will soar beyond anything AT&T can field with its enormous land-based infrastructure—or will they? Are Allen and McCaw and their talented collaborators asking themselves, "What are the unintended consequences of our new venture? Where will we find the next generation of profits if and when telecommunications and data handling costs approach zero?" In short, they ask, as all Green Glass Age leaders must, "Where is the margin in innovation?" If these competitors become bogged down in intricate plans whose assumptions are in flux before they start, that profit margin, like their long-term prospects, will also drop to zero.

Here are three ways leaders can stay ahead of the assumptions curve:

1. *Act as an early-warning device for assumptions gone awry.* In a world where assumptions and situations change quickly, leaders often try to do two things at once: they want to stay close enough to everyday operations to see how the rubber's meeting the road, yet they also want to sit up high enough to regulate the gas, jam on the brakes, and steer smoothly around adversity. A leader can't be—and shouldn't try to be—driver, navigator, and mapmaker all at once.

    Enduring leaders should pick roles that best fit their gifts and temperament, then shift perspective when the situation begins to change. They must also develop a lot of leaders with wide-scanning minds and healthy egos to ride with them. They know that troubles in production will eventually cause rumbles in the boardroom, that anxiety among middle managers can create earthquakes in the field. The leader's job is to soak up signals and pass them on as soon as possible—with utter fidelity—to players at different levels with different views and resources, so that the wisest, broadest interpretation can be made. According to this model, the leader acts as a good observer, scouting out both potential problems and unforeseen opportunities.

2. *Share information in a language that makes sense.* Engineers talk to other engineers in the language of engineering, with all of its hidden meanings and subtle connotations, just as financial people talk finance and scientists talk science. Arcane jargon succinctly conveys oceans of information to some people, but that same shorthand sometimes mystifies outsiders. Even worse, the basic information itself is often distorted by the worldviews and values cultivated by members of a particular discipline. Much of what we know about the world we learn from the journals and scuttlebutt of our profession—not the best source of unbiased information. We even socialize most often with "our own kind," even though a bit of judicious mixing with people from different walks of life would be more stimulating and enlightening. One reason ABN-AMROS Bank of Holland is so successful is its wide-lens view of the world. Each leader works hard at being comfortable with being global minded.

Understandably, though unhelpfully, we see provincial thinking and miscommunication in others before we detect it in ourselves. Who doesn't appreciate a joke about Washington's "inside the Beltway" mentality, the "cultural arrogance" of the French, or the "plastic values" of Hollywood's elite? Less often do we look deep into criticisms aimed at us.

Scaling the walls of these prisons of time, place, profession, and perspective requires more than empathy and an ability to see another point of view as in the aikido blend. It requires a radical shift in our thinking, information-gathering, and communication processes.

David Young, founder of Oxford Analytical, provides just

such a service. His clients are governments and multinational corporations who depend on objective, balanced, real-time reports about political and economic developments around the world that can easily be colored by parochial perspectives. When a request for information in a specific area comes in, Young contacts his ad hoc interdisciplinary team of Oxford dons and other information specialists, who swarm to the task. He explains the process this way: "For every assignment, we try to get the widest possible set of perspectives. Often our leading experts clash in their interpretations; the meetings can be quite lively events. But our clients see that our best efforts offer a wraparound view. Our reports are different from what they might glean from news outlets."[6]

Claude Rosenberg, founder of Rosenberg Capital Management (RCM), a premier San Francisco money-management firm, strives to accomplish the same thing—an end run around the usual biased sources—with completely different tactics. For many years RCM employed the usual methods of investment research: technical analysis, interviews with top executives, scouring financial and industry data. When these techniques failed to predict the recession of the early 1980s, Rosenberg went back to the drawing board and developed Grassroots Research: a market intelligence service that bypassed all of the usual experts and statistics and went instead to the customers, suppliers, and employees of the stock- and bond-issuing companies themselves. He even organized his researchers like a newspaper or magazine staff, calling them editors and reporters instead of managers and analysts.

After more than a decade of operation, Grassroots has saved its clients millions of dollars and made them millions more by alerting them to impending disasters—including the big Philip Morris "Marlboro Friday" sell-off—and to ground-floor opportunities like the revitalization of the U.S. furniture industry in 1993.[7]

The message here is not to subscribe to this or that information service but to do whatever it takes to rise above and beyond your own parochial viewpoint—and encourage your constituents to do the same.

3. *Don't break what you can't fix.* Most leaders work hard to keep their constituents on their toes, to ward off staleness and keep enthusiasm alive. Their motto is "If it ain't broke, break it!" They go out of their way to stir things up. But like all aphorisms, this

one goes badly wrong when it's taken too literally or pushed to an extreme.

In the 1980s the president of another successful, prestigious money-management firm—this one in New York—decided to diversify his company's operations and insulate its revenue from the vagaries of financial markets by expanding from services into products. Two of his ventures were a new mutual fund and a line of financial software to be marketed to the general public.

At first, these new programs took shape in a gradual, orderly way—the same way he had built his core business. New experts were hired, facilities were planned, and general concepts were discussed and refined before significant money was committed to develop the details. When it came time to begin actual operations, however, the usually quiet and industrious company suddenly became a beehive of frenetic activity. Deadlines were compressed—needlessly, according to some insiders—and production targets were arbitrarily raised across the board. Meetings lasting well into the night became the norm, and a crisis atmosphere prevailed. The sense of quiet professional competence that had once characterized the firm gave way to an unfamiliar atmosphere of perpetual turmoil. The costs—for overtime, priority materials, and impulsive purchase orders—were enormous and continued to climb. Work was rushed and quality dropped. Key players began talking about leaving.

After hours one exasperated manager, a veteran of the program from its beginning, finally asked the president, "What the hell is going on?"

The president smiled, got up from his desk and shut his office door, then sat down in an armchair next to the manager.

"Bob, I've always believed in a high-output culture. Productivity—getting more out than you put in—means everything in any business. Now that we've got software and newsletters and mutual funds to sell, as well as advisement services, I want to build a fire under people—to keep them moving."

In other words he felt he had to fix the system—with a blowtorch. He got just the opposite results. His heat resulted in chaos. Fortunately, cooler heads prevailed. The president stepped back from day-to-day oversight of the various projects and let the qualified team leaders he'd chosen do their jobs. The company weathered the storm, but at too high a cost—in both dollars and emotional energy.

Too many well-meaning, talented leaders strain themselves and stress everyone else to create their idea of a high-output corporate culture—even if half of that output is wasted, not needed, and too expensive. Insiders say that Richard Nixon was so certain he performed best in a crisis that he often let international incidents get out of hand just so he could demonstrate his brilliance and garner a few extra headlines. Other leaders with less potential for harm may have different reasons for troubling the calm, navigable waters around them, but the result is still the same: costly, emotion-draining activity, signifying nothing. Some, afraid to collaborate for meaningful and lasting change, dabble in cosmetics: designing new logos, redecorating the corporate office (remember Nixon's decision to outfit White House guards in those Gilbert and Sullivan comic-opera uniforms?), repaint the company plane, or repackage successful products in the latest hot colors so they'll feel more hip and with it on the slopes at Aspen or Davos. Instead of working the numerator and denominator, they put their energies into solving the wrong problems with feverish energy.

Top leaders must keep a closer eye on reality—and keep their impulses in check. They should use the group's resources not just for useful information but for essential feedback as well—to act as checks and balances on their own ideas and behavior. Doing this helps ensure that the inevitable unintended consequences will not only be less damaging but may actually help the cause.

LEADERSHIP FOR THE LONG HAUL

Aikido-style leaders heed and take advantage of the law of unintended consequences by staying aware of changing assumptions and conditions, by working with process as well as product, and by communicating clearly. However, they can do all of these things and still fail if they don't take into account perhaps the most important of their constituents: the people they rely on to implement their plans. In stable organizations, the problem looks like this:

We gain experience as days, months, and years go by, and our needs and desires drift, sometimes imperceptibly, until we suddenly realize that a once-cherished prize has lost its luster. When that happens, our commitment to plans that bind us to our old goals diminishes. It's not surprising that burnout by boredom overcomes people. Leaders encounter this phenomenon most often when they promote people who later fail to perform and when they give raises, praise, and bonuses that fail to motivate. We may then wonder if we should have offered Prozac instead. I frequently hear, "I don't know what's happening, but this team has lost its drive."

This problem is most acute in organizations that enjoy spectacular early success and then have trouble coping with the plateau that inevitably follows. It's as if the adrenaline rush of fame, fortune, and adulation becomes addictive—as indeed it often does. Such leaders and their constituents get wrapped up in the excitement of the planning and team-building process. They feel energized by difficult challenges and overcoming shared adversity. After that, the day-to-day reality of business as usual—learning, backsliding, relearning, and forgiving—can't meet their raised expectations. They have literally become different people, and when those changes get too great, their personal relationships and interests also change, affecting their commitment to plans that were once all-important.

Here are three ways you can help prevent, delay, or avoid these rough transitions:

1. *Celebrate daily life, not just your triumphs.* Industrial-age leaders tend to worship winners, vilify losers, and ignore anyone in between. As a result, their financial statements stress profit after taxes, earnings per share, return on assets, and other economic measures of victory. They think the good life is all about going into markets with a certain number of assets and coming back with more, regardless of the casualties.

    This runs contrary to the philosophy of aikido-style leaders, who subscribe to returns that include such extra values as customer loyalty, employee commitment, vendor partnerships, community health, and long-term stakeholder happiness. These are powerful forces—although they don't show up on a balance sheet—in the short run. Shifting leadership attention away from confining, hard-edged, competitive measures, which may or may not reflect the true contributions of constituents, to the more open-ended, fulfilling aspects of personal, organizational, and community life gives individuals wider comfort zones and more chances to find themselves reflected in the company image. This healthy dojo environment is achieved only through right-acting, appropriate ethics and proper leadership modeling. If it is only surface gestures or acts of manipulation, a good healthy work place will not be achieved. In fact, cynicism and manipulation will become the norm.

Organizational cultures are cobbled together by stitching values and mission seamlessly into the hundreds of daily rituals we take for granted, especially those practiced by the top leader: the transactions on the factory floor, the Monday morning staff meeting, the Friday afternoon bull sessions. It's no secret that many constituents look to leaders for examples of how to behave and what to think on certain issues. When the leader's attitude about a given change is positive and the leader's behavior conforms to stated values, it is accepted and embraced, and the myriad daily challenges that go into making the change work are met with excitement and creativity. But the leader must start by working on inner enemies, for example, a Jabberwock or Flat Earther set loose on the workplace will soon put a healthy culture at risk. Workers resent having their time wasted by fools.

2. *Celebrate incremental objectives, not just occasional milestones.* The more time that elapses between attitude checks, the more time is available for attitudes to change undetected and become entrenched. Even in enterprises that lack clearly defined projects, or work phases, where incremental objectives are essential, leaders and constituents should come together to evaluate and celebrate personal growth, organizational learning, the adoption of a new technique or new technology; to share customer success stories or good experiences with vendors. These mini-milestones give a group a sense of positive movement through time and space, even when formal measures like financial statements and PERT charts show things at a standstill. In fact, these evaluations are especially important at such times, for without a new injection of energy, forward momentum is seldom regained.

As one chief executive of a successful closely held firm told me, "Each of us has risked new ventures, tried new ideas, found a different approach to solving problems, and each of us has failed. But all of us have shared the pleasure of watching the company get better at servicing our customers. There is a shared satisfaction among all of us in simply making the company better at what it does."

Virtually all of the companies I've studied that succeed not just year to year but decade after decade have leaders who stress personal accomplishment, strong relationships, and a flexible corporate culture—often at the expense of short-term, bottom-line results. As Fred Steingraber, CEO of A. T. Kearney, reports in a study of sixty-nine top-performing global companies, "Like athletes, executives cannot be complacent. They must insist on continuous improvement and be alert to competitive changes and challenges. Competitiveness is not a distinction, it is a journey."[8]

3. *Don't procrastinate: mend fences before they fall down.* This evokes the nursing rather than the surgical model of leadership—and the difference is essential. Very rarely do emotional meltdowns strike from out of the blue. Usually personal crises result from accumulated changes that are ignored until they reach a critical mass. Sometimes they are caused by people who fret about minor issues to the exclusion of the things that really count. They then express shock and surprise when those situations finally explode. Inevitably they ask such sad rhetorical questions as "When did I lose my family? Why didn't I take better care of my health? How can I be so successful when I feel so miserable?" These are questions every bartender and therapist hears, but the leader should make it a point to hear them first.

These are also the unintended consequences of avoiding issues that should have been dealt with as they came up. Leaders can help colleagues and subordinates confront these issues and minimize their pain by keeping them on the front burner, making them part of each plan, job, and performance evaluation. We are, after all, much more than the sum of what we do—or even what we feel—at a given moment. The totality of our lives reflects not just our immediate and intended attitudes and actions but our personal history: where we've come from, where we're going, and our place in the network of souls around us. Ignoring such life-determining factors leaves a big gap in the framework of an individual's career, and leaders do so at their peril.

Thinking of our place in this larger scheme of things, I sometimes offer this Tao saying, attributed to Lao-tsu, to my more procrastination-prone friends and clients:

> *Fame or self—which matters most?*
> *Self or wealth—which is more precious?*
> *Gain or loss—which is more painful?*
> *He who is attached to things will suffer more.*
> *He who saves will suffer heavy loss.*
> *A contented man is never disappointed.*
> *He who knows when to stop does not find himself in trouble.*
> *He will stay forever safe.*

THE TUSCAN LIGHT, THE PANORAMIC VIEW

On a soft autumn day in Italy, I sat with my good friend Charles Handy on the terrace of his Tuscan villa, contemplating the vine-covered hills that rose around us. Our topic was business as a mirror of life, but try as we might to stick with specific examples from strategic plans and board meetings, the lilting breeze and rustling trees kept bringing us back to the human condition.

"The struggle is for meaning, I think," Charles said finally. "All work must offer people a chance for dignity—an opening for them to reflect what worth there is inside them, the gifts they have to share. Too often we debase work or think it debases us. Even those in high places take too little of higher value away with them at the end of the day, and that's a shame."

Charles's comment got me thinking about human evolution and mutation. Given the massive social and economic changes facing us at the dawn of the twenty-first century—and all the unintended consequences that will certainly accompany them—why, I wondered, has the art of leadership, particularly in the scientific West, taken such a backward slide?

For something so central to our existence, we seem to take for granted the millions of years of evolution—and the countless experiments in genetic development it involved—that make us what we are. Are we so admirably suited for our purpose that we now can rise above the very power that brought us here—natural selection? Can we substitute our own judgment for that of nature's, compressing into an afternoon or a handful of months or years decisions that previously took aeons? Are our greatest plans merely hubris raised exponentially from the time of the Greeks, or are we on to something better? Are we ready for the unexpected and grateful for the happy mutations that serve us, or are we too eager to claim credit for every consequence?

As the air turned chilly and the Tuscan shadows lengthened, Charles and I stirred from our comfy garden chairs and retreated into the glowing warmth of the house—showing, if nothing else, that common sense isn't entirely dead in *Homo sapiens*. We concluded on a hopeful note, agreeing that as long as we "biological units" could reflect on our own condition objectively but with heart, tapping for our individual and collective benefit the wisdom of the planet, our greatest fears are probably unfounded, even if our fondest hopes continue to elude us, as they always have. Human beings—especially those who show the way, the ones we call leaders—have a tremendous talent for muddling through. Aikido leaders become excellent observers of surprise and know that the person full of intent and aggression and on the attack is more at risk than the one being attacked. The aggressor is filled with anticipated consequences and views mutation as a failure of the planned action. The defender knows that unexpected consequences always come and is alert and ready to take advantage of them.

Conclusion
Leading in the Green Glass Age

> Life must be understood backwards, but . . . it
> must live forward.
>
> —Søren Kierkegaard

On September 13, 1995, seven hundred leaders from many walks of life gathered in San Francisco for what was billed as the Millennium Conference. The central question they asked was what sort of world we'll inherit after the year 2000. The first flowering of the Green Glass Age society we've talked about in these pages. Some time later, another large gathering, known as the State of the World Forum, focused on global leadership and diversity.

What made these conferences unique was not just attendance by a diverse group of scientists, religious and political leaders, and futurists—including Carl Sagan, Bishop Desmond Tutu, and Lester Thurow—but participation by grassroots leaders, young and old, at every organizational level. Two themes emerged from these rare conjunctions of thinkers and doers, dreamers and decision-makers.

THE SHAPE OF THINGS TO COME

First, the conferees agreed that demographic and technological forces are in play that, when taken together, are already completely remaking our world. As these changes evolve, they will transcend anything we've experienced in living memory—and that includes some pretty big changes, from television and air travel, computers and atomic energy, to revolutions in the way we think about human rights and the environment. They say that we are approaching an epochal boundary like the one that separated the Dark Ages from the Renaissance. Admission to this new Green Glass Age society will be limited to the open-minded and well-prepared.

One of the first tasks of those who are privileged to be admitted is to be a Green Glass Age leader who values and acts on principles that will result in more people having more opportunities to share in economic success and general well-being. As Thurow put it, it's as if we could see through history's spyglass the first billowing of the global, ashen clouds that wiped out the dinosaurs. "You're pessimistic if you're a dinosaur," he says, "But if you're a mammal, it's a good thing."[1]

The second consensus had to do with the enormous positive impact these collective changes can have on individuals. In general, the effect will be liberating and democratizing—the culmination of a long and painful historical trend. The true power of computer-linked global-digital networks has been grossly underestimated by users and decision-makers alike.

Intel's CEO Andy Grove, whose ability to cultivate a wide-open "frontier mentality" in his constituents helped his company gain preeminence in the semiconductor industry, puts this revolutionary new tool in even more vivid perspective. Referring to the six-shooter as a key technological device for homesteading Americans—the symbol of a strong individualist tradition in an aggressive, expanding community—he points out that "People used to refer to the Colt as the great equalizer. I think the PC will be the same equalizer. Through the PC, college dropouts can become titans of industry. . . . All you can do is make this equalizer as broadly available in the world as possible."

Grove's views and those of other leaders herald the arrival of the Green Glass Age we've been talking about throughout this book. It's an era of almost inconceivable growth and change—for the world in general and for each of us in particular.

ORGANIZING FOR THE THIRD MILLENNIUM

Those of us preparing to be full participants in the third millennium must slip into our backpacks the single most important provision for our adventure: the aikidoist's knack for restoring harmony where before there was confusion, dissension, and strife. In fact, the *1996 World Competitiveness Yearbook* (an annual report on each nation's ability to create wealth, published by the International Institute for Management Development in Lausanne, Switzerland), while listing the United States ahead in economic strength, technological development, and financial services, ranks us fifteenth in nurturing and using human resources: the education, training, and managerial skills needed to lead our workforce. We must turn our priorities toward using the enormous power that is about to be placed at workers' fingertips to fully develop the educational and community infrastructure and to open systems to all global citizens to grow and participate over the course of their lives.

FUTURE OF THE GREEN GLASS ENTERPRISE

In the autumn of 1993, the *Economist* magazine's "Intelligence Unit" asked over 10,000 leaders from over 650 diverse businesses in forty-seven countries to describe their vision of a successful corporation in the year 2000.[2] They said firms in the next millennium must be less resistant to change, more flexible, and more adaptable—standard fare for awakening industrial-age leaders. But some of their other conclusions might surprise you:

- *Put the customer on top.* The survey showed that special-interest groups, including vendors and rank-and-file employees, will have less influence over the actions and policies in the millennial firm than they do now. This may be partly explained by the fluid "partnering" arrangements so popular these days between major companies and their suppliers and by the growing tendency of employees to view themselves as on lease to their employers rather than enrolled for life. But those factors don't explain the demotion of traditional top decision-makers to supporting rather than leading roles. The chairman of the board will rank third, just behind the CEO, as the most important decision-maker in this new age.

    The entity with the most influence, respondents claim, will be the customer, individually and in aggregate. This represents an astonishing shift away from traditional industrial-age thinking, particularly since overall economic conditions traditionally ranked ahead of chief officers as the factor most directly affecting success. This means that customer needs and preferences will pervade not just the marketing and engineering functions, where they have—in better firms, at least—always enjoyed priority, but in every other department as well, from finance to human resources. Indeed, some respondents predict that customer satisfaction will one day become as important as financial ratios in gauging a firm's long-term prospects—a proposition that Wall Street analysts will find increasingly hard to contradict.

- *Develop leaders, not managers.* Even as these diverse executives called for less bureaucracy, more entrepreneurism, better strategic thinking, more customer focus, and greater diversity in resources, they minimized the importance of managers in achieving these goals. Instead, they put more responsibility for achieving them on leaders—catalysts and self-starters—at every level in the organization, in every job code. These are the people, they say, who create and channel change instead of simply responding to it—the typical management approach. Such leaders will form a new culture of leadership where old notions about team-building, entrepreneurism and self-sacrifice for the corporate good will be obsolete. This marks another profound shift in corporate thinking. Top leaders in this culture will be visionaries, not field commanders—people who according to the *Economist* article, "provide the right blend of discipline and flexibility needed to marshal talent and leverage limited resources in an increasingly competitive global environment."

  How will such nontraditional leaders accomplish this awesome task?

  Respondent Livio DeSimon, 3M's CEO, says it will be by "developing a mind-set and value system that leaves constituents free to question conventional wisdom."

- *Live gracefully with chaos.* Old models of strong leadership stressed order, solidarity, unity of command, bold and decisive action, and most of all, control. By the year 2000, the respondents claim, these imperatives will be passé. While the majority described the millennial firm as mostly entrepreneurial, the second most often used term was "a state of flux." Traditional categories like "bureaucratic," "paternalistic," "autocratic," and even "democratic" were mentioned far less often. This evokes an image of the organization as a kaleidoscope: a collection of ever-changing structural patterns that adapt quickly to new contingencies and that is forever on the move.

How will aikidoist leaders create harmony amid such chaos?

Respondent Robert Cawthorne, CEO of Rhone-Poulenc Rorer, says, "We are putting much less emphasis on detailed financial forecasts. . . . Things in our industry are changing so much that we don't always have the plan worked out, although we know the issues. . . . If you know the direction, you operate in a framework that stops you from going in the wrong direction, but does not smother you."

In other words, the best model for managing chaos comes from nature itself. Aikido leaders must yield to larger forces and blend with the energy these forces bring.

- *Replace numbers with people.* Where does the vaunted information revolution rank in the forthcoming scheme of things? Respondent Korendo Shiotsuki says that "Most systems in the past were used to replace human beings. In the future we see the role of [information technology] systems as supporting the creative work done by human beings."

This represents another remarkable shift in thinking. Traditionally, centralized information technology was used to reduce costs. Computers were "super clerks" that could handle a myriad of data and spew forth detailed reports on virtually any subject, provided that information was historical. In the next millennium, respondents say, the computer will be a real-time support tool for linking creative decision-makers with each other and to their markets: a way not to study the past but to summon the future.

Customer-centered planning-and-doing increases business when times are good and expands opportunities when times are bad—another reason international forecasters say economic climate will eventually play second fiddle to increasingly demanding—and increasingly satisfied—customers.

The Davos Experiment

Early in 1995, I put these ideas about the Green Glass Age to the test at what is probably the preeminent gathering of enduring leaders on the planet: the annual World Economic Forum in Davos, Switzerland, founded by Professor Klaus Schwab twenty-five years ago. Schwab is a true long-distance leader. I have led symposia and discussions over meals aimed at identifying the key ingredients of what I have called in this book aikido-style leadership: practices for surviving and succeeding in the Green Glass Age. Our agenda included work as a vehicle for growth and learning, and how to harmonize our lives—from the inside out—when great responsibilities beckon. We also pondered some imponderable questions: How will global competition and diversity affect basic leadership practices? Will cooperation and competition be blended in the third millennium? How can we all become better learners and apprentices as well as better teachers and mentors? Such heavy fare, of course, requires a light sauce. We also made time to contemplate such lively issues as the necessity for play and ways to renew our spiritual energy in an often dispiriting world. Here are some of the answers we came up with:

- *Use the new technology—the "glass" in the Green Glass Age—to make education more autonomous.* As more and more constituents see themselves as independent contractors rather than employees, they will take increased responsibility for their own professional development, and that, in turn, will place new demands on educators. For example, many universities are creating "virtual campuses," in which students (most of whom are working adults) and professors meet online at hours of their own choosing to replicate in cyberspace traditional classroom interactions. Through the Internet, such campuses literally know no bounds except the barrier of language, and even that will fall to sophisticated translation software in the near future.
- *Build network federations to replace hierarchies.* The intelligent "neural nets" of the Green Glass Age firm will join similar networks in allied areas, making heterarchy, not hierarchy, the organizing and governing principle behind tomorrow's successful firms. More and more, lives will be harmonized through shared

leadership, mutually agreed-upon (versus imposed) roles and goals, and our individual ability to not only tolerate but enjoy the kind of chaos that affords extraordinary opportunities for profit and growth. As individual values and group learning become the basis for decisions, current distinctions based on group identity will diminish. Roles in organizations and in society, including our families, will be elective and consensual rather than arbitrary and assigned. We will live in a world of wider choices, and those choices will mean more to us.

- *Make enduring leaders learners first; then make teachers.* Nobody has all the answers, including those to whom constituents look when things go wrong. Tomorrow's leaders will be viewed as master learners who accompany their apprentices down the long and bumpy road to self-sufficiency, balance, and renewal. With more leader-collaborators to share the load, leaders at all levels will have more time and energy to pursue their passions and find harmony in their lives.

- *Allow leaders and constituents to enjoy longer, healthier, and happier lives.* Just as the great public health programs of the nineteenth and twentieth centuries have extended life expectancy and the human and civil rights movements have made our extra years worth living, so will the "Green" component of the Green Glass Age strengthen the unity between mind and body, making possible even longer, richer, and more productive lives. These gains will be achieved not just through increasingly heroic interventions by medical technology and immunology, but by the day-to-day benefits of healthier living through a better diet, more exercise, and enlightened attitudes toward work and play.

LEADERSHIP: THE PERSONAL VIEW

There is a tranquillity and a joy about enduring leaders that belies the many storms they've weathered and the crises they've come through. Like other performing artists, their tasks become most difficult when they forget to have fun. Playfulness in a leader's personal style bathes constituents like sunshine streaming through gray clouds, raising their spirits, enriching their day. If the light shed by a leader is bright enough, it can obliterate the shadows cast by posturers and poseurs who would turn each transient glory into a monument, one of the false idols that industrial-age leaders love to worship. A joke, a bit of praise, an encouraging word, a friendly piece of advice—all can be communicated in a variety of ways, but never on stone tablets.

Aikido-style leaders put great stock in the common stories they tell. And they are uniform in their agreement about the necessity of such stories to a successful organization. Yet to think that telling stories that are essentially fiction—that is, they aren't based in the everyday reality of the leaders *and* their constituents—will make an industrial-age leader into a Green Glass Age leader is a patent misconception. Their stories carry weight because these are leaders who daily engage in the six practices discussed in this book: They rigorously cultivate self-knowledge. They practice planning as a paradoxical art 365 days a year. They speak the language of mastery, and know that to stay current with the vernacular they need to keep boning up on their language skills. They let values guide them in making their decisions, which means both articulating their values and living by them, the antithesis of the old axiom: Do as I say, not do as I do. And they make sure they let their constituents live by their values as well, to wit: What's good for the goose is good for the gander. They are willing to look honestly at failure and work to turn it into success. Finally, they heed the law of unintended consequences, which involves knowing that some unintended consequences are inevitable, that not all unintended consequences are bad, but even the ones that look disastrous on the surface are often simply wake-up calls to shift balance and change direction.

Although all six of these basic practices are necessary to lasting success, they will be sufficient—all else being equal—only if they play a visible role in the founder's myth that unites and propels constituents. Cultural critic Omar Calabrese believes that the common stories reach deepest into our hearts and minds, essentially "abducting" us with the power of their vision. Such leader-constituent teams, I think, endure the longest and achieve the most. Jean-Jacques Rousseau, who was a musician as well as a philosopher, went even further when he compared the relationship between melody and harmony to that between nature and culture. Melody springs from nature, he says, yet both are bent by man to create a civilization.

The harmony between thinking and being, planning and doing, is what all aikido-style leaders seek. Achieving harmony will reveal the salient features of both the up-close view and the panoramic view of leadership—the things leaders do and why they do them. Unless we know ourselves well enough to get our common stories right—those more-than-rational reasons we work and live together—our enterprises will not endure. To achieve this self-knowledge, you should:

1. Trust in nature, fortune, luck, God, or whatever you think makes the world go round and blend that faith with your best judgment and values. Don't wait passively for manna from heaven, but remember that your search for bounty among the many unintended consequences of past and future acts will be easier if you know, as an article of faith, that the ingredients needed for success are already out there, waiting to be recognized and gathered.

2. Learn the classics, but play jazz. Educate, train, and develop yourself using the best cultural resources our planet has to offer; then use what you know to create new melodies in harmony with the world. Leadership is an art as well as a discipline. Learn from your constituents as you would have them learn from you.

3. Remember: the whole world is your dojo. Seek the light and you will find it!

Endnotes

Introduction

    1. The collapse of Chrysler in the late 1970s that led to government bailout symbolized an industry in decay for over twenty years. David Halberstam's book *The Reckoning* (Morrow, 1986), makes the case that the whole system was flawed.

    2. Kevin Kelly, *Out of Control: The New Biology of Machines, Social Systems, and the Economic World,* Fourth Estate Ltd., 1994, p. 186.

    3. *The Spirit of Aikido.* There are good translations of "aikido" in this book on pages 10 and 75.

    4. An article by Kenneth Baker in the *San Francisco Chronicle-Examiner,* September 17, 1995, featured this description of aikido by Zen Priest John Stevens.

    5. George Leonard, *Mastery: The Keys to Success and Long-term Fulfillment,* NY: Dutton, 1991, p. xiii. George's work on mastery and his wisdom from the mat was a great inspiration for me in writing this book. He is a friend and a gentle teacher.

    6. Ibid.

1. Why Leaders Are Failing

    1. The conference exploring the future of leadership at the St. Regis Hotel in New York was cosponsored by the *Economist* and KORN/Ferry Executive Search Firm, and it was the basis for an *Economist* report on leadership.

    2. Charles Heckscher, *White Collar Blues: Management Loyalties in an Age of Corporate Restructuring,* NY: Basic Books, 1995.

    3. Douglas Ready, *Champions of Change,* Lexington & Cambridge, MA: Douglas Ready and Gemini Consulting, Inc., 1994.

    4. There were numerous articles detailing William Agee's departure from Morrison Knudsen. Of note are those appearing in the *New York Times* in 1995 on February 2 (by Barnaby Feder) and February 9, 10, and 11 (by Diana Henriques).

5. Michael Eisner's trouble in lining up a top team was the subject of many articles. Following Katzenberg, there was another round of troubles over Ovitz. The reader may want to refer to the following: by Bernard Weinraub, "Now Playing: Disney in Turmoil," *The New York Times,* September 23, 1994; by Ken Auletta, "The Human Factor," *The New Yorker,* September 26, 1994; by Thomas King, "Stalwart Disney Is Roiled by Defections," *The Wall Street Journal,* March 13, 1995; by John Huey, "Eisner Explains Everything," *Fortune,* April 17, 1995.

6. K mart's struggles with and response to the Wal-Mart competition were well covered. Jennifer Steinhauer's *New York Times* piece, "Attention K mart Shoppers," December 26, 1995, which was quite definitive regarding K mart's losing strategies. Also see in the *Wall Street Journal,* "K mart Is Considering Options Concerning Pharmaceuticals and Eateries," on May 8, 1996; and an earlier piece entitled "Retail Combat" by Bob Ortega, appearing on November 18, 1993.

7. For a discussion of the collapse of Barings Bank, see John Gapper and Nicholas Denton, excerpts from "All that Glitters," *The Financial Times,* a four-part series appearing September 18–20, 1996.

8. For various discussions of Robert Brennan's (owner of First Securities) program, please see "Crash Landing for Brennan," *New York Times,* June 25, 1995, by Hubert Herring or "New Jersey Unseals the Fraud Charges Against Brennan," *New York Times,* September 30, 1995.

9. The quote from Václav Havel was taken from a speech at Philadelphia's Independence Hall on the occasion of his receiving the Liberty Medal, 1994.

10. Edward Luttwak, *The Endangered American Dream,* NY: Simon & Schuster, 1993.

11. *White Collar Blues,* Chapter 6.

12. Charles Emory is a fictional character.

13. Jim O'Toole was a good teacher and friend for many years when he was at University of Southern California School of Business Management and the Aspen Institute.

14. See Adele Westbrook, *Aikido and the Dynamic Sphere,* Rutland, VT: C. E. Tuttle Co., 1970.

2. The Face of Aikido-Style Leadership

1. *The Spirit of Aikido,* p. 26.

2. Ibid., p. 41.

3. Ibid., p. 20.

4. *Mastery,* p. 154.

5. *The Spirit of Aikido,* pp. 73–74.

6. The Todd Company is my wife's family's enterprise. I have had a privileged view of this remarkably durable firm and many rewarding conversations with key family members over many years.

7. Charles Handy's ideas come to me often in our walks and over meals.

8. *The Spirit of Aikido,* p. 37.

9. See Andrew S. Grove, *Only the Paranoid Survive,* NY: Doubleday, 1996. In an interview with Grove at the World Economic Forum, he made it clear that he was not talking about real paranoia as the title suggests. Eternal vigilance might come closer as bywords.

10. Sun Tzu, *The Art of War,* as it appeared in *The Japanese Art of War.*

11. *The Spirit of Aikido,* p. 39.

12. My sessions with Phillip Moffitt go all the way back to his *Esquire* days and continue through today. I am deeply indebted to him for his general wisdom about the use of aikido in everyday experiences.

13. Terry Dobson, *Aikido in Everyday Life: Giving In to Get Your Own Way,* Berkeley, CA: North Atlantic Books, 1993, p. 8 of introduction.

14. This quote by Lee Iacocca was taken from David Halberstam's book *The Reckoning,* p. 511.

15. Author interview and conversations over time; see note 12 (above) about Phillip Moffitt.

16. *The Spirit of Aikido,* p. 78.

17. Discussion of Nelson Rising and Catellus appeared in *Going Public,* Spring 1996.

18. *Mastery.* Leonard identifies the five key aspects of mastery in Chapters 5 through 9. I have simply paraphrased them here.

19. Mihaly Csikszentmihalyi, *Flow,* NY: Harper & Row, 1990.

20. I heard Jim Whitaker give a presentation at the Quality and Service meeting at Kodak in 1995.

21. Herman Kauz, *The Martial Spirit,* Woodstock, NY: The Overlook Press, 1977, p. 58.

22. I served for a time on my friend Jonas Salk's Epic B. Foundation.

23. Alex "Pete" Hart is a longtime friend whom I have served from time to time.

24. Most of these quotes were obtained when I conducted a series of interviews at Advanta in connection with a workshop I delivered in 1995.

3. The Five Internal Enemies: Locating the Blocks to Leadership Mastery

1. Yagyū Munenori, *The Sword & the Mind,* translated, with an introduction by Kiroaki Sato, NY: The Overlook Press, 1986.

2. This is based on the Greek myth about Oedipus, the son of the King and Queen of Thebes who, raised by the King of Corinth, returns to his homeland, marries his mother, and kills his father. It is the source of the Oedipus complex advanced by Freud and others as the child's unconscious tendency to attach to the parent of the opposite sex and to be hostile to the parent of the same sex.

3. Kazarian's story was first brought to my attention in a *Wall Street Journal* article. Later, Jim O'Toole wrote about him as "immorally abusive" in his excellent book *Leading Change,* NY: Jossey-Bass, 1995.

4. Gershon Kekst is an old friend who was written about in a *New Yorker* article on Steve Ross (see "A Mogul's Farewell," *The New Yorker,* October 18, 1993, by Connie Bruck). Although he is a public relations mover, he rarely puts himself forward publicly.

5. Elisabeth Maxwell's book, *A Mind of My Own: My Life with Robert Maxwell* (NY: HarperCollins, 1994), is a survivor's attempt to sort out a life with a strong personality, who hid his many problems from even his family.

4. Find Your Balance as You Set Out to Practice the Art of Leadership

1. *The Spirit of Aikido,* p. 22.

2. My time with Christie Hefner was a delightful conversation more than an interview. It took place on May 14, 1996, at the Playboy Headquarters in Chicago, Illinois.

3. Ann Bowers is a close friend, and our discussions took place over many wonderful lunches and walks.

4. Michael Murphy, *Golf in the Kingdom,* NY: Viking Press, 1972.

5. Author interviews over time.

6. Alan Jones, *Soul Making: The Desert Way of Spirituality,* San Francisco: Harper San Francisco, 1989, p. 149.

7. Author interview and conversations with Charles Handy took place over time.

8. This quote from C. G. Jung was taken from Anthony Storr, *The Essential Jung,* Princeton Press, 1983, p. 236.

9. Ibid.

5. Master Practice #1: Cultivate Self-Knowledge

1. *Only the Paranoid Survive,* p. 20.

2. Lao-tzu and Stephen Mitchell (trans.), *Tao te Ching: A New English Version with Foreword and Notes by Stephen Mitchell,* NY: Harper & Row, 1988.

3. Joseph Henderson, M.D., who studied with Jung and is still practicing psychotherapy, and with whom I spent many joyful hours digging into everything, shares Jung's teachings with us.

4. C. G. Jung quote from Joseph Henderson, M.D.

5. See M. F. K. Fisher, *How to Cook a Wolf,* San Francisco: North Point Press, 1988.

6. George Leonard and Michael Murphy, *The Life We Are Given,* Tarcher Putnam, 1995, p. 107.

6. Master Practice #2: Practice the Paradoxical Art of Planning

1. James Collins and Jerry Porras, *Built to Last: Successful Habits of Visionary Companies,* NY: Harper Business, 1994, p. 3.

2. The Marshall quote came from Bob Greenleaf, a colleague at AT&T and a great practitioner of and thinker about leadership.

3. Julie Packard appeared at the State of the World Forum and made an excellent presentation about the values at Hewlett-Packard. The quote is from that session in November 1995.

4. See "God's Country," a review by Michael Wood of John Updike's book *In the Beauty of the Lilies* (Knopf, 1996) in *The New York Review of Books,* February 29, 1996.

5. On August 30, 1994, I met with Sir James Black at one of his favorite restaurants for a long and illuminating luncheon interview. The quotes come from that session and other descriptions of "the lab."

6. In February of 1995 I met Richard Bartlett at Davos at the

World Economic Forum. Our conversations and reading his book, *The Direct Option* (College Station: Texas A&M University Press, 1994), gave me this material.

7. Chungliang Al Huang and Jerry Lynch have produced a delightful small book on mentoring that offers ancient wisdom to the would-be mentor. See *Mentoring,* Harper, 1995, p. 45.

8. Daniel Goleman, *Emotional Intelligence,* NY: Bantam Books, 1995, pp. xii and 149. This is a book I frequently recommend for its fundamental wisdom.

9. In November 1996 I went to South Africa for extensive leadership development and planning sessions. Among the many remarkable people I met was J. Brian Clark, CEO of S.A. Telkom, who is a truly inspirational leader. These quotes are from our time together.

10. Meetings with Val Venda took place in my office at the California School of Professional Psychology. He is now a professor at the University of Manitoba and we still stay in touch.

11. The Kinko's Leadership Sessions took place during the summer of 1994 under the direction of John Davis, president of the Owner Managed Business Institute in Santa Barbara, California.

12. Max De Pree, *Leadership Is an Art,* NY: Boston Doubleday, 1989. Many friends became consultants to this great company. For obvious reasons I will respect their request for anonymity.

13. James A. Ogilvy, *Living Without a Goal: Finding the Freedom to Live a Creative and Innovative Life,* NY: Currency Doubleday, 1995. Jay Ogilvy is a longtime friend who has been a great teacher for me and others on the subject of storytelling and planning.

7. Master Practice #3: Speak the Language of Mastery

1. In the later part of 1995 I interviewed Phil White and learned about his passion for effective communications and his views on leadership in the wild days of Silicon Valley.

2. Plato's *Republic,* written around 375 B.C., was his vision of the ideal state. In the parable of the cave we are given rich lessons on the problems of perception and reality and the need for work on the soul to proceed with public work.

3. The interview by Roger Mudd of Ted Kennedy took place during the 1980 election coverage on NBC.

4. Abraham Lincoln, address at Gettysburg, dedicating the Gettysburg National Cemetery, November 19, 1863, as it was printed in G. Will's *Lincoln at Gettysburg,* NY: Simon & Schuster, 1992, pp. 37 and 38.

5. Marina Warner, *Six Myths of Our Time: Little Angels, Little Monsters, Beautiful Beasts, and More,* NY: Vintage Books, 1995.

6. Donald Padwa is a longtime friend and associate. I am currently serving on his ABC board and have heard him pitch his ideas on many occasions.

7. Among the blizzard of articles on AOL's troubles was one that appeared in the *San Francisco Examiner* on January 15, 1997.

8. George Russell has been a friend and client. Much of my information comes from our talks. But, a speech at the Charles Schwab annual conference, Impacts 96, November 6–8, 1996, Orlando, Florida, gave me details about their vision.

9. My work with Waring Partridge and his good associates spanned much of 1996. He has become a treasured friend, along with his lovely wife, Julia, an accomplished leader in her own realm, The King Ranch, in Texas.

8. Master Practice #4: Let Values Drive Your Decisions

1. Ken Auletta wrote two pieces in the *New Yorker* on Sumner Redstone, Frank Biondi, and the Viacom tough guys. The one entitled "That's Entertainment," February 12, 1996, described the Biondi firing. See also "Redstone's Secret Weapon," January 16, 1995. A piece in the *Wall Street Journal* (July 6, 1994), covered the termination of Richard Snyder by Biondi.

2. See Ken Eichenwald, "How a Would-be Mr. Fix-it Left a Company in Ruins," *New York Times,* March 24, 1996.

3. The quote from Václav Havel was made during his acceptance of the Liberty Medal.

4. The comments by David Whyte were made at the 1996 State of the World Forum, San Francisco, California.

5. The Denharts are great friends. I have also played a number of roles in their business lives, including being a director of the company.

6. M. Barone, "The New America," *U.S. News and World Report,* July 10, 1995, pp. 18–23.

7. Jonas Salk, *The Anatomy of Reality: Merging of Intuition and Reason,* NY: Columbia University Press, 1983.

8. Bert Holldobler and E. O. Wilson, *The Ants,* Cambridge, MA: Belknap Press of Harvard University Press, 1990.

9. Win Todd is a director and former CEO of the Todd Company. He is also my brother-in-law and a splendid example of a long-distance leader who keeps on learning over the life span.

10. This conversation with Craig Barrett took place at the Electronic Executives Summit, Silicon Valley, September 27, 1995.

11. The Apple story is one I have followed for a long time. I was privileged to know some of the principal players who spoke under the premise of anonymity.

12. *Aikido and the Dynamic Sphere.*

9. Master Practice #5: Turn Failure into Success

1. A good story of Sam Walton's career was written by Vance H. Trimble and is entitled *Sam Walton,* NY: Penguin Signet, 1991.

2. *Only the Paranoid Survive.*

3. Janelle Barlow and Claus Møller, *A Complaint Is a Gift: Using Customer Feedback as a Strategic Tool,* Berrett-Koehler Publishing, 1996.

4. Ibid.

5. Y. H. Kwong was a grand friend whom I knew during the years he was a trustee of Mills College. His marvelous stories were offered up with each meal we enjoyed together in the mid 1970s.

6. In September of 1994 I met with a professor at Charles University in Prague who offered many remarkable insights about her friend Václav Havel. She asked that her name not be divulged.

7. The author interview with Richard Bartlett took place in Davos, Switzerland, in February, 1996.

8. There have been many articles about Aaron M. Feuerstein, the hero mill owner who took care of his employees after the mill burned. The latest was July 4, 1996, in the *New York Times.*

9. My visits with Pete Hart go back many years. My intense time with Advanta took place in mid-September 1995, when I met with the whole leadership team (about 125 members).

10. My visits with Nadine Gordimer and Elie Wiesel, Nobel Peace Prize Laureates, took place in Davos, Switzerland, in February 1995, at the World Economic Forum.

11. My conversations with Warren Bennis have taken place over

many, many years and always raise my sights, furnish my insights, and delight my soul.

10. Master Practice #6: Heed the Law of Unintended Consequences

1. See Murray Gell-Mann, *"The Quark and the Jaguar: Adventures in the Simple and Complex,"* NY: W. H. Freeman & Co., 1994.

2. George Fisher, *The Art of Taking Charge,* a publication of Heidrick and Struggers, Vol. 1, Number 1, May, 1996. Mr. Fisher has received lots of press attention but this publication was especially helpful.

3. Perry Barnevick, chairman of the board of Abb Asea Brown Boveri, Ltd. of Switzerland, gave me these insights in a conversation in February 1996, in Davos, Switzerland, at the World Economic Forum.

4. Rajat Gupta, McKinsey's managing director, offered this remarkable prediction at the regional meeting of the World Economic Forum in Chicago, Illinois.

5. Bob Allen has been the target for extraordinary media coverage, ranging from mean spirited to dubious. He was called a "hit man" in a *Newsweek* February 26, 1996, cover article. Each step of the reinvention process seems painful, and the press smells blood. I served the company in 1996, helping to create an exciting "start" called HomePlace, which may or may not survive the next reshuffle under the new president, John Walter.

6. David Young has been a good companion at a variety of meetings, where I learned about his remarkably creative network of Oxford dons.

7. Claude Rosenberg is a very wise man who has applied his skills to managing vast sums of money (Rosenberg Capital), but his latest passion is persuading people with high net worth to be much more philanthropic.

8. Fred Steingraber is chairman and CEO of AT Kearney. This quote is from a speech he gave at the Emerson Electric Corporate Planning Conference, St. Louis, Missouri, November 12, 1992.

Conclusion: Leading in the Green Glass Age

1. Lester Thurow, economist and former dean of the Sloan School at MIT, is gifted at inventing "the phrase" which he did at the Millennium

Conference. Also, an unusually gifted writer, teacher, and CEO, Andy Grove, whose book *Only the Paranoid Survive,* has been quoted several times in this book.

2. *The Economist* intelligence report is available on a subscription basis and is separate from the magazine.

BIBLIOGRAPHY

Al-Huang, Chungliang and Lynch, Jerry, *Mentoring,* Harper, 1995.

Auletta, Ken, "The Human Factor," *The New Yorker,* September 26, 1994.

———, "Redstone's Secret Weapon," *The New Yorker,* January 16, 1995.

———, "That's Entertainment," *The New Yorker,* February 12, 1996.

Baker, Kenneth, *The San Francisco Chronicle-Examiner,* September 17, 1995.

Barlow, Janelle and Møller, Claus, *A Complaint Is a Gift: Using Customer Feedback as a Strategic Tool,* Berrett-Koehler Publishing, 1996.

Barone, M."The New America," *U.S. News and World Report,* July 10, 1995.

Bartlett, Richard, *The Direct Option,* College Station: Texas A&M University Press, 1994.

Bennis, Warren, *Organizing Genius,* Addison-Wesley Publishing Company, Inc., 1997.

Bruck, Connie, "A Mogul's Farewell," *The New Yorker,* October 18, 1993.

Cleary, Thomas F., *The Japanese Art of War: Understanding the Culture of Strategy,* Shambhala Publications, 1991.

Collins, James and Porras, Jerry, *Built to Last: Successful Habits of Visionary Companies,* NY: Harper Business, 1994.

Csikszentmihalyi, Mihaly, *Flow,* NY: Harper & Row, 1990.

Denton, Nicholas and Gapper, John, excerpts from "All that Glitters," *The Financial Times,* a four-part series appearing September 18–20, 1996.

De Pree, Max, *Leadership Is an Art,* NY: Boston Doubleday, 1989.

Dobson, Terry, *Aikido in Everyday Life: Giving In to Get Your Own Way,* Berkeley, CA: North Atlantic Books, 1993.

Eichenwald, Ken, "How a Would-be Mr. Fix-it Left a Company in Ruins," *The New York Times,* March 24, 1996.

Feder, Barnaby, *The New York Times,* February 2, 1995.

Fisher, George, *The Art of Taking Charge,* a publication of Heidrick and Struggers, Vol 1, Number 1, May 1996.

Fisher, M. F. K., *How to Cook a Wolf,* San Francisco: North Point Press, 1988.

Gell-Mann, Murray, *"The Quark and the Jaguar: Adventures in the Simple and Complex,"* NY: W. H. Freeman & Co., 1994.

Going Public, Spring 1996

Goleman, Daniel, *Emotional Intelligence,* NY: Bantam Books, 1995.

Grove, Andrew S., *Only the Paranoid Survive,* NY: Doubleday, 1996.

Halberstam, David, *The Reckoning,* Morrow, 1986.

Heckscher, Charles, *White Collar Blues: Management Loyalties in an Age of Corporate Restructuring,* NY: Basic Books, 1995.

Henriques, Diana, *The New York Times,* February 9, 10, and 11, 1995.

Herring, Hubert, "Crash Landing for Brennan," *The New York Times,* June 25, 1995.

Holldobler, Bert and Wilson, E. O., *The Ants,* Cambridge, MA: Belknap Press of Harvard University Press, 1990.

Howard, R., "Values Make the Company: An Interview with Robert Haas," *Harvard Business Review,* Sept./Oct. 1990.

Huey, John, "Eisner Explains Everything," *Fortune,* April 17, 1995.

Jones, Alan, *Soul Making: The Desert Way of Spirituality,* San Francisco: Harper San Francisco, 1989.

Kauz, Herman, *The Martial Spirit,* Woodstock, NY: The Overlook Press, 1977.

Kelly, Kevin, *Out of Control: The New Biology of Machines, Social Systems, and the Economic World,* Fourth Estate Ltd., 1994.

King, Thomas, "Stalwart Disney Is Roiled by Defections," *The Wall Street Journal,* March 13, 1995.

Lao-tzu and Mitchell, Stephen, trans., *Tao te Ching: A New English Version with Foreword and Notes by Stephen Mitchell,* NY: Harper & Row, 1988.

Leonard, George, *Mastery: The Keys to Success and Long-term Fulfillment,* NY: Dutton, 1991.

Leonard, George and Murphy, Michael, *The Life We Are Given,* NY: Tarcher Putnam, 1995.

Luttwak, Edward, *The Endangered American Dream,* New York: Simon & Schuster, 1993.

Maxwell, Elisabeth, *A Mind of My Own: My Life with Robert Maxwell,* NY: HarperCollins, 1994.

Munenori, Yagyū, *The Sword & the Mind,* translated, with an introduction by Kiroaki Sato, New York: The Overlook Press, 1986.

Murphy, Michael, *Golf in the Kingdom,* NY: Viking Press, 1972.

Newsweek, February 26, 1996 (cover article about Bob Allen as hit man).

New York Times, The, "New Jersey Unseals the Fraud Charges Against Brennan," September 30, 1995.

New York Times, The, July 4, 1996 (article about Aaron M. Feuerstein).

Ogilvy, James A., *Living Without a Goal: Finding the Freedom to Live a Creative and Innovative Life,* NY: Currency Doubleday, 1995.

Ortega, Bob, "Retail Combat," *The Wall Street Journal,* November 18, 1993.

O'Toole, James, *Leading Change,* NY: Jossey-Bass, 1995.

Plato, *The Republic,* circa 375 B.C.

Ready, Douglas, *Champions of Change,* Lexington & Cambridge, MA: Douglas Ready and Gemini Consulting, Inc., 1994.

Salk, Jonas, *The Anatomy of Reality: Merging of Intuition and Reason,* NY: Columbia University Press, 1983.

San Francisco Examiner, The, January 15, 1997.

Steinhauer, Jennifer, "Attention K mart Shoppers," *The New York Times,* December 26, 1995.

Storr, Anthony, *The Essential Jung,* Princeton Press, 1983.

Trimble, Vance H., *Sam Walton,* NY: Penguin Signet, 1991.

Ueshiba, Kisshomaru, *The Spirit of Aikido,* New York: Kodansha International, 1984.

Wall Street Journal, The, July 6, 1994 (the termination of Richard Snyder by Biondi).

Wall Street Journal, The, "K mart Is Considering Options Concerning Pharmaceuticals and Eateries," May 8, 1996.

Warner, Marina, *Six Myths of Our Time: Little Angels, Little Monsters, Beautiful Beasts and More,* Vintage Books, 1995.

Weinraub, Bernard, "Now Playing: Disney in Turmoil," *The New York Times,* September 23, 1994.

Well, Edward, *Inc. Magazine,* May 1996.

Westbrook, Adele, *Aikido and the Dynamic Sphere,* Rutland, VT: C. E. Tuttle Co., 1970.

Will, G., *Lincoln at Gettysburg,* NY: Simon & Schuster, 1992, pp. 37–38.

Wood, Michael, "God's Country," *The New York Review of Books,* February 29, 1996.

INDEX

acceptance, 57

Advanta, 60–61, 231–32

advisers, 99–101

aesthetics, 32–34, 167–68

Agee, William, 17–18

Agent Based Curricula (ABC Corp.), 176

aikido, 1–2, 6–10, 11–12, 28
  leadership, 37–61

Aikido in Everyday Life (Dobson), 52

Alder, Dennis, 61, 231

Al-Huang, Chungliang, 145

alienation, 65, 76, 81–85

Allen, Robert, 252

Amelio, Gilbert, 209

America Online (AOL), 176–77

Anatomy of Reality (Salk), 199

Apple, 206–9

Art of War, The (Sun Tzu), 50

Ash, Mary Kay, 145, 230

AT&T, 149–50, 182–84, 186, 188, 191, 192, 251, 252

Avis Rental Systems, 219

Bacon, Francis, 15

balance, 48–49, 90–112

Barings Bank, 18–19

Barlow, Janelle, 224, 225, 226

Barnevik, Perry, 249–50

Barrett, Craig, 204–5

Bartlett, Dick, 145, 230

Basic Systems, 175

Bell operating companies, 251, 252

Ben & Jerry's Ice Cream, 53–54

Bennis, Warren, 239–40

Berlin, Isaiah, 199–200

Biondi, Frank, 190

Black, James, 143–44, 167, 204

Blair, Ian, 204

Bohr, Niels, 162

boredom, 65, 81–85

Bowers, Ann, 95–96, 97

Brennan, Robert, 19

Brown, Jon Mason, 190

Built to Last (Collins and Porras), 139

Bush, George, 164

Cage, John, 188–89

Calabrese, Omar, 269

Capital Holding Corporation, 192

Catellus Development Corporation, 55–56

Cawthorne, Robert, 266

Cellular One, 48

centering, 42–43, 69, 73, 224–25

change processes, 136–37

chaos, 241–42

character, 34–36

Chekov, Anton, 241

Child, Julia, 236

Churchill, Winston, 217, 219

ABOUT THE AUTHOR

JOHN O'NEIL is the author of *The Paradox of Success* and has a corresponding audiotape called *Success and Your Shadow*. After careers as an AT&T executive, a venture capitalist, vice president of Mills College, and president of the California School of Professional Psychology, he is currently president of the Center for Leadership Renewal. He also has twenty-five years of experience as an organizational consultant, corporate adviser, and researcher-advocate in the field of leadership and career renewal.